UNLOCKED

Neil Samworth worked as a prison officer at Forest Bank and then HMP Manchester (aka Strangeways) between 2005 and 2016, when he left the service after being diagnosed with PTSD. His first book, *Strangeways*, was a top ten bestseller. *Strangeways Unlocked* is his riveting follow-up, showing the realities of life behind bars from the prisoners' perspectives. In his *Real Porridge Podcast*, he delves deeper into experiences with his usual honest and humour.

By Neil Samworth

Strangeways
Strangeways Unlocked

STRANGEWAYS
UNLOCKED

THE SHOCKING TRUTH ABOUT
DOING TIME

NEIL SAMWORTH

PAN BOOKS

First published 2022 by Macmillan

This paperback edition first published 2023 by Pan Books
an imprint of Pan Macmillan
The Smithson, 6 Briset Street, London EC1M 5NR
EU representative: Macmillan Publishers Ireland Limited, 1st Floor,
The Liffey Trust Centre, 117–126 Sheriff Street Upper,
Dublin 1, D01 YC43
Associated companies throughout the world
www.panmacmillan.com

ISBN 978-1-5290-6423-0

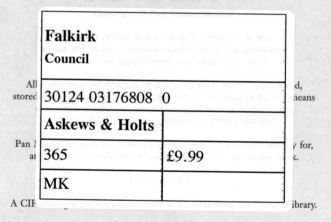

A CIP catalogue record for this book is available from the British Library.

Typeset in Janson Text LT Std by Palimpsest Book Production Limited,
Falkirk, Stirlingshire

Printed and bound by CPI Group (UK) Ltd, Croydon, CR0 4YY

MIX
Paper | Supporting
responsible forestry
FSC® C116313

Visit www.panmacmillan.com to read more about all our books
and to buy them. You will also find features, author interviews and
news of any author events, and you can sign up for e-newsletters
so that you're always first to hear about our new releases.

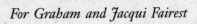
For Graham and Jacqui Fairest

'Stone walls do not a prison make
Nor iron bars a cage'

RICHARD LOVELACE, 'To Althea, From Prison' (1642)

Contents

Author's Note   xi

Preface   1

1   **The Longest Yard**   11

2   **Home Improvement**   33

3   **Borstal Boy**   56

4   **Gangs of Moss Side**   83

5   **Men in Black**   123

6   **Stir Crazy**   147

7   **Criminal Intent**   184

8   **Inside Out**   214

9   **Collateral Damage**   237

10   **Back to the Future**   253

Acknowledgements   273

Author's Note

Where necessary, names have been changed to protect the innocent – and on occasion the guilty.

Preface

At Strangeways, when we wanted a prisoner back in his cell we would tell him to get behind his door. After Covid lockdowns, I now know how they felt!

My name is Sam and Strangeways – aka HMP Manchester – is where I used to work, long before prisons and everywhere else were hit by the pandemic. It was there that, battered from pillar to post, I finally lost the plot and was forced to retire with PTSD in 2016. So by 'battered', I mean physically *and* mentally.

My experience of working in the prison service was action-packed, quite definitely, but it also gave me insight into the nuts and bolts of how our jails are run on both sides of the bars. And for every problem I reckoned I worked out an answer to, there were loads of others that weren't so easy to pin down.

Like the real biggie – what exactly is prison for?

You might think the answer to that is common sense: locking the bad guys and gals up. But I'm willing to bet that by the time you get to the end of this book you'll agree it's really not so straightforward. Do we have prisons so decent folk like you and me and our friends, families and neighbours can kip soundly in our beds of a night? Or is it mainly about punishment, which can be a posh word for revenge, can't it? Where does rehabilitation fit in?

Not counting the Tower of London, England's first jails were built courtesy of Henry II in 1166 or thereabouts – Newgate and what have you, primitive gaffs to make Strangeways look like Club Med. The first state prison proper, Millbank, came in 1816, but it wasn't until 1866 that penal reform became a thing. The Howard League charity was born that year and, do you know what, while there's obviously been loads of improvement since, I reckon no one's still properly got to grips with what we want from our nicks.

In our modern age, they are treated like a political football.

Having worked in engineering, nightclubs and care homes in and around my home town of Sheffield, I found my prison career taking me first to Forest Bank, back then a shiny new private jail in Salford. This was in 2001 and it was a shock to the system, I can tell you. I got to know the types of people who do time – banged up or in uniform – and saw first-hand how woefully managed Britain's prison service can be. Bullying, restraints, cell fires, kids high on hooch . . . you name it, we had to handle it. A vicarage tea party it quite definitely was not.

I spent three eventful years at Forest Bank dealing with troubled and troublesome young offenders and prison staff before, following a brief stint at a children's home, landing a gig at the big house in 2005.

Ah, Strangeways – with its bad reputation, Colditz walls and scary trademark tower, looming over the main road into Manchester.

If I'd found Forest Bank a mindfuck, well, Strangeways was set to be something else again. Although to begin with on K Wing, run by six-foot-two sergeant major-type Bertie Bassett, the best and funniest senior officer – or SO as they are known – I would ever work under, things weren't too bad at all. Well, once we'd cleared up a few misunderstandings, that is.

You can read about that and other escapades in my first book, *Strangeways: A Prison Officer's Story*. But just in case you, like me, are from Yorkshire and therefore too tight to buy a copy, do not fret. A swift recce to remind you of how the jail is laid out is coming soon.

On many of those landings over the next eleven years I went toe to toe with prison reality, took a good few bumps and bruises and worse. I also learned to appreciate 'dynamic security' – a vital skill set, now sadly out of fashion, where staff communicate and interact with prisoners ethically and professionally, making sure they are kept occupied with useful activity while at the same time staying in the loop with what's afoot on the landings. A lot of that has been lost in recent years due to the cost-cutting, falling staff numbers and politicizing that has put our prison service in crisis.

Oh, and there was one Strangeways unit – healthcare – where poorly inmates were sent; mentally incapacitated residents upstairs, outpatients down. I moved onto its landings in November 2008. Over the next seven years we locked up and cared for some of the baddest, saddest and most notorious criminals the UK has ever produced.

On healthcare especially, officers – and the nurses and nurse managers we worked with – copped the lot. Deaths by hanging . . . incidents of extreme self-harm . . . Stressful doesn't begin to cover it; it was enough to rattle anyone's marbles. And when the time came to leave and I was shunted to A Wing, that coincided with a period of so-called modernization that, in

2015, totally wrecked both the Strangeways routine and my own mental health; disastrously so, in both cases.

For me, the end came on the servery one dinner time in a blaze of red mist. I'd only been there a week and a half. A prisoner kicked off, attacking the SO and a female colleague of ours on the wrong side of a locked electronic door. It took ages to open but once it was, and I was able to get through, I lost my rag. Afterwards I could hardly remember a thing about it. Both my knees and right fist were a mess – I displaced a knuckle – but the guy's face was in worse shape. Even so, it didn't stop him threatening staff and generally playing up for another three days while he was kept caged in a special cell.

I'm not proud of what I did. It was unprofessional behaviour, and up to then professionalism was something I'd prided myself on. It's well documented that I didn't get on with everyone – I admit it, there were lots of people at Strangeways I didn't like. However, it's a tough job, no question, and sometimes respect is more important. But after another injury on D Wing a few weeks later, and a lot of to-ing and fro-ing re compensation with the powers that be, it was in the end decided with medical consent that my years as a prison officer in Strangeways or any other such institution were through.

If I thought that would be the end of my problems, though, I couldn't have been more wrong. Even at home I couldn't stop losing my rag. Very soon I had ridiculously high blood pressure and panic attacks.

But then, during Christmas 2016, I dug out my prison diaries, the sort in which every officer details their shifts, picked up a pen and decided to get it all off my chest.

*

The response to *Strangeways: A Prison Officer's Story* amazed me. 'You might not remember me . . .' their messages all start, which I find quite moving. Everyone has a story, don't they? We want to be recognized as human beings, not animals, although there were a fair few of those in Strangeways too, as you are about to hear. The messages are often heartfelt. 'I was really unwell,' one kid wrote, 'very badly behaved, and you looked after me as well as you could. You treated me calmly and professionally. I was horrible and you continued to be how you were.' Whether or not you are suited to prison life is vital. A lot of people there are just ill.

I said to myself when my book came out that if it helped one individual to deal with his or her issues, it would be a success. Well, now I know it helped lots of folk shitloads.

A career soldier messaged me – thirty years, special ops, the lot, several years covertly, yet a very modest guy. 'I thought nothing could shock me,' he wrote. 'Then I read your book and imagined going undercover as a prison officer. Fuck. Right. Off.' One lass who was planning to be a prison officer told me she'd read *Strangeways* and it had changed her mind. Others, though, told me it had revved them up for training; they'd seen it as motivation. 'Sam, will you do another?' asked one new officer. 'I've read it and now know what I'm going to face.' It's good to hear that, isn't it? That people related so positively to my story, and were genuinely interested in the question of prison reform, gave me a real boost.

Then, not long after the book came out, the world was hit by Covid-19, and suddenly everyone knew what it was like to be banged up – or locked down – for days, weeks and even months on end. Okay, so being stuck at home isn't quite the same as a stretch in a Cat A jail. There are no dirty protests for a start (I hope). But it did give us all some insight into what it means to lose your freedom.

And at least people had more time to read. Now people saw their own experiences in it and got in touch by the hundreds, wanting to share their stories.

That led to me opening a Twitter account (@SamworthNeil – Tigger warning: there are cats). I also began a podcast, *Real Porridge*, which has thousands of subscribers on YouTube. Some clips are nearing 100,000 views. I now appear on other people's podcasts too.

Then I went on the *Anything Goes* podcast with James English. That led to a flood of contacts that weren't just prison-based. Ex-squaddies, firefighters . . . all sorts of people got in touch. Many suffered from undiagnosed mental health issues after truly horrible experiences . . . Every single one of them was an individual deserving of having his or her voice heard.

Next, I happened across Shaun Attwood's podcast, where he talks to criminals, often about prison guards. I emailed him and sent a copy of *Strangeways: A Prison Officer's Story* – and ended up on it myself. Two and a half hours in his studio and – boom! More stories flowed in. I've been on Shaun's show twice now; one episode had almost 600,000 views, and that led to even more contacts from former and current officers, prisoners and their long-suffering families.

I get messages on WhatsApp, Messenger, Facebook, my author's page on Amazon, Twitter . . . My mobile never stops pinging. I try to respond to everyone eventually, although it isn't easy because there are so many.

The reason why I do is actually the answer to why I'm

determined to go on writing and talking about mental health and this country's prison system, even if it does mess with my head. My years as a prison officer helped to make me what I am. And it's a life curve I'm still on, even if my physical time in a jail is done.

Strangeways in particular will not let me rest. My darkest days there are never far from my head. Well-meaning mates suggest I put it all behind me. 'Move on,' they say. 'Stop raking this shit up.'

If only it were that simple.

In August 2019, my partner Amy, our daughter and I moved house from Manchester – in the shadow of Strangeways – to Wakefield, on the sunny side of the Pennines. With my own psychological issues, I'd come to hate Manchester. The only reason we'd gone there to begin with was work, and now I was sick of the place. This isn't a Yorkshire–Lancashire thing. Manchester is a lot like London: rush, rush, rush, loads of attitude, swagger – but Yorkshire folk want to chat and make polite conversation. The pace is slower, more peaceful. I love it.

Yet the thing about jail is that, even when you think you've left it, it tends to follow you around. For prisoners and staff alike, you can't shake the place off. It leaves a stain on your soul that won't shift. That's how it is with me, anyway.

Truth is, prison life is just too intense to step away from and forget. Them PTSD symptoms still chip away at my peace of mind. And even before anyone got in touch, I knew others were struggling too, be they former cons (or as I prefer to call them 'ex-customers') or prison officers. Some are still in the service.

To be honest, even as I finished writing *Strangeways: A Prison Officer's Story*, I was in a bad way. The process had stirred everything up. By late 2017, I had a swarm of buzzing bees in my noggin. Although I was excited about the prospect of having a book coming out, I was also angry as hell.

Then at Christmas we lost Amy's dad. Come January and the new year, emotions were still raw in our house. Well, they would be, wouldn't they? That coincided with the pressure of getting the book fine-tuned so as not to alienate all the mates (and one or two potential enemies!) I'd written about in its pages.

Then when the book did launch I had to promote it in London and elsewhere. I was in the middle of appearing on the *Victoria Derbyshire* show when I suddenly realized I'd forgotten to call Amy on her birthday. It was the first time we'd been parted in years, if ever. I did feel guilty about that.

Chloe Tilley was standing in for Victoria that day. She asked if I now felt better. I said yes, but I didn't really. On the media appearances I did they'd put you at ease, make us a brew, buff my face up for the lights, that sort of carry-on. But then I'd be asked about all those villains I'd encountered, like Mark Bridger, the guy who'd murdered the little girl April Jones . . . Usually it was all over very quickly – but not quickly enough to get me back north.

Looking back, I was just frazzled.

So why go through all of that again? Why not just ride my motorbike, or take up golf? Let the horror show drop?

Well, writing a book is a challenge, isn't it, and I like challenges, but more importantly, the problems with the prison service I brought up in 2018 haven't gone away. If anything – and not just thanks to Covid – they are worse. Prison officers have a strong sense of duty, or should have, and maybe there's still some of that in me.

Here is what I see and hear as an ex-prison officer.

Victims. I see families of prisoners. I am prepared to listen, but also prepared to correct them and put forward the officers' side. I've got a proper sense of justice too. Ex-officers and prisoners with PTSD, struggling. I can relate to them as well. Once it's safe to do so, I've agreed to give talks in schools. You who have been on this journey with me know how I value awareness. As in prison, you have a captive audience. The kids I'll talk to aren't in mainstream education and need to learn to make better life choices. I have an unscratchable itch to make the world a better place. It's just how I am.

So now, I've opted to get on my bike – or climb into our camper van – to hear from others who survived Strangeways, just about, or are still dealing with its after-effects. And here's a thing: I didn't get in touch with a single one of them. They all contacted me. That was especially important when it came to ex-customers, most of who, I'm pleased to say, are doing as well as can be expected given the fact that many of them find it a constant struggle to get by legitimately on the out.

As you are about to read, everyone who agreed to make their experiences public has a different tale to tell, personal to themselves but also revealing of the prison service as a whole. In their own words, we will learn how they ended up behind bars; how prison and particularly Strangeways impacted on themselves and their families; if and how a jail sentence changed their lives; their thoughts on issues that only someone who has been inside can fully understand; and how they see their lives going forward.

Given how the Howard League charity I mentioned earlier

has been going for over 150 years, and that we've still some way to go before jails completely get their act together, it's got to be unlikely that this book alone will put that right. But if nothing else, it will hopefully show how our prison population – prisoners and staff – are human beings too, with backgrounds and stories that, had fate not fallen the way it did, might well have been our own.

Without being big-headed, I think the warm response to the first book must have been down to how I used to be as an officer. I was never the big I am. I took folk as I found them, tried to be professional and treated everyone with respect – unless they gave me a good reason not to. In *Strangeways: A Prison Officer's Story* I wrote that one officer alone couldn't make much of an impact. Well, it seems I've had my own eyes opened, because that isn't how I see it now. People can and do change and their words have quite definitely been inspiring.

One lad got in touch, but wouldn't leave his name.

'It was a Friday night and next morning I had my adjudication due,' he said. 'I'd had enough, Mr Samworth.' Doing the nightly count, an officer this kid reckoned he didn't know stuck his head into the cell. Clocking that he seemed down in the dumps, the guard asked if he was all right. The lad just nodded. Not long afterwards, this same officer wandered back. 'Are you really all right, you, lad?'

'I told him to fuck off, Mr Samworth, but he didn't.'

'"What's up?" he said. "Talk to me."'

'So I did, let him have it for an hour. Boom! The idea of killing myself left my head. If it hadn't been for him . . .'

In Strangeways, like everywhere else, it's always best to share your story.

1. The Longest Yard

There is no cheerful welcome sign as you drive up the road to Strangeways. No friendly hand to help you down off the bus and fill you in on all the must-see attractions and characters of interest. And when you arrive in reception, you are quite definitely on your lonesome and very often afraid. Unless you enjoyed it so much last time you've decided to come back, of course, or know several of your new neighbours already, which it must be said is often the case.

The prison is actually split in two – top jail on the hill, bottom jail is where you come in. The wings in both are laid out pretty much the same, four storeys high with a ground floor – aka the 'ones' – and three landings above that – the 'twos', 'threes' and 'fours'.

In the bottom jail are wings A, B, C, D, E and F, the last one an educational unit with its own library. Top jail has G, H, H1, I and lastly K Wing, the biggest. We'd supervise 200 or so prisoners on three landings there.

A Wing – induction unit, although until 2015 it also housed sex offenders, half-and-half. B Wing – drug-free, which goes to show that prison can have its funny side. No wing is drug-free. C Wing was for life sentences. D Wing was K Wing's overflow, really, a hellhole of testosterone and all sorts of dodgy characters guaranteed to keep the most idle prison officer alert. E Wing had Strangeways' very own Cat A unit, that we'll come to in a minute, and the seg', i.e. segregation, where the often violent and truly objectionable customers were secured, like Hannibal Lecter in *The Silence of the Lambs*. Also part of that wing was the VP (vulnerable prisoners') unit, which housed the paedophiles and such, kept away from the rest of the prison population for their own safety.

Top jail: G Wing was for the newcomers, who came in on vans and were processed in reception before a five-day induction course. The two H Wings were where I Wing prisoners went to 'further their recovery' after detoxing. All three were full of addicts and alcoholics and stank to high heaven. On K Wing we got all sorts. Fill your boots.

It's a lot to take in at first, isn't it? Well, stir in a load of street gangs and other hardened criminals, plenty of cunning, violent and generally dangerous people, and imagine it's your first time.

Actually, you don't have to imagine. Let me introduce you to Johnny Mo. He can tell you all about it.

Johnny was one of my prison orderlies in Strangeways, more commonly known as cleaners. He's the sort of lad you want in that job: trustworthy, no mither, the type who just gets on with it. Until he got in touch, the last time I'd seen him was in 2011, when I took him back down to reception on the day he was released.

He is in his fifties now, Johnny, a family man, long-time married and a real self-starter who had no bother whatsoever with the police, growing up on the north-west coast. As a kid he dreamed of being a truck driver and ended up owning his own company, so that shows you the sort of person we are dealing with. He's an achiever.

He's also very private, a normal guy who likes a pint and keeps himself to himself. He isn't keen on having visitors in his house, for example. If you met him, you might think he was abrupt or that he didn't like you, but it's not rudeness. He can just be a bit reserved, shy even. He would happily pay to put you up in a hotel.

Once you get to know him he's likeable, could be someone's grandad. Doesn't embrace technology. Hard-working. Old school. We had him on healthcare for twelve months and he caused no hassle at all. If you asked him to do a thing, he'd just crack on and, when it was finished, find something else to do . . . You literally had to take the mop off him, which seems to have left him with issues now. At home he hoovers eight times a day, proper OCD.

As so often these days, I got a message on my phone: 'Do you remember me, Mr Sams?' Now, as soon as I saw that, I knew who it were; he always called me Mr Sams, did Johnny.

So we met up in Wakefield. In fact, we made a night of it, and fortunately our better halves clicked too. His missus knew my face from the Strangeways visits hall. Movie star looks like these aren't easily forgotten.

It was good to see him again. We all got hammered, laughed all night, and the stories flowed. Then a couple of weeks later we had a rematch on his turf this time, at Fylde Football Club, near Blackpool, and talked for another hour before my recorder's batteries went.

How he came to be in custody would put the willies up anyone.

*

Johnny Mo wound up in Strangeways as part of a drugs conspiracy ring that got caught importing cocaine to the tune of £15 million. However, for him it wasn't quite as simple as that.

His problems began when, with his haulage company, he started doing booze and fags trips, a scam to which he will happily admit, and which in the end was what he did time for. I asked him how much he made doing it and he couldn't say exactly, but put it in the region of a few thousand pounds a month. Good coin.

Basically, when he leased vans and trucks to go over to Europe, any spare space they'd fill with 'duty-free'. I'd heard of this before. When I was in my thirties, working in engineering, my mate's brother did similar. He'd regularly drive up to Newcastle, meet some guys and sell beer and spirits and cigarettes to pubs and clubs out the back of the van.

Unfortunately for Johnny, the group he was involved with, which included his nephew, was also dealing in drugs, which he didn't know. Sure enough, they'd been clocked and caught on film by the drugs squad, HM Customs or some multi-agency police operation. When word came on the grapevine that his truck had been pulled, his heart sank. He knew he was in trouble, but tried to comfort himself with the idea that it wouldn't be a lot. Running booze and fags isn't seen as a major offence. About the drugs haul he had no clue.

Even so, he was worried enough, expected a knock on the door at any point, and this went on for weeks. Every morning he's peering out through the curtains before leaving home, checking under the wagon before he climbs in, looking suspiciously around when he goes to the corner shop. A fucking nightmare. 'It was like being in a room you can't get out of, blindfolded, with your hands tied behind your back,' he said. 'And one where you have got to act normal, even though there is a boxer in there who at some point is bound to punch you in the face.' Every single day it went on like this. He'd sit in the car for a while, or walk up and down the street. His missus would ask him what he was doing. 'Nowt, nowt . . .' he'd say.

Until one day he left home at half five in the morning, went to climb in his cab and suddenly got dragged from the truck to the ground with a gun pressing hard on his temple.

He was taken in for questioning where, unlike lots of people who have form on this sort of thing, he was naive enough to answer their questions openly instead of just saying, 'No comment.'

'Is this item yours?'

Yes.

'Do you know this guy?'

Yes.

And so on. He was Joe Honest. But then the very worst he thought he'd get done for was knowingly lending someone a truck in which they'd been up to no good, and therefore had no issue with admitting to that. What he hadn't realized was that in answering their questions, 'You're going guilty on this, this and this?' 'Yeah', there was no chance of going back to his missus on bail. It was go to jail, move directly to jail, and before he knew it, hello Strangeways.

What was worse, he'd now got double jeopardy. Not only did he have a spell inside he hadn't expected, with the worry of telling his wife, but also, banged up now in HMP Manchester, he realized he was on his own. That nephew of his and the rest of the gang had all heard he'd gone guilty and said, 'Yeah, he's the leader . . .'

Which meant that while he was locked up, the people who had actually been smuggling the drugs were probably sitting at home on bail tucking into their pie, chips, peas and gravy. They'd bubbled him.

Just think. Here you are at Strangeways for the first time – and on the maximum-security Cat A unit at that, which is the bit of the jail where inmates who are deemed a threat to the public, police and/or national security get to live. Now, as I've said before, coming into Strangeways is enough to make anyone nervous, and I include myself in that. I'll never forget my own first day – guts churning, couldn't quite believe I was there – but at least I could go home and watch *Emmerdale*. If your entry point is Cat A, your unease must be off the scale.

Cat A even has its own reception, far worse and much stricter than the usual one. As soon as you are Cat A'ed, you are double-cuffed everywhere. You come in on a ballistic van, not a regular sweatbox, and are kept on your own all the way from court to the E Wing reception. When you get off the van, they walk you five metres, already double-cuffed, with a fierce dog for company. You can't go anywhere; it's an enclosed compound. Inside, they take the cuffs off and walk you through a portal, where you are wanded, rubbed down and strip-searched. Personal property goes through an X-ray. As procedures go, it is rigorous and isolating.

'There were no other prisoners around,' he said. 'I wasn't sat in a holding cell like I had been in court, a busy place with other people about. This was very intimidating.' Those dogs an' all . . . if they start barking, the handlers let them get on with it, don't try to shut them up. They aren't there on parade, quiet and well behaved. It would have all added to the sense of unease. 'I didn't even know what Cat A was until I got there.'

Once he arrived, however, there is no doubt he would've been the centre of attention. It doesn't take the other prisoners on your block long to find out what you are in for. People are saying you're the ringleader of a drugs gang, with all the pressure that comes with it. Seeing as how a lot of people come on as part of a team, he must have stood out like a sore thumb. He would have seemed different to the other lads too: not a gobshite or a murderer or some other kind of major criminal. Up for conspiracy, sure, but he had already gone guilty.

'Everyone on Cat A looks like they can fight,' Johnny said, and he was right, they do. It's Ego City. Just about everyone on there is the big I am. And if they didn't have an ego beforehand, they soon get one inside. So there's everybody strutting about and here's Johnny, a nobody no one knows. Quite often lads recognize each other from the out, or get Cat A'ed as a group. That wasn't the case with our boy. Given his background, he wouldn't have been warned that he'd have to stand up for himself, although obviously feared he would. But as it turned out, his personality played to his favour, which, knowing him, didn't surprise me.

Johnny told me he tried to keep himself to himself as far as he could early doors, but the big plus for him was landing a job almost straight away. That's unusual, as normally officers went with established people on the wing who they knew could be trusted. But Johnny knew how to conduct himself. He's very polite, a good talker, excellent at reasoning and likeable without looking soft. Definite attributes. If he was a prison officer, he wouldn't be the one going toe to toe with people, he'd have the interpersonal skills and sense of humour to keep things ticking over.

'I was asked to work on the servery, one of the best things that could have happened because it acted as my introduction to people. You had the likes of Whitey and Michael Sharp coming through, big hardened criminals, who it gave me a chance to get on the right side of.'

We'll come on to White and Sharp in a bit, but the main thing here is that, pretty much straight off, he had a bit of an identity of his own, upfront and useful. If not friends, he'd have made plenty of acquaintances and had influence through doing little favours . . . 'Is there any chips left?' 'Aye, here you go . . .' that sort of carry-on. That's how prison works and he'd have slotted straight into it.

Which is not to say the place wouldn't still have messed with his noggin. 'The other thing about Cat A is that it was always so fucking quiet,' said Johnny, 'not a lot of noise at all.'

It's true. There'd be no loud music or the sort of racket you might expect on other wings. The mood on Cat A is maybe best described as us and them. You felt it in the air. The rest of the jail could be quite relaxed when you let them out of their cells, even K Wing, the largest and liveliest of the lot. As an officer, you'd just mill about and get on with stuff. On there, E Wing, a very small unit, staff went about in twos.

'And most of the lads didn't give a fuck, mate. They were either looking at big sentences or were already serving them, so thought themselves untouchable. There was always this tension, with White and Sharp especially. Because both were big fuckers, it was almost as if people wanted them to get it on. For entertainment, I reckon, but it felt like anything could go off any moment.'

I know ego isn't a noise, but it might as well be; let's call it mood music. If I were a member of staff, as I was with Sharp once on the twos landing, and told them to get behind their door, they'd just look at you, nothing there, do their own thing. Imagine those last couple of minutes in a football changing room before a big game . . . it's a bit like that but with your adrenaline pumping all the time.

And then there's the smell of Cat A, and E Wing more generally. Compared to other wings, it was very sterile.

'It always smelled of disinfectant,' said Johnny. 'It was a small unit, self-contained, and everyone's cell were very clean.' That was because these guys never got off the unit unless it was to go to healthcare or court and, procedurally, would get moved at least once a month from cell to cell. So it was in your interest to keep yours in mint condition because at some point you are going to be living in someone else's. 'It was hospital-like,' Johnny said, and whether it was orderlies mopping or prisoners scrubbing their floors, I never went on there when I didn't see someone at it. Maybe it's another reason why Johnny hoovers up at home so much now!

Either way, he stayed Cat A for about a year before moving to B Wing, where I heard of his qualities and collared him for a year with us in healthcare. For a Cat A con in particular, a year must feel like an eternity when, remanded while awaiting trial, you have no idea how long you'll be forced to stay there.

But let's get back to Whitey, an absolute monster of a physical specimen. I've endured a tumble or two with him myself, this notorious gangster and member of a well-known Liverpool crime family, aka 'Britain's toughest prisoner'.

'He was there when I arrived,' said Johnny, of a man soon to be jailed indefinitely for conspiracy to buy guns and a threat to kill a teenager. 'Around Ramadan, when I'd just got my job on the servery, I sneaked the last of the samosas back to my cell. Whitey was pretending to be a Muslim at the time and no one was checking back then – he just "changed religion" for the scran. Even so, everyone on the unit called him Hamza because they didn't dare call him anything else. He was a monster and got wind of what I'd done.

'He shouted down from the landing, "You've had them samosas, you little shit!"

'I said, "Was it fuck samosas. It was pies. And anyway, what the fuck's it got to do with you, you Scouse cunt?" Being naive, I suppose. It was one of the biggest mistakes I ever made in jail.'

About ten minutes later, Johnny was in his cell. 'Next news, the door slowly opens and the cell goes dark, this fucking giant of a man standing in the doorway. "What did you fucking call me?" he says. I said, "I didn't say anything to you, Tom."

'He give me a crack on the side of my head, and as I fell, it hit the edge of the bunk bed. Blood was pissing out; I've got the scar to this day. But to be fair, he did only give me that one slap. He could have fucking annihilated me. The bell went off on the wing. Everyone was put behind the doors and Whitey got dragged away. He spent about a week on the seg', and from the day he came back was right as rain.'

As officers, our job then would have been to put Whitey on a charge and ask the victim if he wanted to give evidence. Johnny had other ideas.

'"Go down and be a witness?" I said, "Do I fuck!" He had no option but to crack me. He couldn't let someone on the wing talk to him like that, could he? But don't forget, I was new to this. I had no idea what I was getting involved in. If I'd known then what I know now, I'd have given him the samosas and thrown in a couple of chapatis. Anyway, because I hadn't said anything he shook my hand and we were fine. In fact, I think if I'd asked him to look out for me, he would have done. I was an older guy in there. He's a big tough lion, but how he was with me showed there must be some compassion in the man.'

And as for Michael Sharp, who'd killed ex-cop turned car dealer David Ward while robbing his house, he was a proper hard case too. Sharp had ruled the roost at HMP Wakefield, or Monster Mansion as it's known on account of all the perverts, but it wasn't so clear-cut at Strangeways. Johnny used to play chess with him, which got us pondering if Sharp was tougher than White.

Sharp was about six foot two and around nineteen or twenty stone, so comparable to White in physique. I'd say his arms had a twenty-inch radius, a brutish-looking fucker but with a bit of a babyface, built like a fat powerlifter. Toned up, he could have gone on stage as a bodybuilder. He walked like a carpet-fitter, as if he'd got a roll of Axminster under each arm; he'd definitely fill a doorway.

'He was one of those lads who aren't backward in coming forward,' said Johnny. 'They'd walk straight into your cell – "Who are you? What you in for?" – which is what he did with me. You can't help but notice him. He'd just take stuff . . . your canteen, your food and what have you . . .' In other words, he was a bully.

'He was also one of those who people would stand and talk to, even if they'd rather not. You'd laugh at his jokes even if they weren't funny. You know how it is, when you can't wait to get out of somebody's company. It's uncomfortable, isn't it? Well, Sharp being in front of you was like that. You don't want to be there but you just have to entertain them because of what they are.'

Not that any of that was likely to impress Tom White.

'There was always a niggle between them, but they never went up against each other, did they?' said Johnny. 'Whitey would have won, I think, but there wouldn't have been much in it.'

Think of this as King Kong versus Godzilla, or that *Deadliest Warrior* show that was on TV: 'Who'd win a fight between a Viking and a Samurai?' Anyone with any sense would bow down to White, but Sharp didn't. Only needling each other, mind. Like me, Johnny reckoned there was too much to lose for either of them to really get it on. Quite the ringside seat for a bloke who'd never been to jail before.

'Tom obviously knew that Sharpy was a big strong unit as well and might catch him on an off day, while Sharpy thought the same, no doubt. They were both aware that they might lose face. That's what the crack was in jail. Your reputation was everything.'

My money would also be on White, just because of his brute strength. If he was lifting weights in the gym, the bar might bend but his arms quite definitely did not. Which, by the way, is why American jails and took the barbells, dumb-bell and kettlebells off prison yards. Physical size is a massive problem for officers when they are trying to contain people who are mentally unstable. It's why officers can be scared of lads like Whitey too. Why wouldn't they be? He could snap most of them in half. No wonder a newcomer like Johnny hated E Wing. He did well to stick it out as long as he did and come out sane the other end. 'You needed eyes in the back of your head – at all times. You never knew who you were mixing with,' he said. 'We would get some very dangerous lads on there . . . terrorists, you name it.'

As we've heard, Strangeways' Cat A isn't a big unit. It could house thirty-five prisoners, tops, but there were usually fewer. But what it lacked in quantity it more than made up for in its quality of dodgy types. 'One day I was playing pool with a guy,' Johnny went on. 'Scottish bloke. Strictly speaking, he wasn't a Cat A inmate, he was an attempted escapee, but a decent lad, I thought. We were getting on great. I won the game 3–0 and, as I turned away, he smashed his cue on the back of my head. "That was for taking the piss," he said.'

Off went the E Wing alarm bells . . .

'They locked the joint down and dragged him off to seg', but brought him back three hours later. What's more, he went back in the cell next door – and you can talk to your neighbour through the toilet.

'"Johnny," the cheeky chap said. "I'm sorry about what happened in there . . . but you wound me up, beating me."

'"Fuck me," I said. "It was a bit over the top, wasn't it?"

'"Suppose so," he said. "Couldn't lend us a teabag, could you?"'

With the seg' and VP also on there, E Wing is basically a Cat A jail within a jail, and therefore keeps every duty officer on their toes. Yet even there, the modern way of putting inexperienced and unsuitable youngsters in charge was an issue. And of course, hardened criminals soon twig on to that.

'You'd get these raw twenty-five-year-old officers, lasses quite often,' Johnny said. 'If it had kicked off big time, they'd have been absolutely destroyed. Prison officers aren't all big lumps like you, are they, Mr Sams? There were sex offenders on the VP unit too, bad lads down the seg', and our lot on top. Inexperience isn't what you need.'

No, it isn't. I wouldn't want any young son or daughter of mine taking such risks, would you? And in the years to come, it would get worse.

When I started at Strangeways, you had to have been on the job two years to be trusted on E Wing. Then, from August 2015, when the so-called modernization came in, they began to rotate it – overtime shift here and there – and the cons ended up running the joint. One day, a lad was kicking off about salad. He was an inch away from one officer, up in his face, screaming and spitting. I'm thinking, *Just drop him, or this is going to kick off*. Then he went in this female officer's face: same thing, invading her personal space. Know what they did? Phoned the kitchen for another salad. Wow! No bottle, and he knew it.

But don't just take my word for it. Here's Johnny again . . .

'Some of these people are on thirty-year stretches for horrible things. You've young 'uns managing lunatics. You need experience on a wing like that. Screws can't be bullies. They do need interpersonal skills, but also physical presence. If not, they will get eaten up.'

For Johnny, though, things got marginally better on B Wing and then much better.

'You came and rescued me, Mr Sams. I'd spent three weeks banged up twenty-four-seven on B Wing, which was meant to be drug-free and had an easy-going atmosphere. I'd come from E Wing, which had a reputation, so they didn't want me loose on the landings.' Until a certain Yorkshireman came down to see him. 'My door opened and you were stood there. "I believe you're looking for a job. I'll come back at five o'clock, teatime, and bring the orderlies we've already got." You shut the door, locked it and that was that. I thought you wouldn't come back. But you did.'

I've learned to be a good judge of character. Thirty seconds, I knew.

'You brought the two lads, locked them in with me and fucked off for ten minutes while they talked about the job. Then you took them off again and said, "Get your kit together. I'll be back in half an hour." In fact, you were gone an hour, so I got nervous again, thinking, *Fucking hell, they didn't like me.*' Before, like a big breath of fresh of air, the key went in the door and there was my happy smiling face.

Next stop: 'A different fucking planet.'

If E Wing had been an education for Johnny, healthcare was something else again. Not quite as physically intimidating, perhaps, but with an atmosphere and cast list little could prepare you for.

Take Wobbly Bob. How best to describe *him*?

He was an outcast from society, basically, a lad from the traveller community.

Wobbly Bob was usually on normal location. When he touched down on healthcare it was often because he'd been acting up. The nickname wasn't meant to be cruel; if anything, it was a term of endearment. He'd done more than his share of drugs and alcohol, which had left him unsteady on his feet. That's what the prisoners called him, and the staff took it on too. Bob himself seemed quite happy with that. He was a bit of a sorry figure, and you could tell it made him feel accepted.

This time, he came in on Christmas Eve and was being a proper arse, restrained in reception and brought up to us under restraint.

We took everything off him, but it wasn't long before he'd smashed the telly we let him have. About ten o'clock on Christmas morning, he went off on one again. Now, due to my 'dynamic security' philosophy I'd got to know him well, so I set about talking him round. He stopped banging his head on the wall, which was reasonable, but then he took his tracksuit top off and tried to strangle himself with it.

'For fuck's sake, Bob, pack it in,' I told him as he stood there in his prison boxers and T-shirt. 'We've taken everything off you – do we have to take your friggin' clothes too?'

Our usual nurse manager, Bradders, was off that day, so a nurse manager called Sandy – or 'Matron' as Johnny called her – took charge. So I was giving him this colourful chat and Sandy was stood behind me, with a bit of a cough by the sound of it. Eventually, I calmed him down. 'No more fucking about, or I'll have no choice but to wrap you in a suicide blanket.'

I stepped out of the cell and who should be there but the jail's number-one governor, Dickie Vince. Now, I liked Dickie – we all did. He was one of the few governors who'd come in on Christmas Day even when not on duty, go to every wing and shake every staff member by the hand, wishing you a merry Christmas. He knew us all by name too. Impressive.

This, though, was awkward. I realized now Sandy hadn't got a cough: it had been a signal. Meanwhile there I'd been effin' and jeffin'. 'Governor!' I said, thinking on my size elevens. 'Happy Christmas!'

'And also to you, Mr Samworth. Is everything under control?'

'Quite definitely, Governor,' I said, and off he wandered.

Johnny laughed as we remembered that, and it brought to mind what followed too, because Christmas Day is often a shitstorm inside. This one wasn't, and that was mainly down to Sandy's generosity with her colleagues and, it has to be said, good sense and experience in dealing with everyone else.

The usual routine was, get the prisoners out, give them their medication, let them have a shower and deal with people as best we can. We'd try to get as much done as possible in the morning so, you never know, we might have a peaceful after-noon of it. It's a lousy time to be in jail for anybody, is Christmas, either side of the door.

Sandy was in the servery and she'd decided we staff were going to have a special feed. The thing with Sandy, though, was that she was never going to use supermarket brands; she'd rather raid the nearest farm shop. There must have been sixty quid's worth of bacon, sausage, beans, tomatoes, mushrooms, the full nine yards. She invited the nurses from outpatients downstairs, plus us lot, officers, healthcare assistants and such. She cooked all morning and put it under a hotplate to keep it warm.

When it got to dinner time – aka lunchtime for my southern readers – we served the prisoners as usual. The smell of what was coming to us, meanwhile, was incredible. She'd cooked everything . . . the full Monty. I was drooling. An army marches on its stomach. God knows how it must have smelled to the inmates, those who weren't orderlies anyway. Well, there has to be perks with the job, doesn't there, and they'd get their bit of turkey later.

We had three by now: Johnny, Morrissey and another lad, Smith. Prisoners weren't supposed to share our grub, but there'd be plenty left and Sandy decided it shouldn't go to waste. So after the roll count and locking everyone else up, as you do, it was off to the association room, where the nurses had pushed the tables together, thrown on a paper tablecloth, a bit of holly, and there sat Johnny, Morrissey and Smith, about to tuck in with the healthcare staff. It was quite the scene.

Now obviously, everyone was supposed to be locked up while we ate, and I did think for about ten seconds, *What if the top governor comes back?* But then I thought, *You know what, it's Christmas Day. If we get a bollocking, we get a bollocking.*

In the afternoon, we had all the prisoners out, playing pool and cards – not for money, that's not allowed. There wasn't a bad word. The day was a real tonic for everyone. If anyone had kicked off, it could have got naughty, but Sandy and the rest of us knew they wouldn't. There's your dynamic security in action.

In many ways, Johnny Mo's story is unusual. True, when he arrived on Strangeways' E Wing he followed the same pattern most first-time prisoners do. Stomach churning. Worry about what might be happening to family outside. Fear. Depression. Misery. Paranoia. Stress. Uncertainty. Loss of personal control . . . I could go on. When you've been inside before, you at least know what to expect but, as he's told us, when it's a brand-new experience it can be hell on earth.

What wasn't so usual, though, is that Johnny's story had a bit of a happy ending, and at Strangeways, and in the prison service generally, you'd have to say that's very rare indeed.

In the end his honesty saved him, because he obviously got believed. Once everyone else involved had been locked up and it all went to trial, he again just told it how it were, and the prosecution presented no evidence to pin the drugs on him. At the finish, his total of two and a half years served was for the fags and booze. While remanded for a drugs conspiracy, he wound up simultaneously serving his sentence for the lesser crime.

And now, ten years on, despite a few lasting limitations like not being able to have his own trucks, he seems to be over the experience and doing all right, so much so that he can even find some of it funny.

Darren Spensley is a lad we will meet again. But he too got sent down fresh as a daisy, having never been in serious trouble.

As we've seen with Johnny, in what can be a hostile atmosphere, violent outbreaks are a constant danger. *Who are you looking at? Want some?* You could get in a brawl at least three times a day if you wanted to, quite definitely. When Daz and I met up recently, he recalled an incident in the showers at HMP Kirkham, a Cat D prison near Preston.

'It was only my second week inside, so I cried myself to sleep most nights,' he admitted. 'But as soon as that door opened, I was the biggest, hardest lad on the wing. I'd left my shower gel (Topaz, 69p a bottle; put a pint of it on your hand and you'd get three bubbles out of it) in the Bronx, as the shower block at Kirkham was known.

'When I got back to my cell, drying myself off, I realized I'd left the Topaz and had best go back for it. "Awright, mate," I said to this big hairy naked guy. "I left my shower gel – it's the orange one."' You could climb from one cubicle to another; no locks, just a glass pane door, no privacy or security.

'He was a right brute. "Fuck off, dickhead," he said. "It's my shower gel now." I was nearly in tears, stood there in my towel. I realized that we were going to have to get at it.

'"Give it me back," I said. "Listen, newbie," he said, "fuck off or I'll do you in." So I went for my gel and he went for me. Well, that was that. The towel fell off and there we were, the two of us, wet through and at it, big-style. Before long the shower was full of blood – his – and this goon was out sparko. I got my shower gel, fucked off back to my cell, and from that day never had a bit of hassle in that prison. If I'd lost my shower gel that day, I'd have been scrapping every week. I was there just short of three years and nine months.'

From there Daz went to Forest Bank – or Wacky Warehouse, as older cons called it, because all it needed was a ball pool and slide – and eventually to Strangeways, where he met yours truly. It didn't take long for me to spot his value, so Daz got made a cleaner too.

And on healthcare anything could happen.

'Do you remember the traveller lad who came on the wing, for protection or something?' he asked. 'Tall lad, phone up his arse.'

I did. On healthcare, we had an SOs' PIN at our disposal so we could give patients a phone call and pay with our credit, legit. One day, an officer saw that this bright spark was taking advantage. Did he deal with it? Did he fuck! He said, 'Sammo, come and sort this lad out.' So off I goes to the social room and there he is, the traveller, with the phone up to his ear this time. 'Oi, off it!' I said. At first he tried to ignore me, then slammed the thing back in its cradle. 'Do you know who I am? I'm a fucking street fighter, me.' I just ragged him off back to the cell. No messing.

But the time Daz remembered – when this kid had a phone up his backside – was in the laundry. After fishing it out, he asked Eric, who worked there, to hide it and Eric said, 'No. This laundry is my domain. You're putting fuck all in here.' So off the kid went to the gym and shoved it under a treadmill instead, before leading us to it and saying, 'Look what the cleaners did,' in revenge.

That was another risk for unwary prisoners – bloody-minded wily bastards you just couldn't predict. Senseless to thee and me.

'Worst thing, though, was when I was walking to visits with him, in my case to see my missus,' said Daz. 'We hadn't got very far when it began: all these shouts and insults from the cons who saw us go. There was a right deluge – "You dirty horrible rapist, you filthy fucking nonce . . ." It was obvious they were after stringing him up; I'd no idea what for. When we got to the other end I asked the lass who was taking us what the fuck that had been about. She admitted she shouldn't have brought me down alongside him, because he was a VP [vulnerable prisoner], and now they might think I was one too.'

In fact, a lot of people were after this kid's head. Strangeways, of course, held lots of Salford lads, and he'd shot one of them on the out, bigged himself up about it. '*I've done him, I've done him.*' He was sent to healthcare because the seg' wouldn't have him.

'Well, that didn't help me, did it?' said Daz. 'They were all, "You fucking nonces," just because I was with him. You get tarred with the same brush.'

It might not have been as openly threatening as E Wing but, as we will see, healthcare carried a fair few dangers of its own.

2. Home Improvement

Not everyone is inside for violent crime, of course. Now and then the prison would land some real fish-out-of-water white-collar types who were no physical threat to anyone. Often they were family men who had somehow fallen into shit way over their head. Mr Big locally, perhaps, but now floundering out of their depth. Imagine how *them* fellas must've felt on their way in.

That said, in my entire time at Strangeways I probably met only about a dozen white-collar criminals, all told. And Lee Robson wasn't one of them, because he was only in there three weeks, and that was as recently as 2019, three years after I'd left the service. He is another lad who got in touch after reading about my own experiences.

Lee, a canny forty-year-old Geordie kid, and his cousin, Harry, got themselves jailed for defrauding investors. At one point they were rich enough to bid for a large property in California. Had they got it, it would have cost them up to fifteen million quid.

So how had they got their hands on that sort of dosh?

It was on account of what the judge called 'a complex web of business failure', before adding that a twenty-one-month sentence apiece should 'serve as a stark warning to other rogue directors and traders that the Insolvency Service will strenuously tackle financial wrongdoing in order to protect members of the public.' In other words, he made an example of them. Well, that's how they saw it anyway.

And if coming into Strangeways was a shock, it wasn't made any easier by getting sent down *eight years* after the company in question collapsed, by which time Lee was married with two kids.

When we spoke and he agreed to share his tale, Lee's only real concern was that it might be a bit dull compared to the rest. Well, it might lack guns, jailbreaks, fighting and such, but boring it quite definitely is not.

Born and raised on an east end estate in Newcastle, Lee went to a nice Catholic primary school and spent his time as most kids did in the 1980s, playing football, knocking on doors and running away, climbing on garages, jumping gardens – nothing worse than that. Funnily enough, while at high school, he also played rugby against King Edward's, a posh lot my team of sixteen-year-old roughheads met on tour from Sheffield. Small world, eh?

After school, he won himself a psychology degree at Liverpool University, intending to be a sports psychologist, but by the age of twenty-one or so had begun to dabble in property investment instead. Liverpool is where Lee also met his future wife, who is from Manchester, which is why they both live there now. At this point, by the way, prior to the property career, cousin Harry became a Seventies dancer in a Newcastle nightclub for £30 a night.

'I joined him that summer, for a bit of fun at first, until I worked out how we could invest the extra cash.' The cousins went into property full-time, and soon decided to expand the company.

'We got up to about thirty-five houses of our own,' said Lee. 'Student digs, used to rent them out. We bought them to renovate and refinanced them when they were finished, took the cash and bought another one.'

The years that followed sound heady and pretty carefree. As the money from their property investments piled up, they started to become known around town.

Simple example: if they were buying a house for a hundred grand in 2004, and renovating it for twenty, having spent a hundred and twenty, they'd then refinance it for a hundred and sixty, pull forty grand out and buy another one, thereby building their portfolio. But as soon as the noughties recession kicked in, property values fell and so that plan pretty much came to a halt.

'When the refinancing stopped, we started to take money from individual investors to fund the purchase of the properties. And we kept doing that for about two years, perfectly fine.'

Then, though, they tried to set up a pension fund, which I'll not bore you with the mechanics of but was basically about the investment of pensions in property. The rental income would give a return and, in ten years' time, say, the portfolio would be sold, with 40 per cent of the profit coming to Lee and Harry, and 60 per cent going back into the pension funds.

But then the collapse of the housing market worsened matters and before long the entire enterprise went tits up.

'The pension fund got pushed further and further back,' said Lee, 'until 2011, when the whole thing collapsed. We were left with a load of investor debt. We lost all the houses and, as we weren't FCA, Financial Conduct Authority, registered – you don't have to be by law – we didn't have the protections from them we could have had.'

The investors certainly had no comeback on their cash, which if you are FCA-registered you do, up to fifty grand. 'They lost a lot of dough, while we lost all our houses. Bankruptcy came in 2011.'

The media is a double-edged sword, isn't it? Bankruptcy got them in the local papers too. 'I didn't realize it at the time,' Lee said, 'but I was wounded. Newcastle's a small city, so it made the front page of the *Chronicle*. It was embarrassing. I lost confidence, businesswise. If I could keep out of everyone's road, I'd not have to face anybody in a shop or anything.'

In fact, a *Manchester Evening News* report states that 'a previous company, run by the pair renovating student housing, had gone bust in 2009, owing more than £3 million to investors,' after which they'd set up a new firm, again 'offering investment opportunities and also buying and refurbishing student properties.' Be that as it may, Lee and Harry's money-making ambitions were sunk, but almost another decade would have to pass before things really came back to bite them on the arse.

Along with starting a family, for Lee the intervening years were spent working as a street performer with Harry, including three summer seasons in Blackpool. Then, in 2014, he got into e-commerce via Shopify and such. That's still how he earns his corn today. 'Harry and me went back to wor comedy act, dancing like knobs, which was how we'd financed wor first student house in Liverpool, actually. Now, though, I'd no choice. My wife was pregnant for the first time and we'd no money.

Harry is still a street performer, but these days with fire and knives. He has always been very athletic.'

Until, in January 2018, a letter dropped on the doormat. 'By then, my kids were five and three years old and I'd never had a sniff of any more trouble. My life had moved on.' When Lee opened the letter to read that HMRC was taking them both to court he burst into tears, 'and I don't cry often, if ever. It was pure panic. If I could have run away, I would have done. It was a hell of a shock. Crown Court was alien to me.

'This sounds like a side point, but we'd saved to take the kids on holiday in February. I realize there's bigger things, but it ruined that entirely. I read that letter and my head was gone. I didn't know what was going to happen, didn't know the court process. How long would I get if it went wrong? How would I defend myself?'

Lee described the eighteen months until being put away in July 2019 as worse than the actual sentence. As with Johnny Mo, it was the fear of the unknown. How would he explain it to the kids? 'That is all I'm arsed about, my wife and kids. I'm normal. We like to go to the beach with the kids and the dog.'

And throughout that long wait, 'there was a load of stuff with barristers getting it wrong, realizing wor case wasn't as strong as they thought. The HMRC had us on technical points, and on the morning of the trial they offered us a deal to knock £600,000 off the indictment.'

Lee's mam and dad had taken it all really badly, worried sick. His missus was too. The lad decided he couldn't stomach it any more, went guilty, and was sentenced to twenty-one months, with six to serve.

I wondered if he could point to a moment, back in the day, when he might have avoided the nightmare that had followed.

'August 2010 was when I really started to think, *This is going wrong, this*. That was when we started getting investment through desperation. I was twenty-seven, still a kid really, trying to keep things going. Looking back, we should have recognized it was failing and shut up shop there and then. But we were very naive, and actually what we got sentenced for was all the investment we took in after that point.'

While I was working as a prison officer, I'd gone bankrupt myself. It was 2011, and my and Amy's circumstances had changed. I ended up with one of these IVAs – Individual Voluntary Arrangements – where they put everything in a pot. One day this guy comes to me and says, 'Let's do a proper breakdown of your income and expenditure.' Went through everything – car tax, insurance – and came back and said, 'You are £350 shy a month.' I had to tell them at Strangeways. I remember the court thing, filling in forms, absolutely cacking it. And on paper that was just small fry; we didn't have thirty-five properties to contend with and loads of investors and tenants righteously banging on our door.

'The mortgage companies had taken back all the houses,' recalled Lee, 'so my bankruptcy papers were massive. Interview after interview . . . the complexity of it all took ages. But part of the reason we'd got so carried away is we had this big London law firm working for us.

'I first engaged them when I was about twenty-four. I know now I was too young to be doing anything like that – didn't have a fucking clue, really. This lawyer was telling us we were wonderful, had a brilliant business model, blah blah blah . . .'

Understandably, he was easily persuaded.

'We also had a guy who stress-tested the business model, an economist from a massive financial TV channel. These people were better placed than me and had about thirty years' experience on us. I was sat at these meetings thinking, *Well, if they're telling us this is shit hot, it must be shit hot.* So we carried on longer than we should have.'

And in fact, before Lee and Harry started investing pensions in residential property, you hadn't been able to do it at all. It was only with the launch of a new Strength in Places Fund (SIPF) that it had become allowed. 'It was a new concept to open pension avenues that weren't there before.'

The pair received advice that they should stop taking on new investments after their original companies failed, but chose to keep going. Along with prison time, it also got them the longest ban from being company directors – fifteen years – the HMRC had ever handed down. 'Two lads from Newcastle who couldn't afford to defend themselves . . . it was a feather in HMRC's cap to say we've slammed these bastards. I was out of my depth. I've still got about six years to go.

'Your solicitor appoints a barrister for you,' Lee went on. 'I asked the barrister, "If we go to trial, can we win?" "Yes, we can. But trials can go either way. I can be convinced but the jury can go against you. Can we win? Yes. Will we win? Can't promise you. If we lose, are we going away? Yes. Maybe for as much as nine years . . ."'

Now we've arrived at one of my big beefs with our justice system: plea bargaining. It might surprise a few to know that we have it in the UK as most would think it just an American thing, but no. In Crown Court, the defence can ask the judge what the likely maximum sentence will be if their client pleads guilty; and the earlier the plea is entered, the bigger the discount, although in England and Wales the maximum is one third. In magistrates' court, the prosecution and defence can come to a deal where the defendant pleads guilty to some charges and the prosecution drops the rest, which encourages people to cop for crimes they haven't done. In my opinion, both are completely flawed.

To begin with, their barrister seems to have played it by ear. 'He said we just had to find a balance,' said Lee. '"In the next eighteen months this is going to go all over the place . . . it's going to go up, it's going to go down, it's going to change, a bumpy ride . . . buckle yourself in . . ."'

'I took my dad to that first conference,' he continued. 'He wanted to support me, but it was a mistake. As a parent, all you want to do is fix it for your kids, and he couldn't. I regret having had him there.'

In the end it went really crazy. 'The prosecution barrister's mother died just before the trial,' said Lee, 'so he didn't turn up. He sent a junior who didn't want to go up against my barrister, as he was known to be very good, which is why they offered us a deal that we would never have got had that set of circumstances not happened. The first indictment had been £900,000, dropped to £300,000.'

Lee's barrister said there would be a 10 per cent chance of getting a suspended sentence, although anything within a range of twenty-four months would be difficult. 'But he said we were lads of good character, there was no greed involved, no evidence of a penny spent on ourselves, no posh watches, fast cars – it had all gone into the company. In the end we did get below twenty-four months: we got the twenty-one, but it wasn't suspended.'

Lee and Harry went for sentencing on Thursday, 11 July, but the judge ran out of time, so remanded them overnight to come back the next day. 'The story made every paper that morning. Our barrister reckoned the judge hadn't been able to suspend it without looking soft.'

Next stop: Strangeways.

Going off to court having gone guilty was horrendous. The judge had told them, 'Pack a bag,' so Lee knew he wouldn't be coming home. 'I cried like a baby leaving the house,' he said. 'It was the complete lack of control. Awful.'

I asked Lee if he was frightened.

'I'm not a macho man by any means, but no. Not for myself. I was scared for my wife, because she'd have to run the business, house, and look after the kids on her own. Actually, I was scared for my kids, too. They wouldn't know where I was. I was scared of what people might say to or about them.'

Lee was sentenced on the same day as five lads who'd been on a plane to Vegas, got pissed and ended up wrestling. The plane had had to divert and they got locked up for longer than Lee, who got to be good pals with them because they hadn't expected to end up in Strangeways either.

They would have met in the holding cells at court which, in the hopefully unlikely event that this happens to you, is where you'd end up, talking to other people who are shitting themselves. You then all go on a bus and, unless you're Cat A like Johnny Mo, get siphoned off into holding cells at Strangeways reception with lads you've been to court with, so immediately you've got something in common.

For Lee and Harry, though, even that wasn't straightforward.

'I know somebody who works at Forest Bank. She told me the day before, "Your bus will be going to Forest Bank, the local prison for Manchester court. As soon as I know you're coming in, I'll put your name on reception, get you in the same cell as your cousin. Don't worry, it'll all be fine."'

Imagine his surprise, therefore, to be told as he came aboard, 'You're not going to Forest Bank, mate, you're going to Strangeways.' Even that little crumb of comfort had gone straight out the window.

In Strangeways reception, meanwhile, with its portrait of HM the Queen on the wall and music blasting from the radio, Lee, Harry and their fellow arrivals got their first taste of prison cuisine.

'They gave us fish and chips. The fucking peas were like bullets, but I was starving so I ate it. We were sat talking to this lad who was giving it loads. He said he'd been to ten prisons, in for kidnap. He was stood on seats, banging the cameras, kicking the door, fine with us but being a knob. He'd been shifted from Durham, he said, because he'd phones up his arse, hoped he wasn't going to be on some wing or other here as he might meet someone he banged out – in his mid-twenties, giving it all that!

'Then this other guy arrives, a Manc lad on remand for robbery. He pitches in, "If any black bastards like this give you any shit, come see me on A Wing." The kid who'd been mouthing off sat straight down, no more said. That was when I thought, *Fucking hell, I'm here now. This is it.*'

You can see why he would, although truth to tell, their Manc 'rescuer' too would have just been grandstanding, trying to put the frighteners on the newbies. Put it this way: there are plenty of lads inside he would *not* have been coming out with openly racist shit like that in front of. You did get such characters in Strangeways, though thankfully they are in the minority.

'It was a hell of an awakening. An officer comes in with four green files. "Cook!" he says. That's my cousin, Harry. Then he reads another name, and another, and another and off they all go to the induction unit, A Wing. It was bad. There were eight of us in that holding cell, and I'd hoped Harry and me were seen as a unit, but no. "We're meant to be in the same cell," I said, but it cut no mustard.'

Lee and the other three were then hived off to I Wing, which if you remember is mainly detox. 'I was going in the top jail and walked up the main drag, nervously looking around with my bag of gear. When we got there it was like the land of the dead. It smelled disgusting.'

I couldn't help but laugh at that, remembering the first time I walked up the main drag to K Wing. Pennington's Back Passage, we used to call it, and that had its own smell – not quite as bad as I Wing's, mind.

'I felt like I was watching a TV show. The gate that leads into the hexagon was locked, so we were waiting around. I saw these old blokes shuffle through on Zimmer frames to get their meds. *How bad do you have to have been to be that old in here?* I thought. *What've you done?* I later learned they'd come off K Wing, which while I was there was where they housed the nonces.' That's why it was locked.

'When they went, we were allowed into that central area

and they opened the door to I Wing, but it was silent at first. It must have been half eight or nine at night and everyone was already banged up. The pool table had a cover on. I was looking around . . . Wow!'

Lee and the lads he was with – a pair of addicts among them – were processed in the little office area. He was told he'd be sharing with a lad called Nasir, doing twenty-two years for drugs and guns. Turned out Nasir was also 'a listener', a job that, like cleaning, was given to more trustworthy types, as they would visit lads around the jail who were struggling mentally. Even so, nothing can prepare you for when you first walk into your cell.

'I expected it to be small, but not that small,' Lee said. 'This guy had been in ages so had gear everywhere. Shitloads of food, he had, packs of noodles, twenty shower gels – it was like an off-licence. As I walked in, he was praying. I didn't know the etiquette, so just sat very quietly until he'd finished, thinking about how narrow the room was.'

Prayers done, Nasir seemed a bit standoffish at first, but once he realized Lee was all right, they got talking. He told him about his case and Nasir told him about his. 'Twenty-two years! I got claustrophobic for him. My head started to go.'

At this stage, by the way, Lee still didn't know his sentence. This was on the Thursday night, while he was remanded overnight waiting for it. 'Nasir was telling me, "The fucking judge I got is the worst on the circuit, outside guidelines all the time. I should've got twelve years, not twenty-two. He's a cunt. Everybody on this wing has been sentenced by him. Who've you got?" It was the same bloke, of course.'

Nasir then slid the door flap back, called a guard over and

asked if he'd give them a call at 6.30 a.m. for court. 'I was grateful for that. He made us a cheese toastie with the toastie maker he'd got under his bed, gave us a Penguin, a cup of coffee, then I went to bed.'

Not that he got much sleep. 'Itchy, scratchy blankets, the blue concrete pillow, fucking ceiling right in my face . . . All the windows were smashed and I was freezing. When I got up I looked in the mirror while I was cleaning my teeth: *My kids will just be getting up now.*

'I'd already had enough. One night.'

In court, at least the judge half apologized. 'He hammered us for about two hours and for the last hour sang wor praises. "I know the damage this is going to cause your wife and children," he told me straight to my face, "but my hands are tied."' Each of them received a twenty-one-month sentence that, with good behaviour, might mean actually serving a third of that, seven months. 'We'd been in custody since May, so I calculated it in my head: home for Christmas, and that became my mantra.'

To Lee's relief, at Strangeways he went straight back in with Nasir, and soon it was Saturday morning, when he had his first experience of I Wing being busy.

'I opened the door and there's people everywhere, going for meds or a game of pool. Everybody looked pale. But then somebody shouted, "Are you the Geordie?" I said I was, aye, so he comes over for a chat straight away, knew people I know, went to a school near mine. Just the sheer connection of him being from the north-east and talking about familiar stuff was such a relief.'

Before he went on the landing, Nasir, whose nickname he

learned was Nas, had told Lee to be wary of the wing nutcase, a lad called Evan. 'On the nets all the time,' he'd said, referring to how inmates make a nuisance of themselves by jumping on the safety nets strung across landings. 'He's kettled people, poured boiling hot water on them. An absolute fucking nutjob. Stay a million miles away.'

'This Geordie kid and me were getting on sweet as a nut until it came time to get banged up again. "Anyway," he says, "nice to meet you, mate. I'm Evan." Next time I saw him he was on the nets. And not long afterwards this lad called Perry, in for terrorism, hit him on the head with a can of tuna and got escorted off to seg'.'

On the Saturday night, they got banged up at half past five. 'My cellmate goes, "Have you ever had a face pack on?" No. "Do you want one?" So he got us another Penguin and we watched a romcom with J-Lo on Film Four like we were at the beautician's. I'd have gone home at the drop of a hat, but it could have been a lot worse.'

That said, it took three days before he really settled, because that was how long it took to get properly in contact with his family.

'The whole phone PIN system is wrong,' said Lee. 'You get a one-minute phone call at reception to tell your missus and kids you're all right, but your head's gone then so you can't say what you want to. And once you are on a wing you need a registered PIN to use the phone there, and it could take weeks for it to be sorted.'

On the Sunday, his cellmate was getting all dressed up. 'He got *GQ* magazine for the aftershave samples and saved them for his visits. I'm thinking he'd be out for two hours and I'd be in a cell on my own for the first time, which would be completely weird. But when the guard came to get him he told me that I had visitors too.

'I was surprised. My sister had phoned up and sorted it for my missus and dad. So I went there with a lad called Wayne who had put a shotgun up a prostitute's fanny and blown it off. He was on A Wing, so I got him to ask about Harry and said to tell him I was all right.'

Prisoners become resourceful, you see. So here Lee was, networking like a good 'un, and he had only been in three days.

That first visit was emotional, but he at least knew they were coping. 'My phone PIN came through on the Monday, so I could ring home too. Harry didn't ring home once in the first fortnight, so I got a message to him through Nas to tell him to go to church so I could check he was OK. The following Sunday I saw that he was, and things just got easier.'

I wasn't surprised to hear that Lee applied for and got jobs on the servery, in the laundry and as a cleaner straight away. 'My cell door was open all day, I was that busy. I got to clean my clothes when I fancied it, take whatever food I wanted . . .'

The survival technique he came up with was to try and get on with everyone, prisoners and staff, whatever that took. 'I saw loads of fighting in my time there, but I was never a person who was going to go in and cause bother or owe anyone any dough. I was never going to try and sell stuff. I was focused on staying out of the way as much as I could and just getting through it.'

That's good advice, if you can get away with it, though easier said than done, of course, especially the bit about borrowing from other inmates. Never, ever do that. Also, even for officers, it pays to try and be a bit humble in how you are dealing with people.

'I was in with a lad called Ricky Grey,' said Lee – someone who only the other week was on the telly in a BBC documentary that exposed this Manchester crime gang who'd torture people with blowtorches and 'punish' women by raping them. 'He was barmy, Ricky, built like a boxer, massive. "He's built like he could kill you with his bare hands," the detective in the show said, and he was.

'He was offering the guards out, did not give a shit. But was he bothered about me? No. He was sound as a pound with me, because I wasn't any threat to him at all. Prison became a real education.'

Unusually, Lee stayed on I Wing until the time came to be shipped off to a Cat D jail, even though the other three he came in with were soon sent to A Wing, the induction wing, just as Harry and the three with him had been on arrival.

That could have been because he was safer there, a nice guy standing out as he did like a sore thumb. It might also have been because the prison wanted to keep him away from his cousin for some reason. Or that there has to be one listener on every wing and Nas had caused a stink about his last cellmate, but got on fine with Lee. Either way, he ticked every I Wing box except drugs, so stayed.

When Lee got told he was leaving Strangeways he was quite definitely surprised. 'As you will know, Sam, every inmate is an expert in European prison law, so you get plenty of advice. Playing pool on the wing, people would say, "Six months? You'll be whole sentence, pal. It's not worth them spending their dough on a bus to get you out." Others would tell you you'd be gone by Monday. "They don't want you in. You're taking up space from someone who could be a threat." And then others would say, "You'll probably do half the sentence here and then you'll be going to Risley, a Cat C."

'When it happened it was a shock. Tuesday morning, getting on with the laundry. I'd do the ones on a Monday and Tuesday, twos on a Wednesday and Thursday. I was listening to talk-SPORT because Rafa Benítez was leaving Newcastle and I was fucking devastated about it. Unbeknown to me, due to the noise from the radio and dryer, this officer was shouting at us from the end of the wing. I went up and he told me to pack my bags. I thought I was moving to another wing . . . *fuck, I'm settled, I know all the lads* . . . but he meant Kirkham.

'At first, I panicked – for two reasons. One, I didn't know if my cousin was coming too. And also, I'd got weirdly comfortable. I was phoning the kids by then every morning before school and every night before bed, so had that to look forward to. Bit of a routine.'

So there you go. If anyone sees jails as a deterrent, they're not. They very quickly become a way of life for everyone. For Lee, the worst thing about moving was that it again felt like losing control. 'It might be an odd thing to say but, for me, my worst moment at Strangeways was probably leaving.'

This isn't unusual. As an officer, I used to see a lot of lads on big sentences gutted about being uprooted. They get nice and comfy.

'All the way down to reception, I've got my see-through bag with all my shit chucked back in and I'm asking if my cousin's coming too. Nobody knew. I went for the strip search all over again and got put in a holding cell with five other lads, all moving south. So I'm thinking, *Fuck, am I in the wrong room here? Am I off to London?*

Then he got moved into another room and there Harry was, waiting for him. 'Yes! Me and him were hugging and catching up. By then I'd seen him at church one Sunday, but you couldn't talk there. There was another guy called Victor, big thickset guy from Leicester who had done twelve years already for firearms. He goes, "How long have you two been in then?" Three weeks. "Fuck off," he says. "And you're that excited? You've only just come in off the street."

'The van took us to Kirkham via Forest Bank, and we dropped off at Risley, so the journey took something like five hours. I'm six foot five and it was a really hot day in July, so I could see why the vans are called sweatboxes. When we got there, though, you were given a key to your cell door and you got your own toilet and shower.'

That might sound like luxury, especially after Strangeways, but let me tell you that many lads who have been imprisoned a long time just cannot handle it. Some commit crimes just to be sent back; I've seen it happen. They are being tested. Lee, keen to fit in wherever he got sent, was never going to be a problem, but even he could spot the issues and threats that open prisons like Kirkham have.

They do lovely samosas in the visits hall at Kirkham, which is in the village of that name in Lancashire. Lee admitted to stuffing his face with them and had 'Mars bars coming out my ears. I felt sick when I left, I'd eaten that much scran.'

Cat Ds, though, are still prisons. Open or not, people tend

to forget that. At Strangeways, with the sort of customers we had around, I never once dropped my guard, ever. Actually, that's not true. I did once and ended up blindsided, cracked on the jaw.

For prisoners, as Lee is keen to stress, probably the most shocking thing about being sent down is the absolute loss of personal control. You are cuffed on and off the van, undergo strip searches, have to do as you're told, and while things do loosen up a bit in Cat D jails, where you are given more leeway in your movements, they still come with dangers of their own and can in a lot of ways be even more unsettling.

'The holiday camp thing is a load of bollocks,' said Lee, who still visits Kirkham to this day on account of a project of his that we'll come on to in a bit. 'Last time I went, the sun was shining, there were ducks on the pond, and I thought it didn't look too bad. But when you are in there, you can't go home when you fancy it, or pop out for your kid's birthday party, and all those things add up. For me, it was just a dead environment where I couldn't grow at all.'

In fact, he told me his first couple of weeks there were worse than Strangeways. 'You can see the road. They may as well send you home. I wasn't even locked up any more. What a waste of time.'

But you have got to have something at least like a Cat D jail. You could never send people who have done twenty-year stretches for murder or whatever back on the street without easing them into it, to see how they get on in their own head as much as anything else.

'I didn't sleep well,' said Lee. 'The beds were shit – there was a metal end and I could never sleep flat. But we had curry nights, played cards. I'd make a cheesecake . . . It had a farm shop that my mam, dad and missus called in at. They sent me a message to say they'd just had a look, thought it was very nice, and hoped I was all right. The relief of knowing they'd been there, fifty yards over the road . . . But it's not going to be the same for someone without that sort of family network, is it?'

In such a relaxed atmosphere, the lads made friends quickly – people they still talk to. 'Everybody's doors were open and you'd be in and out of each other's cells. Everyone was bang into *Love Island*. I'd never normally watch anything like that, but because it was on at a specific time and everyone was talking about it, I got hooked.' They all became experts on tennis too, as Wimbledon was on. Soon HMP Kirkham felt more like working on an oil rig.

Cat D jails are mainly a waiting game for your first release on temporary licence (ROTL). First, you'll get a 'townie', when you are out for the day. High-risk lads have to go on that with an officer and complete a certain amount before they can leave on their own. Once you've done that you get your first over-nighter, and then they come in four-week increments – one night, two nights, three. The most you get is Friday to Tuesday, and your last one is a four-nighter.

'One bloke I was in with, from Chorlton, robbed a load of jewellers and supermarkets dressed in a burka. He spent four years at Strangeways before going to Kirkham, and had to do more townies with an officer than I did because he was high-risk.'

And speaking of risk, it isn't only the public who have that to worry about. In Cat Ds, you have to keep an eye on your neighbour.

There was a lad at Kirkham when Lee was there called Hank Brown. He had killed a member of a local crime family. His route to ROTL as a high-risk lifer was very long and, obviously, there'd be gang members from all over coming through. They were also worried about what might be in for him on the out.

'There were rumours someone was trying to engineer a route to get at him. I've since read up on Brown and he'd been quite a force to be reckoned with in his day, although all I saw was a grey-haired old bloke who one way or another was at the back end of his days.'

In short, when you're involved in major criminality, Cat D is a dangerous and quite ruthless place to be. Lee being green was a good thing probably, because he wouldn't have clocked the extent of it.

'One incident surprised us with a lad I worked with in the kitchens, a level-headed, fairly passive kid from Birmingham. A bus came in from another jail, and word got back to this kid that there was a certain individual on it who had made a mug of him at the last place they'd been at – filled him in, I think. My workmate only had a few months left to serve, but the minute he knew this character's pad he marched straight in. Stabbed him with a knife and twatted him with an iron. That was him shipped out straight away. Finished.'

Make no mistake, Cat D jails can be way riskier than Cat A or B. At Strangeways, if you've got hassle with someone, you can get it on because you know in a matter of minutes it will get broken up by the officers. In Cat D, fights erupt and there can be no one there to deal with it. You could go in someone's billet, kill them, and no one would know. We once had thirty-six gangbangers from rival gangs on K Wing at HMP Manchester, over three landings. It was tense as fuck. If you took that situation to Kirkham . . . well, I dread to think. Consequently, as soon as there's an incident at Kirkham, the horn goes off and everybody's banged up just to be on the safe side. Billets are checked and locked for hours.

You might think that, having gone through all that, Lee would never want to hear the word 'prison' again. Well, you would be quite wrong. For a start, there's that project of his briefly referred to earlier. At Kirkham, he now hopes to run education courses to try and help prisoners come to terms with what they will face on the out, which I am keen to get involved with myself. And more generally, he is actively trying to get the prison service to improve its communication to new prisoners prior to their arrival in jail, by way of leaflets and posters and what have you.

Lee said court and the uncertainty of sentence were the worst part. He also agreed with me that the prison service should have a video on its website, telling people what to expect when they arrive. That shouldn't be difficult to organize, should it? 'I wasn't myself for a few months, and had the best support you are ever going to get. My wife took control at home; great parents; great in-laws; money coming in . . . So if I struggled, how badly are people who don't have that support structure going to do?

'Some days I get up and think of court when, every day, we had a cloud over us. Newcastle might have won 3–0. I'd be in the park with the kids, sun shining. Didn't matter. There was always a "but". In jail, that went away. All the officers in Strangeways were sweet as a nut.'

They will have been. He didn't cause them any bother.

'The only thing they said was, "How did you end up in here from running a business?" All I could tell them was I didn't realize that what I was doing was going to land us in there. Most people who end up in prison know the endgame if they get caught. I didn't.'

3. Borstal Boy

Sometimes I lie awake at night, thinking. No, scratch that. I lie awake *every* night. There's something about the wee small hours that drags your shit bang into focus, isn't there?

Recently I realized that, for me, HMP Manchester and Forest Bank were the middle section of my own movie. Gritty and action-packed, and me co-starring with some right characters both sides of the doors, even if the mood overall was grim. Yet it's only now, as I move towards life's final credits, that I've begun to see the full picture.

While working as a prison officer in the north-west of England, I came into contact with people from right across the UK. Writing a book about it threw that net even wider. The stories I've heard since have hammered home that, while Strangeways is pretty fearsome, the routes people take to jail are similar up and down the land.

Take a bloke we'll call Mr B. Subtle, as that's how he became known inside on account of how he would run the landing. If some lad began to reek a bit, rather than soft-soap anyone he'd say, 'Here's some gel, get a fucking shower.' He wasn't an officer, mind, far from it. This geezer was a prisoner, and had been in some form of custody or other since being a boy, the polar opposite of Lee Robson.

Mr Subtle was born in 1969, so is in his fifties now and, having been out since 2017, is trying hard to make a fresh start. It hasn't been easy for him, as he seems to have enjoyed jail by and large, got himself nice and comfortable with the lifestyle. And why wouldn't you when you've spent over two thirds of your life in the system?

For the vast majority of prisoners, the start to their movie was far worse than the middle. Terrible childhoods, abuse, horrendous events at every turn. By the time they are teenagers (youth workers do fantastic work, mind), they are already broken men and women.

Yet people rarely look at the whole picture. They don't see how most inmates get to where they are, or try to understand how they might have lost the plot. For a time, I know I didn't.

And yet, since getting to know Mr Subtle, I realize that if our early lives had been reversed, we could now be in each other's place. Okay, so he's from the south-east while I'm a Yorkshireman, but he's an ex-working-class rugby player like me, so we get on well, and our thoughts on the prison service and its issues are uncannily similar.

Strangeways never had the pleasure of Mr Subtle's presence. His jail time was spent mainly in and around Kent, and more recently HMP Norwich, but his experiences are quite definitely widespread.

Dark hair combed back, of wiry build and a bit drawn in the face with something of the football manager about him, nowadays Mr Subtle gets upset when he thinks about the chaos he's caused and people he has hurt. Watching my vlogs about inmates getting bullied and knocked around can be very upsetting for him, because he was once the villain doling it out.

He was told he had a borderline personality disorder, and is still on medication, but while he was serving his last sentence he got classed as a model prisoner. He had a hand in everything – mentor to struggling kids, top job as a listener . . . But as he freely admits, while running around here, there and everywhere across various wings, this belated force for good was also trafficking drugs.

Mr Subtle is a complicated bloke and, if you keep an open mind, you'll learn why. Lads like him have never felt what society thinks of as normal. Their chances of jail time are way higher than anyone who grew up unconditionally loved and surrounded by good examples.

The guy is living proof that the start of your life will shape you.

'I had a lot of anxiety as a kid,' he said, last time we talked. 'I was an attention-seeker most of the time. Youngest of six – three sisters, two brothers. Mum and Dad had me when they were in their forties, and she died at fifty-nine, him five years later. Quite young to lose them . . .'

In his own middle age, Mr Subtle was diagnosed among other things with disassociative identity disorder, which is where folk have more than one distinct personality and behave differently according to which one's in control. Brought about through past trauma, it can also make you deluded, depressed and fuck with your memory. 'So my memories are of things I've been told or have tried to put together myself. Some are like videos. I can plug it in and play back the whole fucking lot.'

Growing up around Thanet in Kent, he had behavioural issues very early on. At nursery and in the infants at primary school, he'd have his scran in the headmistress's office, a disruptive presence. And then came sexual abuse.

'This geezer owned a toyshop down the road from us. He had a son, this bloke, who'd left home. He kept this lad's bedroom exactly as he had left it, like a ten-year-old's. That was where he took us, me and my mate who lived two doors down from me. It happened there a few times.'

I should warn you: what follows isn't pleasant. In fact, it's worse than a disgrace. But Mr Subtle was keen that we got the fullest picture.

'He would masturbate us, me and my mate. Maybe he did that with others too, or worse. I don't know. We weren't ten years old yet, so couldn't come. I'll never forget how he'd go on about ejaculating. He said it was like when you want to go to the toilet for a wee and keep holding it and holding it and holding it and then you let it go.

'There's certain things that will never ever leave me, ever, and that's one. Him sitting on his fucking sofa, on the corner of the chair, with his fucking cock out of his brown Arkwright coat. He'd a Freddie Mercury moustache too . . . Just talking about it brings back the smell.'

The shop was part of the community, windows full of toys and games. As you went in there was a counter to the left and steps behind that which went up to the man's flat. To the right was shelving for toys and a door to the basement.

'Then you had another row of shelves down the middle. In the late 1970s to early 1980s, when I was growing up, shops like that had no CCTV, just concave mirrors high up in the corner. And when you opened the door he'd usually be upstairs, so a bell would ring and then he'd come down.'

Mr Subtle wasn't sure how it began, whether this nonce got to his mate first, who then took him along, but knew they 'worked out a way to deal with it. Don't ask me why – you'd think we'd have run a fucking mile – but we'd go back every other fucking day, especially in summer. Airfix models . . . sometimes he'd give us them, other times we'd rob them, bit of both . . . But we began to suss out our advantage. I suppose it came down to kids' survival instincts.

'What we realized was, if we both went in together, by the time he's come down, one of us could hide. Then, when he took one of us upstairs it left an empty shop. Except it wasn't. There was a slight alcove where the mirror couldn't pick you up.'

So one of the boys would hide there while the other went up. 'It would only last a few minutes, so we didn't have long to nick bits and pieces. We also worked out how to get a couple of quid out of the till so as not to raise suspicion. Then you'd open the door, the bell would ring, he'd come down and while he was looking around the other kid would fuck off too. We saw it as to our benefit. We groomed him, the cunt. Couple of wank jobs . . . I actually find that funny now.'

That's not how most people would see it, of course, and neither have Mr Subtle's therapists, psychologists and psychiatrists. But then, as he admits himself, he has never been most people.

Not long after this abuse Mr Subtle developed meningitis, and was in a very bad way for a while. Soon he was plagued with anxiety, still climbing in his mum and dad's bed up to twelve years of age.

'It wasn't until 2008 that I started to deal with all this, thanks to thirteen hour-long sessions with a fantastic Canadian therapist in HMP Norwich. Cor, mate, that's why I love being a listener. I know the importance of allowing someone to talk their shit out. Even so, I can stand at the sink sometimes myself, washing up, and tears come out of fucking nowhere.'

It was after the meningitis, at around ten years old, that he began to sniff glue, petrol and gas. 'We had a lot of glue-sniffers round our way. It's something different, is how it starts. I can't look back and tell you how I felt. All I know is there was plenty going on and I got involved in all of it. I began to drink alcohol very young as well. It's important to remember that, because this is coming back later in life.'

It wasn't that the then Master Subtle wasn't bright. 'I was very intelligent, did well at junior school, tried to buckle down. At home, I was on my mum's apron, bit of a Mummy's boy, but otherwise never felt settled. After the meningitis was when the anger really set in.

'Thing is, I had such a deep love for my mum and dad. My dad was a Royal Marine, 3 Commando, and won a light-heavyweight boxing championship in the Marines. I'm a chip off his block. None of my brothers and sisters was like me. They're grammar school. Behaved 'emselves. That was how it was going through school – *You're not like your brothers . . . you're not like your sisters . . .* No, I'm not. I'm like me.'

At one point he joined a youth club and started playing for its football team, changing his name to Carl. 'We were a fucking good team – I was getting write-ups in the local papers. My family would ask, 'Who's this Carl?' I just didn't want to be who I was any more.'

A trained psychologist might say he was escaping into another personality but, true to form, Mr Subtle reckons he just 'turned into a little shit. Our secondary school was one where teachers at training college would cry if they were sent on placement, slap bang in the middle of a council estate.'

Our man reckoned it was a great training ground for prison. 'The amount of people I saw inside who went there – it was like a school reunion sometimes.' Soon he was in the care of the local authority, en route eventually to HMP Eastwood Park, which in those days was a male juvenile detention centre. 'In fact, I spent my sixteenth birthday in jail.'

But when he'd arrived at secondary school, all had gone well at first. 'First year, great, but then it all turned upside down. Three of my cousins went there, two of them boys with a reputation as bad lads, constantly brawling. So after being told I was nothing like my brothers and sisters and to apply myself, suddenly I am just like my cousins. *If this is who you think I am*, I thought, *this is who I am going to be.*'

Halfway through his second year he was spending more time at home than at school, constantly suspended. 'I'd burgle the school once a week, go in on Monday and say, "Want to buy a Ferguson video?" We went in through a science block skylight, a mate and me, never got caught for it. In fact, since then I've done a lot of bird for my mental health issues, not so much for my crimes.

'Anyway, we were on this roof, arguing as usual. We didn't do houses, unless it was for revenge or someone's insurance job. As a lot of schools were on council estates no one noticed smashed windows, but we'd still cough politely to "cover the noise up". My mate used to have a dump inside, one of our traditions, but the squabbling – "I'm going in first." "No, I'm going in first" . . . This particular night I was supposed to be going first and got a waft of that toilet chemical smell. It was pitch-black, so I said, "Go on, then. You go down." He landed in the bog.

'That was the time we got a forty-eight-inch TV, and back then it wasn't flatscreens, there was this fucking great back on it as well. Heavy cunt. We got it out through the window, but that set off the alarm. Didn't matter. No one gives a fuck around there. We must have dropped it on the sports field five times. Old Bill turned up, siren going – we just left the telly in the middle of the field. These were the type of people I'm starting to hang about with. Older than me. My role models.'

You won't be surprised to hear he wasn't exactly a hit with the teachers either. 'One, who took us for English, wouldn't let me in the classroom. One day he called me over to one of them lecturer's desks, slightly risen for a bit of extra authority. The fucker was seven foot tall anyway, didn't need it. "Once again, you've not done your work. Can you tell me why?" "Because you keep sending me out of the class, sir." "And why do I keep doing that?" "Because you're a cunt, sir."'

The whole room erupted – while the teacher went apoplectic.

'The headmaster wasn't there that day, and he was an odd one too. He used to cane you and then start crying, the prick. So I went to the deputy head, who had a voice like the lion off *Reading with Lenny*. It wasn't long before the end of the school day. I was expecting the cane off him, but instead he locked me in a stationery cupboard.

'Now, I'm not too pleased with this situation, so started kicking off. He's on the phone to my old man. "Can you hear your son?" "Where is he?" "In the cupboard." "Well, I don't fucking blame him. Tell you what, between the hours of nine and three thirty, he's your problem," my dad said, and hung up. Twenty minutes later I was still kicking and screaming blue murder when I heard a key in the door. It was the caretaker and headmaster. The deputy head had fucked off home.'

That got Mr Subtle a two-week suspension. 'But then this other teacher came out to talk to me while I was having a fag with my mates at lunchtime, and I started throwing half-bricks at him. That got me a letter home saying I was banned and not allowed within 200 metres of the place. When I did go back, I got bit by a hamster in Rural Studies, so killed it.' That led to another suspension.

'I come back from that and was on the first floor, by some oak shelving under the window. One kid was giving me it about killing this hamster, saying I was sick, so I pushed him out of it and he broke his arm. That was the thing that got me expelled.'

From there Mr Subtle went to a pupil referral unit. 'Now, I was intelligent, me, top of the class in all sorts of subjects quite regularly. Nowadays I've got a lot of time for people with learning difficulties, but back then it was less politically correct, and you're a product of your environment, aren't you? Motorized wheelchairs . . . we had everything. Some could only just hold their head up, and that was the class they put me in.

'They'd given up on me long before I'd given up on them. I suppose you could say me and school just did not get on.'

Eventually, he got kicked out of the referral unit for beating on a kid who refused to pay up from a bet in their pool group.

Young Mr Subtle then had a home tutor for a while, but

when that didn't work out went to a school run by probation officers in Ramsgate. 'That was basically a bit of work in the morning, and in the afternoon we'd go bowling, roller-skating or rock climbing. Went to Snowdonia in Wales, did Duke of Edinburgh – fucking great. I enjoyed that.'

You can see why he would. At last, someone was pitching things at him he could take to. Not that Mr Subtle is one to make excuses for his behaviour. He admitted he wasn't nice to know.

'Our estate was responsible for about 85 per cent of the crime rate in the area. We were proper at it. We'd rip off shops. Two bits of ID – a gas bill and electric bill would do it. You'd break into an empty property, loads around, and get the bills off the mat, piece of piss. On the day your stuff was delivered to that address, on credit of course, there you were. "Can you leave it outside, mate? We're decorating."

'Learning from adults, we were. We'd compete, boys against girls, to see who could rob most in the town centre. I got caught in a stationer's shop once, nicking a roll of Sellotape. These are what is known as "inquisitive crimes", and in no time you are doing other stuff – commercial burglaries . . . Sunday to Thursday we were at it all the time. On Friday and Saturday we took a couple of days off.

'But nicking cars was our big thing. That's what led to me going away properly for the first time.'

Mr Subtle was fourteen when he carried out his first armed robbery.

'It was a wages snatch on an industrial estate. Unfortunately, we were silly. These vans used to go around all the factories dropping the old brown envelopes off, and we waited until this one was on its way out. Still got fourteen grand, mind. We had handheld crossbows, which are very fucking scary, especially when you've masks on. That said, if you use the right wording in a mask, the weapon don't matter.

'The last armed robbery I done was by knifepoint from a shop. I was working from experience by then, in and out, don't fuck about. Control it. Same with shoplifting. Don't walk about making yourself look a cunt, searching for cameras. Go in, grab what you are after and walk out. Simple. No one's going to notice. Except this time, unfortunately, they did. It was caught on CCTV. The video is still online, or was last time I looked.'

As he says, his behaviour came from hanging about with people for whom it was natural. 'I don't come from a city, I come from a seaside area – Ramsgate, Margate, Broadstairs, Thanet – but we still had the same people you'd have in Manchester. Donal MacIntyre called us one of the most violent parts of the country.

'There was a lot of fighting between estates, very working class and with a fishing industry that was fucked. Ramsgate didn't like Margate. One arm of my family specialized in starting fights in nightclubs – 'rent-a-riot', they were called. Tough area. We'd a massive brawl once on the seafront, and when it stopped everyone smashed up the cash machines in the arcades. Ransacked. A few got nicked, and I got banned from the seafront – indefinitely!'

Mr Subtle was given his own juvenile delinquent officer, but what chance did he have? 'We'd drive up to London on petrol bought with bent credit cards. It was easy to do – you just swiped them back then. I was six foot tall, so we'd get two hundred fags as well. Dressed half decent, with Mercedes keyrings or whatever. I knew the difference between right and wrong, but it didn't apply in our environment. "Don't fuck it up" was doing the right thing – or you'd get a beating.'

One day, he was drinking at a pub with his mate when word came that a girl they knew had been thrown out of the youth club and hurt her arm. 'You don't do that, do you? My mate had a rounders bat in his car, so I went to sort out the cunt who did it, but this lad beat me to it and cracked the youth worker on the back of the head first. As the Old Bill turned up, skidded and got out their old-school blue car, I've fucked off – once you've legged it as a kid and you know your area, they ain't getting you. I've run up the bonnet and over the top and, as I've gone, booted off the light. That's it. I'm gone. On the run.'

Staying with mates, he robbed cars to make money. 'Even today, walking ten minutes down the road to the supermarket, I could lift at least six items from the stuff people leave in them. I was an opportunistic criminal – it's always there. It's not like drugs, where you have to go and find some; just a walk to the shop will do it. As I tell people, that hasn't changed, but my attitude has. I still think like a criminal, but I just choose not to act on it any more. Being aware of how easy it is stops me from doing that too, in a funny way.

'Anyway, my mate had a Lancia Beta and I was on the run. Through the night we had a chase with some horrible bastard police, who stalled, and we lost him. At one time we had six to eight police forces looking for us. I've dropped one mate off, and me and this other bloke stayed in the car, parked down a country lane. Across the field we could see the main road, with a police car on it. I looked again and it had gone. This was four or five o'clock in the morning.'

All of a sudden he heard a knock. 'There was Old Bill at the window. Soon another car arrived and an officer we knew got out. We were prepared to go quietly, but this new cunt threw me against this pebble-dashed wall. "Fink you can get away from me, do yer?" I'm fifteen at the time, bruv, and this is a grown man copper. I got done for doing a runner and the youth club GBH. *Fuck it*, they thought. *We've had enough of him. Put him away.*'

He was sent to what he calls a children's home first, although to me it sounds more like an old-fashioned borstal. Either way: rough.

'It was where I first witnessed bullying, which I put up with for a bit before I snapped. You started in a secure unit, where you weren't allowed to wear trainers inside. All the doors were locked. Windows only opened an inch. No one ran away. It was near Maidstone, but if you google it, you won't find anything. All the records seem to have disappeared! I was there in 1984–85.

'My key worker, he weren't too bad. There was sexual abuse going on, but for me it was more about violence. Frank Bruno was fighting Bonecrusher Smith in May 1984, and it was on late. We all wanted to watch, but it was nine o'clock bed. We didn't like that, so linked arms, singing that we would not be moved. They got out a fire hose – big, powerful thing like you see in jails – and put it on us, a load of fucking kids! Fucking hurt. They won. We went to bed.'

In the gym they were allowed to play murderball, and it was kicking off all the time. 'Me and another kid, Les, were working in the kitchen, and my key worker had fallen out with him. He told me he was leaving the kitchen for ten minutes: "Have a word with Les, will ya?" And when he was gone I battered the kid. I feel bad about it now, but that was the environment. You didn't make decisions based on morals and principles. It wasn't a rational world we lived in.'

It was mixed sex too: 'Boys on the second floor, girls on the third floor. First-floor dining hall, offices, toilets and showers. It was a beautiful building, an old Victorian manor house, out in the sticks. Stables had been turned into staff accommodation, but some lived with us in the house. One guy was an ex-boxer with arms like tree trunks . . . The stairs were squeaky and I got caught coming down from the girls' floor. Jesus, did I get a battering.'

Meanwhile the kid he shared a room with was getting picked on. 'This bully had also given me a couple of digs in the jaw. I allowed it for a few nights, until one night he comes in, gives my roomie a slap, and then moves towards me. I stood up. "I see you, you cunt," I said, and done him with a pen in his cheek. Nothing ever happened to me again. Throughout my life, I don't let anyone take me for a cunt.'

And from the 'children's home' he was soon off to Blantyre House Detention Centre, which looked like an old Tudor building.

'I was still on these charges, deferred. So I've gone back to juvenile court, three magistrates then, and they've gone behind to reach their decision. I'm sitting there, my mum and dad behind me. The chief inspector was the prosecutor in juvenile magistrates. It was a small room, a police station and the courts next to each other.

'Suddenly, this constable comes in the door and says he's here for the prisoner. I hadn't even been sentenced yet. Sure enough, when they come out, two months for assault, ABH in the end, and a few other bits and pieces – possession, things like that, cars obviously, concurrent on one charge, another two months for that . . . So four months I got: short, sharp shock. I went to run out the court, but got caught by the chief inspector and this PC. Mum, Dad and my sister were in bits . . . But that was me gone, off into youth custody.'

It was about then that he started hearing more about his dad. 'Turned out, from all the stories, he'd been a right nutter in his day. So no wonder I turned out like I did, although why all my brothers and sisters didn't, I don't know. It all came out when he died. He had all sorts of issues: PTSD from his service – he was in the Suez Crisis, Korea, all that. Got kicked off Malta for beating up two of the King's Guards. Anyway, he's telling them, "If I see any marks on my son . . ."

'My mum had given me twenty B&H Gold, so I'd nineteen fags left and a pink shirt on. The same constable who'd driven me to the children's home drove me to the detention centre.'

Blantyre House was built around a parade ground. It must once have been part of an army boot camp or something. Mr Subtle was told to get out of the car and stand on a drain while he was read the rules of the establishment, and kept forgetting to say 'Sir'.

'I was told to run to the entrance door as fast as I could. It weren't that far – other side of the exercise yard. But as I got close, the door's opened and there is this giant of a man taking up the doorway – back then, screws wore the lot: tunic, belt, tie done up, cap right down to the nose, you could just about see their eyes. He had this big black beard. Boom! Right in the gut. "Get back. Not fucking quick enough. Do it again."

'That was my welcome into grown-up custody, although I still hadn't yet turned sixteen. That night, I cried myself to sleep.'

Mr Subtle spent a week on the induction landing, learning. 'Thing was, on the run I stayed in some pretty dodgy places and got scabies. I had to be covered in white powder. I had it on my nuts. Remember Y-fronts, before boxer shorts, small or XXXL? The induction cells were single-occupancy. I'm standing there, button-up jeans around my ankles, flapping water up from a potty onto my nuts 'cos they was burning something chronic. They used to check you for crabs an' all, shine a torch on your pubes to see if there was any movement. You'd queue up – "Next!" – like in a school hall.'

Mr Subtle got himself a job as the library orderly, and learned how to march. 'First week, they beasted us. You'd have to wake up in the morning and do your bed pack. You'd do your ablutions, get your breakfast and get ready for work – all with your mouth fucking shut. You don't talk unless spoken to. After two weeks you have a grading. You start off as grade one: itchy jumpers, matching cuffs and collars that denoted your grade – grade one was green or blue. Everybody worked. They'd fill one of them big metal bins in the kitchen with water and potatoes and we'd have to sit outside peeling them.

'We had breakfast, lunch, tea and association in the dining hall, which had one telly that we could only watch at weekends. The place held about 120-odd, 147 max, in two dormitories, east and west.

'Grade two was for orderlies and so on; grade three was your trustees. Better job. In the dining room, their tables were under the telly, and they were always first to be offered seconds. It was all about routine – you even had to walk in a certain direction. Same with exercises: we all went round the same way. I made grade three, and we'd get all sorts of comments as we went to the servery – "Greedy bastard", "Don't fucking eat mine" – all of that. The others saw you as privileged.

'I got used to it, though. Fucking loved it. Met a white Jamaican from Romford. Him and me got on like a house on fire. We even sorted out a nonce, fifteen years old. We heard a rumour he'd messed about with his sister. I don't know if it was true or not, but we done him up the arse with a toothbrush.

'Two of the screws laughed about this toothbrush incident – "Good. He deserved it." If the screws didn't like a kid, then he was fucked, because he got no protection. That was how things were back then.'

One thing about Mr Subtle, though: he doesn't see himself as a victim. He hates people who go on social media to complain about how badly they were treated in jail. 'They were doing time for a reason, mate. All right,' he said, 'I didn't deserve what happened to me as a kid, but I was a cunt and I accept that. Fuck me, I deserved everything else. Did I deserve kickings from the Old Bill? Probably. Did I give as good as I got? Probably. I got through. I survived. I was there. I don't have to fucking exaggerate.'

The fact is, though, here was a kid who had very little chance of a life on the straight and narrow from the off. I asked Juli, a social worker friend of mine who sees first-hand the impact of childhood abuse, for her professional opinion. Here is what she wrote:

- The baby who has been removed from parental care because of safeguarding concerns. Her mum is alcohol-dependent and can't keep her safe. Mum's dependence on alcohol helps her to dull the pain of having been sexually abused by her father as a young child.

- The fourteen-year-old boy excluded from school due to his poor behaviour. He refuses to work with outreach educational supports because they want to visit him at home and speak with his parents. He doesn't want anyone asking questions as it will make his stepdad angry. He's scared someone will find out that his stepdad uses him as a punchbag. Who'll protect his mum if he's taken into foster care?

- The man in prison due to years of criminality, mostly crimes involving violence. He lost contact with his young son because it was felt he'd be a risk to him. Two months ago, his child's social worker came to visit him because he was asking for contact. He disclosed that his anger is because of an older brother sexually abusing him when he was just six years old. He was powerless to stop him.

'Traumatic experiences in childhood,' finished Juli, 'are directly linked to instances of depression, anxiety, shame, guilt, anger and self-harm, plus relationship and sexual difficulties. This trauma exposure also significantly increases risk of addiction as a means of coping with the pain.'

From youth, there has not been a decade when Mr Subtle hasn't been inside for some misdemeanour or other. Until this one, anyway. But then we're only a couple of years into it, aren't we?

Having spent his sixteenth birthday in detention, a lifetime in and out of adult prisons was shaping up to be inevitable. And sure enough, on and off, he had spent fifteen years in such institutions before his most recent release in July 2017, the twists and turns of which have given him plenty to draw on for his current life as prison reform campaigner, TEDx speaker and internet blogger.

'I'd had every chance given to me before custody, courses and what have you, never taken any of them. When I was young I saw it as an adventure. You are with your mates, your own kind. You don't get put in these places because you are Farquin Tarquin, Pupil of the Week. You get put in them because you are a little shit. Therefore, it's little shits around little shits.'

Once he started to be surrounded by older men, kids began to annoy him. 'I'd do 'em over the head with a bird table, things like that. An hour of PT, an hour's woodwork, normally making bird boxes . . . how many of them I've made throughout the system I've lost count. You've probably got one in your garden. Community service – some of the other stupid programmes I've done. It was all about taking up the time. You got punished: "We are going to make it awkward, no rhyme or reason behind it." No therapy behind it, no reforming work.

'We got to look at educational cartoons – spotting your exit signs, where could you have made a better decision, things like that. It was before its time, if I'm honest, the sort of thing they do now. It was admirable stuff in its way. They got us to film things as well, but the problem was, as soon as they showed us their video equipment a mate and me would go back and rob it. That's how much we gave a shit. Fuck me, you'll get no worse than a detention centre. If that's not changing anybody, nothing will.'

Mr Subtle's thoughts drifted back to his detention centre, as they often do, because he had liked the discipline. 'You need it,' he said. But did he think it made him tougher?

'Oh, yes. I tried to join the army the first time I got out, Second Tank Regiment, but when they saw my criminal record they didn't want me. That was a blow, but I wasn't going to change. At detention centre, I got stronger, into weightlifting. You had to do double your body weight in the clean and jerk and one and a half times your body weight in the snatch. You'd get bronze, silver and gold certificates. I got silver. Within about six weeks I put on a stone and a half.' In their porridge, they were fed oatmeal meant for pigs. 'In fact, the pigs stopped getting our leftovers in their swill before we stopped getting their oatmeal in our breakfast. Genuinely!'

His first YP – Young Prisoner – jail proper was HMP Canterbury, aged seventeen. 'It was a maze, like Strangeways by the sound of it. That was an eye-opener, walking through. The noise, smell, sheer size and look of the place, atmosphere . . . I can feel it now. Twenty-two or -three-hour bang-up then. Little fucking radio, hanging out the window trying to get an FM signal, your piss pot and that was it. You had three to a cell in the 1980s – and today they go on about overcrowding!'

That was when prisons got so full that the cells in police stations had to be used – Operation Gridlock, they called it.

'We used to love staying in police stations because they didn't give you frozen food like they do now. You'd get your fish and chips from a chip shop. They'd leave your cell door open, TV at the end, and there was only about eight of you . . . Oh, so much better. Weekends were brilliant. You'd have your junkies coming in, banging doors and screaming. They'd let us out to have a word with them. Obviously we were all in for murder, even if we weren't, and the Old Bill would play along. It was like a camp trip out of jail.'

Years later, Mr Subtle would find himself at Blundeston Prison in Suffolk. 'I had a £110 pair of Timberlands, and they took them off me because they had a "metal bar" in the sole. They took your scrunchie – what you scrub yourself with in the shower – because someone tried to take their own life with one.' While back on his first night in Canterbury he found useful weapons on the servery. '"You can't bring X, Y, Z in, mate, but here's a metal tray!" Haha. I've put some fucking scars on people with those trays. They end up like razor blades. You could shave with the cunts.'

So anyway, Canterbury, teatime – banged up. 'Next thing I know, there's a knocking and it gets louder. "Beast! Beast! Beast!" The whole jail was at it as the nonces were served their dinner. I'm getting goosebumps again. That was my introduction to men's prison.'

Some of Mr Subtle's tales are head-spinning – so much so that it's next to impossible to keep up. In 2002, he lost the plot while working as a debt collector, and ended up charged with GBH on a 'customer' and six counts of ABH on police officers, yet still got bailed and did a bit of plea-bargaining to get his sentence down. That was also the year he got sectioned for twenty-eight days and put on medication for the first time, which he only came off very recently. Nowadays he's no longer on meds, smokes a bit of weed, no more. It helps to keep his head clear, he says.

'I was on risperidone, which is used to treat psychosis but also anger management: five mil morning, five mil at night. One mil of it a day is poisonous. My CARAT [Counselling, Assessment, Referral, Advice and Throughcare] worker told me I was poisoning my kidneys and liver. "Do you think you need 'em?" I was on all sorts at the time – antipsychotic stuff you give serial killers, the works.'

He arrived at HMP Norwich in around 2010. 'I've worked screws, mate, in my time – mobile phones, drugs – but as it went on I didn't need to any more. I'd had all that. But I might say I could do with a ceramic plate, or cup. Pens, notebooks – I'd have some of that. All the pretty female officers, I used to leave them alone. I'd go for the ugly ones . . . 'Cor, miss, I love what you've done with your hair . . .' Haha – I'd have them bringing me slices of cake.'

Another officer complained to him that a nonce had moved in as a neighbour at home. 'Later on, he comes up to me and whispers, "Some blokes turned up, threatening him in masks. Anything to do with you?" I says, "Mr C, how would I know they lived at number forty-two?" "Thought so," he said. "There's a gift for you upstairs." I've gone up and there's four ounces of burn – a couple of two-ounce pouches. That's how it works in jail.'

So at what point did something click? Was there a defining moment when he decided to change? It seems not.

'No. It's never, ever been about rehabilitation. For the system, it's about keeping you off the streets, out of trouble, until they put you back out there again, doing the same thing. And as for me, I've got older, I'm bigger and have more about me now, haven't I? Kudos. I've jumped above my older mates because I've done jail time. For the likes of me and the people I've spent my life around, prison is a badge of honour, not a deterrent, isn't it?'

That said, changed man or not, Mr Subtle is in a position where he knows he can make a practical difference for others, not to mention a legitimate career for himself. He can quite definitely see everything wrong with the system, no bullshit attached. And why wouldn't he be in a position to do that with all his experience? As he said at the start, he might have been a bad lad – may still be deep down – but the one thing he is not is naive. He has been on probation, in hostels, under supervision, in prisons, and banged heads with the lot of it. All the system's failings he's lived through. I'm guessing he'd be reluctant to admit it, not wanting to paint himself as a victim, but that upbringing of his must surely be what's driving his current passion for education and reform.

Mr Subtle is someone who is going to have a say whether you or the authorities like it or not, particularly about probation and how that can be rebuilt, from the ground up, and made fit for purpose.

His main gripe is with the MAPPA system – which stands for Multi-Agency Public Protection Arrangements – under whose auspices he fell due to his history as a violent offender. In other words, due to him being high-risk. There are three MAPPA categories:

1) All registered sex offenders.
2) All offenders who have had custodial sentences of twelve months or more for a violent or 'other' sexual offence and who will be under probation supervision on their release.
3) Anyone else assessed as posing a risk of serious harm to the public which would be best managed in a multi-agency setting, i.e. police, prison service and probation service.

But let Mr Subtle talk us through it.

'I was last released on 9 June 2017 from Norwich,' Mr Subtle says. 'A month or so before, on Thursday 11 May, my probation officer come up to see me. I'd been sent down for forty-five months, and had done just under two years. Because my crime had been in Norwich, they wanted to reintroduce me into the community slowly and put me in a hostel that was out of the area.'

He kicked off about that and probably too much because they put him right on the edge of the south-east area in Luton. 'On Napier Road, you want to see it . . . It's just up behind the police station, as featured on *24 Hours in Police Custody*, the Channel 4 documentary where they follow coppers in Bedfordshire. Lovely spot . . . drugs, red-light prostitution, and so on. We'd go out in the morning and I'd have to come back every two hours to sign in – that "high-risk" bollocks. Thing is, though, it was a MAPPA hostel or AP [approved premises] and that really makes you feel like a nonce.

'The thing with APs is everyone thinks it's all sex offenders and it ain't. That's the issue – they tap you into it. In jail, they separate you and the VPs. Yet when we come out into the community we have to live with the fuckers. Believe it or not, one place, not Luton, is opposite a kids' park! If you was going to put an AP anywhere, it wouldn't be there. There was also some woods nearby. That joint is known as Paedophiles' Palace, bruv.'

This is a huge issue with some ex-customers. I knew a lad in Strangeways who was put in a hostel sixty miles from Manchester, near enough. Visiting his family was impossible. He was in there two weeks before realizing what the score was because someone in town made a comment to them about being nonces. His mate went back to the hostel and filled some of his 'housemates' in. Got five years.

'On the day I got out, a Friday, ten o'clock in the morning, I asked them in reception to get me a taxi. "You don't need one, there's someone outside to meet you." It was one of my support team, who took me off to see probation, sort the paperwork and what have you, and then I got myself to Luton.

'I did not want to be there but there was no sex offenders in, so that was something. It was situated on a corner with a nursery opposite, another head-scratcher. At the end of the road was a T-junction, with a couple of off-licences to the right and a ceme-tery, proper deprived area. Less than 100 yards down the road there was a mattress where one girl used to take her clients, in a little cubbyhole with a bricked archway. You'd come out in the morning and there'd be people sat on the wall, guys trying to sell you drugs, birds selling themselves. Cars would come by, "do you want to buy this, do you want to buy that . . ." It was mental. If anywhere was going to set you up to fail, it was this place.'

This guy has seen a LOT of probation officers and does not

like them. He'd rather see out his sentences when he could, didn't like to engage with probation and preferred to do courses inside. In my view, people should have to do their probation with a family member or friend.

'When I went to my first AP, John Berg House in Norwich in 2009, one day I heard a lot of noise, something was kicking off. This car pulled up and four guys jumped out, coming for one of the residents who they reckoned had been selling drugs on their patch. That's how bad it was – and probation put me in there!

'The hostel was a huge building on a main road. If people were walking the opposite way to me as I approached the door, I'd keep walking straight past to the top of the road and double back – never go straight in. And when you came out, people would shout that you were a nonce from motors going past.'

That would have been when he had a bit of a showdown with the boys in blue.

'Because I had a history with the armed police, they even had a name for my arrest, Operation Bolt, prepared for hostages and all that bollocks. All I done was lose the plot one day, bit of a row, nothing to get excited over. But as soon as they came to arrest me . . . game on. I refused to come out; threatening that if they come in, I would kill the lot of them. That sort of shit. Just lost it.

'I couldn't handle the Old Bill, couldn't walk past a policeman in the street without thinking, *G'wan, you cunt*. And as I got worse, the arrests got worse. A decent copper talked me down but I only gave up so I would go to mental hospital and not prison.'

And where did he end up? 'Prison. Back to prison. "You're not mentally unwell, you are a violent individual."

'Well, okay. I did get six months once for chasing a copper down the road . . . all right, I had a carving knife in my hand, but I didn't touch him. He'd attacked me with pepper spray.'

Meanwhile, nearer the here and now in Luton, one bloke in that hostel discovered spice, of which more in the next chapter, so they all got started on that. 'We were getting it for £15 for three grams, falling all over the place. People were getting taken to hospital but we just didn't give a fuck.'

Somehow, his licence finally finished in April 2019.

Nowadays, Mr Subtle is on various trusts and committees and spends hours in Zoom meetings, starting to get recognition for his knowledge and role in the Prison Reform Trust network group. Through the Open University, he studied for a Bachelor of Science degree in Criminology, passed in 2022, having in July 2020 earned a Safe Return to Work (Covid-19) City & Guilds credential.

Not that his efforts to improve the prison service don't get frustrated from time to time. They do. A lot of high-ups still take the piss. They want your information but won't give anything in return. A lot of people in power would shit blue lights if they were locked up, but still speak about matters of which they haven't got a clue. This lad has. He's seen it all and done plenty of it too.

I came away from our chat with two main thoughts.

One: beware of taking anyone at face value. There is always more going on beneath the surface than you know or perhaps can even understand.

And two: the prison service ignores stories like Mr Subtle's at its – and our – peril.

4. Gangs of Moss Side

Think of Moss Side and I bet you straight away think of gang members. Strangeways held loads, bringing a whole different context to what could already be a dodgy and complicated environment.

Gangbangers, as they were known, would be found on every landing, just about. They could be a nightmare to deal with, especially when you had a load of them in from competing crews.

As with Mr Subtle, these were kids who had grown up in and around crime, steeped in violent street life. They were into everything: drugs, booze, feuds, death threats . . . The vast majority were a handful.

The territory of these gangs actually extends from Moss Side to the likes of Old Trafford, Fallowfield and Hulme in South Manchester. Two of the biggest and best known are the Gooch, based on Gooch Close to the west of the Alexandra Park estate, and their deadly rivals the Doddington gang, who used to be known as the Pepperhill Mob.

The Gooch's membership is mainly Afro-Caribbean, and there are all sorts of other offshoots, various Crips groups and what have you, all of them dealing in the trafficking of drugs and weapons, kidnapping, money laundering, robbery, prostitution and no end of violent activity. If names like Fallowfield Mad Dogs and Moss Side Bloods make them sound like Los Angeles tribute acts, don't you believe it. These lads mean business and wreak absolute havoc.

Lee Marvin – that's his real name – grew up around the gangs of Moss Side, although never wanted to join any. It was a surprise to me that he didn't have to. But no, it seems Manchester's gang leaders can tolerate a certain amount of individual initiative, a bit like Omar in *The Wire*, I suppose. But as we are about to discover, only a *certain* amount.

First thing to say about Marv is that, for him, there was soon no difference to being in prison or out on the streets. Strangeways was no deterrent because, for a good twenty years at least, life carried on the same either way. You'll see why as we go on.

A tall and stocky lad with a big afro and laid-back manner, his attitude to life is all the more remarkable given everything he's been through. Maybe that's what has helped him to survive. This is a lad who does his own thing. But as we know, kids who come into this world unwanted have to learn to look after themselves.

Although he's what might be thought of as a natural gang-banger, Marv would have none of belonging to one side or the other. 'Back in the day, I got asked if I wanted "DOG" tattooed on my chest – "Doddington Original Gangsters". I said no, as if I took my shirt off, I'd have made 50 per cent enemies already. All of Gooch would have wanted to kill me. I knew and got on with nearly all of them. That was the problem.'

James Miller, one of the main players in Doddington and

currently doing thirty-five years, once told him, 'You're a proper game lad, you,' and them boys are fucking ruthless. Guns, you name it. He said a polite no, wanted to stay independent.

In spite of being a lone operator in their world, Marv has been shot, stabbed and battered in his time, and nearly died. In and out of jail, he has, by his own admission, also been a crack-head for twenty years. In fact, if you were looking for examples of people who seem destined to wind up behind bars, you couldn't do better than Marv. He was actually born in prison – HMS Styal, in fact, for female adults and young offenders in Wilmslow, Cheshire. His mum was 'a bit of a rogue', his dad not around much. 'She had me in the mother and baby unit.' Not long after, she gave him away.

'My mam didn't want to think too much about that, because I don't think she wanted to do it – I've still got the letters she received from probation when she was let out. She was asking, "Can I send him gifts, birthday cards and stuff?" I don't think she realized that, in the 1970s, you was never seeing your kid again. The authorities wanted to keep them at a distance.'

That said, Marv didn't get signed off until he was nine months old, while she was out on probation. 'I think I was her little secret that she left in Manchester, because she was from London.'

She had a drug habit too, which at some point led to her refusing a leg amputation, Marv says. You can see why. I mean, who would want their leg chopping off? Although there's a good chance she'd have been injecting dodgy needles into it.

'From prison I went to an orphanage local to the jail, so you can imagine how many kids they took from there. They weren't very nice to me at all, and I can prove it. All this time later,

I've still got a scar in the middle of my back from when they burned me with a cigarette.'

Marv was in the orphanage from the twelfth week of his life (new mothers had until then to choose whether or not to keep their babies) until that seven or eight month mark. Taking them away like that sounds pretty brutal, and maybe it is. But it's also far from straightforward because being brought up outside jail might be better for their child's development and would see them placed with law-abiding parents.

There's also a chance that some judges might be wary of imprisoning criminal mothers as it would also punish the kids, and some women, of course, are smart enough to play on that. In theory, when caught, they could deliberately fall pregnant to avoid a prison sentence.

'It's a hard one,' Marv drawled. 'If you're a bloke coming home every night with a big parcel of drugs, the woman's on your shoulder, in there with you. It could be her business, and you're just the fucking puppet in front but as a man, you'd take the charge for her if the police came knocking. Women, like men, can be very, very cunning. But my views on women being in prison . . . they are not nice places to be with a baby. If you know you are going to lose touch with it, that would not be nice.'

It can also leave the baby with an inferiority complex.

'When I was a young 'un, committing crimes, I'd think I wasn't a worthy member of the human race. In Manchester city centre, I used to go down all the back streets like a little rat. I wouldn't go down the main streets where members of the public were – to me, they was just the people I'd rob off. If I saw a car unlocked, I'd jump in it without a second's thought, never think of the consequences. Having spent a bit of time crime-free, I now realize the destructiveness of just robbing a wallet. It causes drama. If I lost mine, I'd lose little sentimental things, as well as credit cards and what have you. With a missus and kids of my own, I understand that now.'

In the orphanage he says he was in a shop window. 'It was like they were trying to sell me, and that was made harder because I was mixed-race – or as they called it then, half-caste. My mum had a Greek Cypriot background. I later found out it was one reason she gave for signing me away – fear of taking this illegitimate baby home to her family of orthodox Christians, really religious. Another, I learned when I finally met my birth family thirty years later, was she thought I was going to be adopted by a couple of doctors.' In fact, his 'new dad' was a factory worker and his 'new mum' was unemployed.

'She knew deep down who my real dad was, I'm sure, but she reckoned not to. Later, I got to know him too, and he told me I'd have been dead if she had taken me to London. She used to sit in drug dens there, including one where the girl whose house it was had a baby in the cot. The baby died while everyone in there was getting high. He was adamant that would've been me.'

Mainly, Marv thinks, not taking her son south was his mum thinking she was giving him a better life, when nothing could have been further from the truth. 'From the day I was signed off, everything went downhill. I would much rather have sat in a crack house with my real mum than go through what happened to me when I was adopted.'

The male half of the couple who took Marvin home was Jamaican and strict as fuck, an attitude Marv put down to the man's own upbringing.

'He never knew any better. But I also think he was pissed off that my adoptive mum couldn't have kids. He had three daughters in Jamaica who he sent a few quid over for, and then he had me, not really his son and a bit wayward from the off. It was in my adoption file that I'd been born in foetal distress.'

Marv's adopted mother was a white Welsh woman. 'When they went to the orphanage, they could pick any baby they wanted. They told me she wanted me straight away. The probation officer says on the file that my "saucer, almond-shaped eyes" did it. She told me I had beautiful eyes and was the smiliest, happiest baby in there.

'Before the three of us left, a social worker noticed the burn on my back, and my new mum said they had to sign it off as a "wee burn" or I couldn't have gone. There would have been an investigation. One of the first things I remember in my life is my adoptive mum saying, "I never burned you, son, it wasn't me," because she used to smoke a lot.' Marv lifted his shirt and showed it me.

Marv also had an adoptive sister, five years older than him. 'The only reason I was brought into that family was she wanted a little brother. She died of a prescription overdose in 2020.' It's clear he still feels bitter about that. 'She used to call me out all the time for being on drugs, when behind closed doors she was at it herself. But that was all right, wasn't it, because they came from the doctor . . .'

As he got older, young Marv still showed signs of distress. 'Going to sleep at night, I'd count up to 900 and keep bouncing my head off the pillow. When I finally got to sleep, I'd dream of mopping the floor and I'd wet the bed.' That made his dad angry. People never look for *why* you are doing something, do they?

'My adoptive mum used to try and hide a lot of it from him. He'd go to work at night and be home at two o'clock, so she'd try to clean it up. He took to checking my underpants, to see which ones I had on.'

The bed-wetting didn't stop until he was eleven years old.

When Marvin was twenty, and in prison by then, one officer told him, 'You're a comfort eater, you – missing something big in your life.'

'He didn't know my background, but he was right. I was missing my mam.

'I was pretty unhappy as a kid. Ran away a lot and the police would bring me back. I got from Ancoats to Cheetham Hill once – two miles – then lost a sandal down a hill with a kid called Alex who is also dead now. A policeman let me wear his helmet in the car.'

'So yes, I was a bit of a rogue, spent a lot of time on my own. I used to play in empty houses and mills. One day I pushed open a door, saw a glue sniffer doing his thing and ran off to sit in my bedroom. Next day, I go back and find empty bags on the floor. I smelled it straight away and it hit my brain in a wave. *Oh, this is good.* I started breaking the bags up, trying to get a buzz. I then started messing with empty glue pots and putting my fingers in around the edges of Evo-Stik tubes, trying to copy what this bloke had been doing. I was only seven at the time.'

As well as glue-sniffing, he also saw someone doing butane gas, so started on that too. One Saturday morning he stayed in the house while the rest of the family went shopping as usual. 'It was 20p for a tin of gas; get 10p spends off your dad and put it with someone else.'

He also began to get into scrap metal – collecting cans and getting a pound off the scrapman per bagful. 'The scrapman was a really nice fella, although scrapmen was really gangsters back then, weren't they? It was a cover, the scrap, a way of money laundering. They'd give us a few quid 'cos they knew we was off the estate. We used to get copper boilers out of abandoned houses, because there were a lot of them around our way. I made a few quid off that too.

'On the butane gas, it was beautiful. I used to escape out of this world. Then I started shoplifting in the city centre, robbing toys and whatnot. I'd got this little computer thing for Christmas, and one day met this fella who said he had a mate who would let me have some games for it, took me to see him. He turned out to be a paedophile.

'He put me through a right bad time in my early teens – but the thing is, he even used to come to my mum and dad's house to pick me up. He'd raped me a couple of times and I couldn't speak. Gobsmacked. I was a child – didn't know what to say. Would anyone believe me? Was it normal? He was a proper dodgy bastard, deep into that stuff. He lived in the flats opposite, and from his balcony could look into my bedroom window. "Do you mind if he helps me do some deliveries?" he'd ask them. And off we'd go into the pits of hell.'

Marv managed it with drugs. 'The gas was my escape. Full can in my mouth. I'd go to this place in my brain, nursery songs. It felt like I was alone with it. I knew there was no one else like me, and didn't feel I could speak about it. He said he'd get me locked up for lying.'

The family lived in Ancoats, quite a poor area of Manchester, and despite the dad's long hours, they never had any brass. 'You are living from pay packet to pay packet, aren't you?' said Marv. 'It's the way society gets you in debt, so they've got slaves. If everyone realized that accumulating material possessions was just a trick, the workforce would fall, wouldn't it, because people would put their feet up and chill in the garden every day. They have you in a knot from when you're seventeen – get a car on finance, get a house on finance, we'll give you a loan for a new pair of trainers or the latest handbag, but then you're working your arse off for it and you've got no choice but to work, else you lose it, don't you?'

And because you are working, you think you deserve things.

'You start buying things on credit, but they're not yours, are they? If you own your own house, you're only one pay cheque away from being homeless. Even if you don't pay your council tax and pay your mortgage, you can lose your house. You are debted up.'

Again, I remembered our own time in Little Hulton, mentioned in chapter two, when we got two months behind with the rent and they threatened us straight away. We'd been in the house five years, paid every month, but got in a bit of a financial pickle, a bit late one month, and there you go.

'Same with cars,' said Marvin. 'You can finance a car for three years, pay religiously – but miss it a couple of times and they are coming for that motor. They have tracking systems now, so you can try and hide it but one night it'll vanish from outside your house. Call the police: "Finance took it back." That's why criminality is rife. All that advertising for the fancy items – people think they need to keep up, and if they can't afford to buy it, they'll nick it.

'I was always the tallest, so the boys would go, "Marv, let's get this car in the avenue." We'd jump in and push it down the road. I was never behind the wheel, didn't learn to drive, but I'm not fussed. Those who did were dead in their twenties from joyriding and stuff.'

He reckons he had acquaintances rather than friends. There was just one lad who was a mate. He learned to be a car mechanic at fourteen, and he's a doorman in town now, and they are still close. But no one else. It doesn't take Frasier Crane to work out that Marv covered himself in armour.

'Mainly I got to know the people I'd take drugs from – or with. I had trust issues, and kept people at arm's length. Still do. I don't want to take other people's problems on. I've got enough of my own.'

So glue, gas, and then he discovered cannabis before, aged sixteen, he progressed to LSD. Then whizz. Then Es. Crystal meth. Basically, anything he could get his hands on. 'I'd buy amphetamines off a fella, then coke – never stopped – then went to spice. I tried heroin, but it wasn't for me. I don't like the sleepiness. I'd rather be alert. My DNA was telling me not to touch that – my mum, screaming from the other side.' The speed was made in a local mill, coming out like paste and stinking like cat piss. 'Nowadays I'm drug-free, but that cocaine high was the most beautiful feeling you could put in your body. You feel on top of the world. The release is just heaven in a rock, or bag. But the powder never gave that to me. You never got the feeling you got off freebase crack, which has all the impurities out, crystallized.'

He also started selling stuff, Es and whizz to begin with.

'I've only ever had two jobs in my life: selling drugs and, when I got expelled from school, my sister got me a job in a textile factory at Newton Heath. Obviously, I spotted a flaw in the system and got to robbing straight away. It was one of them old mills, five floors with a massive storage warehouse.'

Marv's job was to go to the floors where people were sewing, fill a box with all the ends of material and other rubbish and take it back down and across the car park to this storage building. After putting it in there he'd go back and do it again. The stores where the products were kept – quilt covers, pillow-cases, curtains – were on the third floor. 'I got on it straight away. *This is fucking easy, this.*'

The trolley was one and a half metres wide. He'd separate a square of space in the box from the material around it, stop at the third floor, run to the stores, grab a few items and put them inside, cover it all over with rubbish and wheel it down-stairs. Then, instead of putting it straight in the warehouse, he would throw the good stuff over a canal wall. After work, he'd go down the bank, collect the stuff, carry it home and sell it on the estate. Foolproof? Quite definitely not.

'I was there eleven days until I got nicked for it. The manager comes running out. "I've fucking caught you – I knew you was doing this!" Phoned the police. I got arrested, theft from a workplace, got a caution, sacked, and never got a wage because it was a week in hand.'

By then, though, Marv had already had run-ins with the law, not far from Forest Bank and Strangeways, where he'd end up. He said his first proper arrest came when the lad he was with took a gold signet ring off someone in Manchester city centre. 'The guy went and phoned the police, telling them the robber was black and had no socks on. So they found him and I was arrested as well. In the police station I went for a wee and a copper said, "If you was older, I'd kick the fuck out of you, you little bastard." I got a caution for that.

'I also got probation for my first-ever street robbery when I was thirteen, going on fourteen. After school I had to go to an office and used to sit there playing pool with the probation officer. Since then, he's gone on to run the whole of the North-West Probation Service. Really good guy, Mr Wright, heart in the right place. I'm glad he's done well.'

This would have been around 1987, before the Moss Side gang wars of that period really got going. 'All the kids who turned into big-name gangsters were around. We had the Cheetham Hill Boys, the Moss Side Boys, one of the Maynards. Every Thursday night all of us used to go to hip-hop night in Ashton. Groups of local lads used to lie in wait and brick the bus. We'd have to pull the seats off, use them as barricades. Sometimes the bigger lads used to jump off and chase them . . .

'Good times, and this is what used to mystify me. We had all these lads who were mates in the city centre, but who'd go on to be well-known gangsters, serial killers and arch enemies up the road.'

At the time, Marv was still living in Ancoats. 'I was going to little dance clubs and stuff when the rave scene started. At sixteen, I thought I wanted to be independent, met my first baby mum during those few days in the textile factory and moved into her flat. I wanted my own things about me, my own place in the world. I'd never had that.'

The lass lived in a block of flats a hundred metres from where he grew up, in the middle of his estate. 'I was selling whizz, bits of weed, from the tenth floor. I was away from my adoptive mum and dad by then, but regretted it from the minute I moved in. I didn't love her and we didn't get on. I wanted to get away, but she fell pregnant. I wasn't ready for a child, but you put your dick there . . .'

It was also around this time that Marv did proper crack for the first time, aged seventeen.

'I remember it clear as day. I used to sell Es and whatnot and had seen this nice girl on the dance floor. We started talking and I had a pocket full of sweaty money. She asked if I wanted to go back to hers. I did, sure, and in her house, near my estate, she offered me some. I'd tried cocaine before, but only a couple of drags in a spliff while rolling with Salford kids on the club scene. Moss Side gangsters . . . Cheetham Hill gangsters . . . Salford gangsters . . . the main boys hung out together. But then money started coming into it. There was a load to be made from the doors. The Salford boys would jump the counter, rob the champagne and give it out to their boys, know what I mean?

'It started getting a bit crazy, and you had your Noonans, who were on the doors, trying to stop it. At least that was how they wanted it to look. They had this image as a load of Robin Hoods, public-spirited, though everybody suspected that wasn't quite how they carried on in private. The oldest, Damien, was the best – he was the one who built that family. When he died, that family died. Damien was the main boy from when he ran the Hacienda door.

'I remember seeing him one day when I was a raging addict, crackhead. I was waiting to buy crack outside a pub in Hulme. I've seen him and he's seen me and said, "Oi, come here." I was with this lad who said, "What the fuck does Noonan want wid'ja?" I said, "Fuck knows," and walked over. He went, "How are yer? Y'all right?" then pulled a wedge out and give me £20. I was waiting to buy crack from a Yardie but would have to blag it for £17.50, as I was £2.50 short. I says, "Are you all right, Mr Noonan?" all polite, like. "Look after yourselves," he says, "chill out." I'm guessing he wanted me away from the front of the boozer. So I've had to run around a corner to this phonebox to tell this Yardie, "Do not come to the Gamecock now. Noonan is outside. If he sees you selling me drugs he will beat you." I've never forgot him doing that little gesture for me, whatever his reasons, and I used to do the same.'

As Marv got older and made a few quid, he said he'd go see the kids in Ancoats and give 'em twenty quid. 'One had a raggedy pair of trainers on. Took him into town and bought him a pair with a stolen card. Done that a few times. I have kids come up to me now – "Marv, I remember you, mate. You was fucking mint, you.""

But let's get back to the crack. 'This girl, she come in with a pint pot, foil on it, crack on it, very organized. Tried it, fell in love with it.' He started on crystal meth only a few years ago. 'It's exactly the same buzz, same intensity. I spent all my money with this girl that night and next morning, ten o'clock, went to my best mate's house, the one who's a bouncer now. "I've just found a new drug," I told him. "Fuck me, mate, it's on fire – we need to buy some." Hyper, I was. At the time it was so new you could only buy it in Moss Side.'

Still selling weed, him and his mate agreed they would only do crack on weekends, but on Mondays Marv would sneak off and spend £80 for four lots on the sly. 'I'd smoke it dead quick.

He'd be buying it too, without saying. Messed up our friendship for a bit. Super addictive.'

His first time in grown-up prison, though, not counting as a baby, was for robbery when he turned twenty. Still involved drugs, mind.

'I found out some kids were selling heroin on my estate, in Ancoats. They were from Middleton, used to buy weed off me. I'd some lad with me and I said, "Carry this," and I passed him a machete. So I knocked on the door. "Patrick, what you up to?" and pushed my way in. There were five of them. "Why are you selling smack on my estate?" One had a bracelet on, which I took off him, along with all the money in the house. Then we walked out the back door, and the lad I was with threw the machete on the ground in the garden.'

When Marv had gone, these lads phoned the police, saying they had been robbed. 'Didn't say they was drug dealers, though. Said that was me, and the machete was later used in evidence. I got bailed, was outside the supermarket one day and seen one of these lads going in. So I flipped his legs from under him and put him on the floor with my knee at his throat. "You little bastard. You're selling smack and getting me locked up for it." He phoned the police again, and I got done for breaking the terms of my bail – remanded into custody for it.'

Wow. He's not a very ethical drug dealer, is he?

'I got done for robbery times two, my first-ever sentence. Went to jail for twenty-seven months.' The prison in question: HMP Hindley in Bickershaw, near Wigan. 'The cell when I got there had nothing in it, just bars, door and a bed frame. We had to drag the mattresses in ourselves. The walls were full of spit, piss and graffiti. A white piss bucket in the corner was stained yellow. At first, I thought I'd gone to hell.'

In some ways he had. This was when Greater Manchester's prison estate started to fill up with all those violent gangsters: lads like Luke Taylor, of the notorious Pitt Bull Crew. His brother, Aaron, had fallen victim to a gangland shooting.

'Yeah, that was when it started going crazy, and I'll tell you why. Because of all that money in nightclub doors. When we used to roll in town, you were the man if you were in the latest hip-hop trainers, could dance and had yourself a tidy bird. But then the doors started coming into it, and they realized how much money there was to be made off the rave scene. You think: a thousand people paying a tenner each is a quick ten grand. And that was for a lad who owned a club. Suddenly, there's ten grand in his office.'

It doesn't take a genius to work out what happened next.

'People was just going in and taking it, so then he has to start paying others to protect his cash, doesn't he?'

Marv recalled one nightclub in particular, the Conspiracy, 1989, before his prison career got going.

'The Thunderdome in Ancoats had just been closed down, due to gangs and stuff. The police kept raiding it. I used to make my own Es and sell a bit there, rhubarbs and custards, red and yellow. I'd get cold capsule tablets, sleeping tablets, crush 'em, put in a bit of whizz. A mate and me would make enough a night.' Marv said they made a fortune. 'Tenner a pop, twenty pounds a pop . . . Es were £20 each. Then they started dropping in price: two for £35. Then people started to sell 'em for £15. Then they went down to a fiver.

'We was going in clubs and even Tony Wilson, the king of

Manchester, would come up to us: 'All right, lads, how you doing? Still selling the pills?' It was all just a laugh and a joke for a while.'

One Saturday morning, though, when Marv had just got home after being out all Friday night, his door was suddenly bashed in.

'Police. I'd been followed from the nightclubs. They'd been watching me selling drugs in the clubs and took the door off its hinges. But I had only been selling fake pills. None was real Ecstasy. I admitted it in interview. Still got convicted for possession with intent to supply, though, times two. Possession of cannabis too, because I had a bit of weed there I had to go guilty for. I got a combination order for that.' His solicitor told him, 'You do not know how lucky you are.'

'I just thought it was a joke – went to court thinking, *I'll be home soon*. My solicitors fought for my freedom. They said 99 per cent of people go to prison for what I'd done, but because I hadn't yet been in jail, it didn't happen' – until the robbery a year later, anyway . . .

'When I finally did end up in jail, it was on my birthday as well. I'll never forget the smell of the bars. I was addicted to crack by then, but in those nine months inside I never once seen or touched it even. I was sure I was going to give it up. *I'm not gonna touch it again* . . . But, do you know, the day you get out, you forget about prison. The minute you are in reception and you step out of that gate, it's like you've been asleep. All that energy you built up to get clean goes out the window. I bought crack with my discharge money and within hours was back to square one.'

That happens a lot when people get no training in how to

transition. They just walk straight out into it. 'I turned back into the same crackhead,' said Marv. 'But looked better. That was all.'

He went to see his adoptive mum and dad, wired out of his head.

'My dad had a go at me but I wasn't listening to him by then, didn't like or respect him as a person. I was getting a reputation around the place and he didn't like that. As far as I was concerned, he could fuck off.'

Marv had vowed never to bully anyone weaker. 'I was around prostitutes all the time when I was young, as our estate was next to the red-light area. This old working girl told me, "Marv, two things you must never do and you'll be all right. Never hit a girl, and never take her money." I could be intimidating, a tall black lad, but had a heart of gold. I would never steal off the girls, and they got used to me. I treated 'em with respect. I never bothered them for sex – that was their job. It's like if you know a painter and ask them to come paint your house for nowt in their spare time. You want a day off, don't you?'

The girls used to ask him to clock the registration plate of any cars they got in – 'so the punter saw that I'd seen him and couldn't beat them up or worse. They'd wave as they went past. Sometimes they'd pull notes out of their knickers or bra and hand the cash over to me, saying, "Mind my last punter's money."'

Or they'd ask him to score some crack for them. 'I'd help them do robberies, pretending to be police. She'd take them down an alley and I'd come around the corner with a flashlight: "Ey, ey, what you doing?" And because his pants are round his ankles, she'd already taken his money out and put the wallet back. We never stole those, and we never took wedding rings. We were conscientious, looking back. Even bank cards, we wouldn't fuck with them, and they were worth a lot of money. Why? Well, if you took their wedding ring, they'd have to admit to it at home, wouldn't they, bring the police in, and same with a wallet. If you just took money, embarrassment kept them quiet. I also had a bit of compassion.'

Out of prison, Marv moved to a squat in Moss Side. 'I wanted crack, and was soon living from empty house to empty house, on my own.' Some local boys recognized his face from the old days in town. 'Boys were coming up and saying, "What you doing around here, you?"'

Obviously, with the gang thing at its height, that could have quite definitely been a problem. He was on Moss Lane East, the old frontage to Moss Side, where all the drug dealing went on.

'I got paid for bringing punters in. Cars would go past with lads from Doncaster or somewhere else out of town. They came from all over – Stoke, Midlands, Yorkshire – to buy a parcel. I'd whistle to slow them down – I was used to doing that for working girls, making connections. Yardies would ask me to get some shots and they'd dish them out in Broadfield Road park. I'd say the punters could leave the money in the car if they liked, to put them at ease, so they didn't think they were getting robbed. Then I'd drag them over to the dealer, who would be sat safe and sound in the park. I was getting paid for that.'

Once he was in a car with two lads and one pulled a gun. 'He stuck it in my face and said, "If you tell anyone I'm buying this, I'm going to kill you next time I see you." It was two o'clock in the morning. He was just out off a nine-year detain, a gangbanger done for a shooting in Moss Side, but also a closet crack smoker, which on the street is looked down upon. You're at the bottom of the pile.'

Marv reminded me that Biggie Smalls did a song called 'Ten Crack Commandments'. One of the most important: don't get high off your own supply. If you are smoking crack, you can't be trusted with anything.

Even though he was still in Moss Side every day, Marv's base was now in Wythenshawe, where his baby son's mother lived. 'What I'd do every couple of days is go and give them money – hundred quid, hundred and fifty. It was important to me, my moral compass. Then I'd fuck off. I tried to keep my drug habit as far from him as possible, but then my habit was affecting him because I didn't raise him. Soon I was in and out of prison, although my adoptive mum and dad still had that link because he'd come down to their house at weekends and stay, so he was still being raised by my family.'

But one kid in Moss Side really saved his bacon.

'At the time, I was also going onto Doddington estate to rob punters, drug users . . . easy meat. Me and my mate, who is doing life now for stabbing a student in town, we'd stand there, the car would park up and he'd skull-drag them out the car, fingers in their mouth, thumb under their chin. He was violent – "Give me that money." I'd use my brains. We robbed a couple and then got a warning from the Pepperhill Mob: stop robbing on the estate or it will come back to bite you on the arse. Not good for business, you see.

'So I think we'd already pushed our luck, because one Saturday morning I'm on Moss Lane East and a car comes past. There's a lad in it called Jason Winters, one of the Pepperhill crew. "Marv," he said, "your time has come here now, mate."'

Winters told him to get in the car.

'I'd known him years. He said, "We've come to a bit of a dilemma, Marv. James wants to see you now." This would be James Miller from the Doddington gang, who we mentioned earlier, and he's not happy. "He's going to knock you about a bit. But listen: he's been shot in the head, just come out of hospital, two big scars from his neck to the top of his head. I know your game, Marv, but hit him back and you'll get shot."'

'I'm thinking, *Oh shit*. Winters was giving me a heads-up, a proper squeeze. He made me an offer. "Right, I'll drop you at Wythenshawe instead, but you've to stay away from Moss Side." I couldn't do that. It was where the crack was based, where all the money was, my bread and butter. "Or you can front it now and I guarantee you won't get shot." So I told him, "No, fair enough. I'm in the wrong. I'll front it."

So off the motor went to Doddington estate and the Pepperhill pub. 'We get in the avenue and, sure enough, James Miller is standing there with an English bull terrier. It had been nicked from a scrapyard, so was a proper vicious beast. There were also about twelve lads behind him, masked up. I still knew who they were, recognized the fuckers. You can tell who people are with a mask on, can't you?'

Clearly this course of action had been decided on already – *Here's Marv. He'll get what's coming to him today*.

'They drove me into the avenue and I got out of the car. "I'm so sorry, mate . . ." I started to say, but then whack! He smacks me one in the face. "Dog! Get him!"

'Well, this fucking animal chewed me to fuck. Ripped my legs to shreds . . . look.' Marv showed me the result. A fucking ton of scars, bite marks everywhere. 'The dog's biting me like fuck, and as this is going on Miller's smacking me himself. The only other person hitting me was his son, Kyle, who's become a friend of mine since. Back then he was hitting me with a Lucozade bottle, trying to smash it on my head.'

Marv said he started screaming, not that he felt anything, being high on crack. 'You don't start laughing, do you? I thought screaming would stop them, but it didn't. I jumped into a garden and they threw the dog in after me. Then they got some fireworks out and started firing air gun repeater rockets at it. The banging sent it crazy. I got a good ten minutes of that, blinded by the flashing, maybe longer. I was flopped, man. Have you ever been bit by a dog? Oh, it's horrible – worse than getting stabbed, and I've been stabbed. Dogs dig in and rip at you like you're just a lump of steak.

'So, eventually I've staggered out the garden – and this is where my crack use came into play. He's like, "Don't come on this estate again, robbing fucking shots, or you're gonna get it." So I started to hobble off, thinking my legs were going to explode with the pressure, still worried I might get shot, but otherwise relieved it was over. But then, being a dickhead, I turned round to go and apologize again – "James, I didn't mean it . . ." – and he's gone, "What have I just fucking told you? Dog! Get him!" Oh, my God. I'm at the end of the avenue now, trying to get away. I got around the corner, and this is where the kid, the closet crack smoker who I won't name, saved my skin. At night, he'd sell drugs with the rest of his crew then come and see me.

'I used to break into houses in Moss Side, furnished on rental, but no one living there. I'd get in and they were mine. They had fire doors you could open by slamming them. This kid used to come and ask, "Marv, have you got anywhere where we can have a smoke?" So we'd sit there, him and me, and he'd say, "Don't tell anyone I'm smoking or I'll kill you." It's all right to sell, but not use. Crazy, innit?

'Anyway, he's torn round the corner after me, turned round to make sure no one was watching, grabbed the dog and said, "Marv, get off now, man – go, go, go!" So me, I went. I didn't go to hospital, mind. Just sat in an empty crack house, smoking to deal with the pain.'

It came as a shock for me to discover that not every Yardie or drug pusher belonged to some gang or another – it blew a bit of a hole in the whole Manc gangster myth.

Marv revealed that a few older lads operated on the fringes. Others – a nephew or brother of a gang member maybe – had their money-making activities tolerated too if they were on their own turf.

'Got to be gangsters? Oh, no, no. Moss Side is very small. There's only one road separating Gooch and Doddington.'

Marv told me of one kid who was always getting 'kidnapped' by the police. 'They used to throw him out in the middle of Gooch estate, but the boys there wouldn't shoot him because they knew the boys in blue had just dropped him off! They'd give him a squeeze and let him go.'

Moss Lane East, where Yardies and non-gang members stood, sounds like a bit of a free market, similar to roads where take-aways pitch together. They could sell bits as long as they didn't get too big for their boots and stayed in their own lane. That's obviously where Marv fucked up.

In Strangeways, as I say, I worked among loads of gangbangers who have grown up a bit now, said they were done with it, families and so on. I wondered if that meant things were quieter on the out.

'No. There is still a lot of animosity. You've got to remember, before prison these guys were killing people. There are kids growing up who know who shot their dad, know what I mean? A lot of fellas go straight 'cos they've no choice. If they get seen in certain places, they'll be dead. The only way to escape it is to move out of the area.'

Well, that or retreat inside your head. We had this character in Strangeways who once took LSD, and it damaged his mind. He'd put his clothes on inside out, shoes wrong way round, was always stood on the landing cadging cigs. It sent him simple. But if any of the other inmates tried to bully him, he would beat them to fuck. Not that there couldn't be kindnesses too, if you want to call drug pushing that.

The day after Marv got chewed, he ran into a kid with a gobful of gold teeth – 'a really nice lad, with compassion for me. I'd see him on a morning. He went into the newsagent's for a paper at five o'clock, saw me, told me to wait, went back to his flat for crack, walked past and threw it on the ground. He knew I was just in and out of houses.' That would have been so he wasn't seen passing it on.

What none of them knew, however, was that they were being filmed, and had been for the last nine months. James Miller got ten years, his son six, others got years too. The surveillance was done from a house that has since been knocked down and turned into a community garden.

Marv, meanwhile, still had a habit to feed.

'On Moss Lane East, back in 1994, there was a guy called Noel, who everyone said was pure money. At that time in Moss Side you could buy a house for five or six thousand pounds. A burned-out derelict house cost three grand, and he was buying them up.' Our man Marv, meanwhile, was one of those busily emptying them. 'Toilet seats, showers, plug sockets – you name it. I had a kid who'd come with a van and buy it all – furniture, the lot. He'd unscrew everything he wanted. There's a lot of guys who were at it back then who now have very large property portfolios.' As the millennium approached, Marv would get about £100 for the contents of an entire house and spend it all on crack. 'I didn't make a bean; smoked the lot. Vast amounts.'

It wasn't just houses. He'd do whatever it took, including fleece those customers of working girls in town. One favourite, a lesbian he said was really into him, spent what she got on crack and smoked it with Marv. One punter, who liked her to trample all over him, kept her in new clothes and actually bought her a house in Wigan. 'It was obvious he was infatuated with her. She used to take all the clothes back afterwards and get the cash. He offered to buy her a diamond ring, so we did a deal with the jewellers to con him on that too and made £500. You'd think she would have used that house he got her as a way out of her situation, wouldn't you? Live there, maybe stand on him twice a week, but no. That's not how an addict's mind works. Bottom line, we smoked every penny away.'

And it goes fast. Think darts players can calculate quickly on their feet? They are nothing to these guys. When he's working out prices, Marv would give Einstein a run for his money. Listen to this story about Dessie Noonan who, as we read in chapter two, was stabbed by Hank Brown, one of the inmates at HMP Kirkham. (Don't worry if you struggle to keep up – so did I!)

'He used to come to this crack house next to the swimming baths in Moss Side, where I was living with a guy called Toddy. He always had a driver, Noonan, and did then, two days before he got killed. He reckoned the police just took £400 off him, gave someone £20 and said to bring a Jamaican Yardie to him, as they generally had the best gear. Noonan bought fifteen white. He got the guy to open every single one, put the crumbs to one side. You get 0.2 for £20, so ten points is a gram. You get five £20 stones off a gram. He gave the rest of us about a gram of bits, kept the rest for himself and was putting £20 stones on the pipe. Know what that means? You're smoking £20 in a go. As quick as you take a drag of a cig, the smoke coming off it, that's £20 gone – real money. Thirty seconds . . .'

If I have a pint, a pint and another pint, at some point I'm gonna be fucked, aren't I? With crack, you're not. You want more. 'You never stop,' said Marv. 'Same with smack, you are going to fall asleep eventually, aren't you? Skunk, you'll wipe yourself out. Crack, you just keep going, chasing it all day long. I'd think of money in terms of how much crack it would get me, nothing else.'

Having eventually joined us at Strangeways, Marv was soon a mover and shaker – another example of how, for the hardened criminal, jail quite definitely holds no fear whatsoever.

'As soon as you go in it's about faces you recognize. Straight away you'd get the bits and bobs you need. I got a lot of respect because I was a bit crazy, used to do the hits and stuff. I was the debt recovery agent in Strangeways.'

By then, losing his freedom wouldn't have mattered to Marv because for a great proportion of his prison career and especially at HMP Manchester he was on crack. And for the addict your next fix is all that matters, whether you're holed up in a derelict house on Moss Side or the twos landing in Strangeways. He was completely consumed by that product for a good two decades.

It's also why prison is no deterrent to lads like him. He knew everyone inside just as he knew everyone on the out; pretty much every criminal on just about every landing . . . Wythenshawe lads, those from Cheetham Hill, the lot. The Salford boys, he knew them too, collected debts for them, as he says. And because he wasn't affiliated to anyone, he was sitting pretty, could move in every circle. In Strangeways, he already had a reputation and was able to slot in with no great disruption – business as usual.

By his own admission, although a big lad, Marv is not the hardest man on the planet but what he does have is presence and he put that to good use, became a bit of an enforcer. That meant he had no trouble getting whatever he needed, be it phones or drugs; he's a dab hand at networking. Lads like Marv make a lot of connections in prison, which they can – and do – continue to use once they are dumped back in the concrete jungle.

Nor is Marv the sort of prisoner you'd find on a detox wing, which, given his addiction, might be a surprise to some. Here's why.

When coming into Strangeways reception Marv is not going to ask for help and would turn down any offered. He'll either bring what he needs in with him or know where to get it and how to move it around to his advantage from the off. Other new arrivals, who might have been in police cells and are rattling by now, might ask to see a section officer, nurse or doctor . . . 'Are you an addict?' 'Yeah.' Little fish in a big pond, they are. Having declared addiction in reception they'll be given an amount of methadone, a drug used for opioid therapy and pain relief, and be bundled straight off to I Wing. Marvin, staying shtum, would go on normal location, safe in the knowledge that he wouldn't have any problem getting what he needed.

What's more, he wouldn't need to pay for anything either. 'Yeah, Marv. We'll sort you out. Can you go and have a word with that lad because he owes us . . .' It would have gone like that.

No prison was ever going to get Marv clean and anyway, even if it had, it wouldn't have stopped his criminal behaviour. He was quite literally born to the life, as we've seen. His criminality fed his crack abuse and vice versa, and helped to shape and maybe worsen his behaviour. If it hadn't been crack driving him in and out of jail, it would quite definitely have been something else.

So for him a spell in Strangeways was not that big of a deal, just one part of his everyday experience, one of them who is in so deep with so many dodgy types that at some point jail becomes inevitable. You might be buying crack off someone being watched by Manchester Police – a lot get lifted that way.

There were always operations on. In Moss Side, the coppers had maybe ten houses, either derelict or with someone moved in, and they'd clock people for months. You won't catch lads like Marv fighting or with drugs in their cell, none of that. They know how to play the game.

On one occasion, our old K Wing SO, Bertie Bassett, took him into his office and sat him down in his chair. 'Here you are,' he said. 'I've been hearing your name a lot, and since you run the place . . .'

In prison, Marv was one of those I was not going to catch in a cell, beating someone up . . . We all knew him – cheeky chappie on the landing. 'What you up to?' 'Nothing, Mr Samworth,' nice and polite, like. When it comes to bad behaviour, his type know how to fly under the radar, look like they are just getting on with their jail time while up to all sorts in reality. Pleasant-natured, never had any real confrontation with staff, none I can remember anyway. Even as an addict, or maybe *because* of that, he was, and is, a very shrewd lad.

So how do drugs get into prison? I asked.

'People on remand,' explained Marv, 'they've got co-accused on the street. As soon as they meet in the dock, parcels are passed. It happened to me. I had a gang of armed robbers from Ancoats doing that. They were getting multiple ounces of heroin at a time – fortunes, it was worth. They had people from the top end of the jail buying a quarter off them, seven grams, selling it for £1,000 – an eighth for £500. One ten-pound bag of heroin in prison, you're probably making fifty quid. Five wraps off it, yeah? I had kids who would buy a weight of drugs off the lads say to me, "Bag 'em all up." So I'd be sitting there doing the wraps, go and give them out, and people would spend their money willingly. They'd be waiting for me. "Marv, give us mine . . ." I'd flick it under their door.'

For most it's about passing the time, but smoking heroin and crack are big no-nos inside. 'Closet smokers lose respect, as people know they can be bought. Mind you, people knew I did it. There was crack in Strangeways. It did used to come in. There was lots of ways of getting it in Forest Bank too. There was a shop outside, and people used to order magazines for inmates. You'd pick a mag off the shelf, give it to the shop-keeper, he'd bag it up, put a sticker on it with your name on and put it on a pile with all the others going to the prison. I knew kids from Salford who'd fill magazines with drugs. Cut a hole inside, have it looking exactly like the ones on sale and pretend to go to the counter with one of them but switch it. Next news it would be on a pile waiting for their mate in the prison wing office.'

Now there's a thing. I do remember magazines coming in . . .

Marv even did a bit of work for Liverpool gangsters Nicholas Johnson and Isaac Clark. 'They got robbed by this Oldham firm who took their smack. They gave them it willingly – "There's the gear, don't take the phone" – but lost the phone anyway. So these Scousers come down to our landing: "Oldham firm robbed us, we'll pay to get our shit back." They were getting boulders of drugs in over the wall, and offered me a quarter of weed for every Oldham kid I banged out. Every night there'd be a shout: "Anyone want to see the medics?" I'd go down there myself and chat to everyone in this big waiting room: "I know your face, where are you from?" If they said "Oldham", bam! I'd go and collect my weed.

'I knew people in debt. I'd probably smoked some parcel

with them. Maybe they owed £400 to someone, couldn't pay it. Their bird's been dropping money off on the out but now doesn't want to pay the bill, so he tries to move wings. I'm paid to hurt him, but here's what I'd do. I'd go to the cell. "You know you're wanted, don't you? You know you're in trouble. I'm supposed to beat you black and blue. But I don't want to do that, so here's what we'll do. I'll give you the lightest dig I can over your eye. I'll skin it like we'd do with rapsies and a deck of cards." Pop the eye, bang, it would open, claret everywhere. You run down the landing, full of blood, and that would be me getting paid. I'd give 'em a bit of parcel to keep 'em quiet, work with 'em.'

To some, rapping a bloke on the eyebrow with your knuckle might still sound brutal, but don't forget, if someone told Marv, 'I need him sorted,' and he came back and said, 'I've pulled his ear,' well, that's not going to be acceptable, is it?

Marv also agreed with the point I made to Lee Robson: don't borrow anything. 'Yeah, everything's double-bubble back, isn't it, and worse? If you don't pay one week, it's doubled the next, like on the street.'

Sometimes Marv actually wanted to go to prison, to try and get a break from the crack – and also from life! 'I was born there; it felt like home. Sometimes I'd be on the street and think, *I need a bit of jail, me*. I'd pull a stupid theft. Nick a rack of clothes, say, three months if I got caught. That was the mentality of a lot of people – *if I get caught, I get caught. If I don't, I don't*. You get away with it, so do it a bit more, until you do finally get collared.'

After three or four years in Moss Side, Marv was caught for robbery, possession of a firearm and something he couldn't recall.

One night, on remand in Strangeways, he watched *Granada News*.

'It said, "Raid in Moss Side – drug bust", with pictures of doors going in. I recognized all the houses. Next day I got ordered to the police station, told I'd been filmed. A taxi had come, two girls working undercover for Greater Manchester police got out: "Can you get us crack?" "Yeah," I've told them. "Give us your twenty quid . . ." I've gone in the bookie's, bought a piece of crack off some lad, split it on the counter, wrapped one half up and given them the other. That's me nicked for supplying crack cocaine. The camera didn't lie. Twenty-six of us got arrested. It was called Operation Noel as it began over Christmas.'

One time on remand he went to court with scran he'd got from lads on the wing, to give to someone in exchange for a ball of crack. That was the plan. The kid had him on, saying that he couldn't get it out of his arse, so Marv of course started panicking. No way he could get all the food back, so if he didn't get the drugs, he'd be twatted! At the very last minute, this contact slipped him the goods. 'Most stressful morning I've ever had.'

In all, Marv smoked crack from the age of seventeen to thirty-seven, had two hundred convictions and went to jail over twenty times. He's been stabbed – 'Going through Broadfield Road park with Frankie, a mate of mine. He asked me to buy him a can. "Nah, man," I said, "I'll give you some crack instead." But he's an alcoholic and stuck a knife in my side. "You should have bought me a beer," he said.'

He's been bitten by a police dog – 'I was smoking crack in an empty building. Someone had seen the lighter going and called the cops. I hid, but they set their dog on me. I thought the Miller dog was bad, but this was worse. The copper knew me and left it on for ages. They took me to hospital, where the nurses treat me like shit.'

He was nearly killed with a weights bar – 'I robbed a mate's PlayStation from his house. Sold it to another mate for crack. I'm sat in a car in Wythenshawe and all of a sudden this fucking bar crashes in on my legs. My knee's ruined. I had an X-ray; the cartilage is gone. He tried to ram my eye out too, so I've a big scar under that.'

He's even got a scar on his tongue. 'Got caught pickpocketing in Blackpool. The bouncer leathered me, split my tongue and it bled for three weeks. Every time I touched a pipe the blood would fill it up, but I still carried on smoking, making like Popeye, blowing it out. I had to sleep on my front or wake up choking to death.'

Oh, and before we let him go back to his now quieter life, let Marv tell you how he got shot for robbing a Moss Side dealer.

'A mate of mine said, "Do you want to start selling for me?" I said I'd give it a go. "There's ten white, £20 each, I want £100 back. You have £100." The minute he walked away I've smoked my five, so now every penny I make I've got to give to him. Then I smoked the other five. I've seen him again. "Ollie, sorry, mate – I smoked 'em all." He's only a little lad, but said, "Marv, you can't do that. What am I supposed to do to you? Have ten more. Just get your smoke out of it and give me £130 back. But don't fuck about or I'll end up shooting you, Marv." As soon as he'd gone I smoked the lot. I'm thinking I'll just graft and get the money back that way, but every time

I made money I was thinking, *Am I gonna give it Ollie or am I gonna go smoke?'*

No prizes for guessing which way that went.

'I left Moss Side for a bit, to stay out of his way, and hung about in town with the working girls, getting bits and bats off them. Then this lad said, "Marv, let's go buy some white," so I got in the taxi to Moss Side with him, put my head down so I wouldn't get spotted. Charlie, his name was. Anyway, he's gone into a nightclub that was in the middle of the estate, full of drug dealers drinking brandy and Coke. And while I'm waiting, someone has spotted me and told Ollie I'm outside.

'I'm fucked now. Caught. I could have told the taxi driver to fuck off, but I thought, *I can't run now he's seen me, blatant.* So I got out the car and said, "Ollie, I'm so sorry, mate." He's said, "What did I tell you, Marv?" He's a bit wavy off the alcohol. "Come and talk to me round here." So I went and he's pulled this big heavy revolver. Boom! Later on, forensic evidence showed that the gun had been used in multiple shootings.

'I think he missed – with the first shot. Then he hit me in the leg. It went right through. "Don't fuck me again, Marv. You better sort something out." I don't think he was trying to kill me.

'My leg was burning like it was on fire, but that didn't bother me. Do you know what I did? When Charlie got back in the taxi, I got in too and said, "I've been shot." Charlie, like a dickhead, has jumped out of the car shouting, "Who the fuck just shot him? Come on – fucking shoot me!" I'm saying, "Charlie, he literally will. Get in the car." But as soon as he did that, the driver left his keys in the ignition and ran off.'

So Charlie drove it instead, right past Manchester Royal Infirmary to a nightclub in town. 'We've got to the nightclub, walked in past the bouncers, who we knew, and my leg is pissing blood. I went straight to the women's toilet and began smoking crack. This is how mindless we were. I could have been dying, but crack was more important.'

All of a sudden, Marv says, a woman came in. '"Aaargh, there's blood!" There was an' all – big pool of it. I was bleeding out like fuck. "It's all right," I told her. "It's only me." She went and told one of the bouncers.' He told Marv he needed medical help, put black bin bags on the floor of his car and set off with him to the MRI. 'On the way there I still had a piece of crack. But I wasn't giving that away so I asked him for money to get some scran. He gave me twenty quid. I wasn't thinking that I might die – I was thinking about where my next pipe was coming from once I got out of the hospital. The doctors said I needed an operation; I said I wanted the bullet for my son, to put on a gold chain. They said, "Shut up, you daft cunt," or words to that effect, and asked the regional crime squad to come see me. "What happened?" "Dunno. Drive-by. Walking down the motorway and someone shot me."'

He discharged himself as soon as he could walk with crutches. 'We was on the phone later, Ollie and me. "Marv," he says, "I really didn't want to do that, you know." I've seen him since, in Strangeways. We laughed about it. I was thinking, *I've got him now. He's on a wing with me, trapped. I could beat him. Rip his head off. But I'm not gonna.* You've to think ahead to when you get out. Ollie is a high-ranking gang member, and I'd have a firm on me then, wouldn't I? It was just part of the game.'

*

The last time Marv was in prison was around 2012.

'I got nicked for theft. My mindset was changing by then. I'd met my partner Ciara and told her I couldn't do it any more – just sick of it. I was starting to hate myself. I needed to get off crack.'

So what helped him do that?

'Spice. I was on K Wing and this Yorkshire lad had some. He gave it to a Lithuanian kid, on basic, and he started doing roundhouse kicks on the exercise yard. I was locked up with a Scouser – clever boy, who used to get little parcels of weed on visits and we'd smoke it, low-key. The lad with the spice was giving away loads of it. He gave me a decent amount in a ball and the Scouser warned me not to do it all at once, just a tiny amount. It lasted until the day I got out.'

Marv found a shop in Stockport, the only shop in the north-west that sold spice, where three grams cost £20, but got to know the lad and was soon getting three packets for £25. I do remember it making its way into prison about that time. Marv feels responsible for bringing spice to Manchester. 'Nobody on the street had it until I started going up to people saying, "This is better than crack." It was loads cheaper, and lasted longer because you got more. But it was far stronger. For four or five years afterwards I used to sweat profusely for no reason what-soever. Apparently, it cooks something inside your body.'

His partner Ciara, listening to our conversation in the couple's flat while looking after their baby son as we talked, a nice family scene, had been locking him in before going to work, in case he got on the crack. 'But I didn't want that any more. This was stronger. I was sat there squeezing my bits as hard as I could because it was sending me crazy, off my cake, and I knew it. I would hallucinate and fall asleep during conversations, but still got everyone to try it. If a newsagent sold weak ones – which they could until it was banned in 2016 – I'd suggest some stronger brand like Exterminator.'

I think Marv's being a bit harsh on himself about bringing it into Manchester, but spice is certainly at epidemic proportions now. In Strangeways, they'd be up to the sort of stuff you can see online: a spice version of those reality TV 'bum fights' they used to film with homeless people. There was a lot of that going on.

'People would say to me, "Get two lads in a fight or in a washing machine and we'll video it." It was the maddest thing ever. It was like Manchester was the spice centre of the world. Piccadilly Gardens on the news with people falling over . . . medics checking they were alive. I feel responsible, because spice wasn't around before I started championing it. Nobody was smoking it in town. I was telling beggars to try it. It would have got out anyway, but I still feel terrible.'

He never did it at home, 'except once when she caught me at it in the shed. Knocked one of my front teeth out and I swallowed it. That was the first and only time. We've been together fifteen years.'

Getting off drugs was difficult. 'I could only stomach rehab for half a day. The spice is what got me off it, but then I started losing my mind on that, nearly killed me. I threw it down the toilet in the end. I sat there one day, skinny as a rake, and thought, *I could die at any moment.*'

If anyone can take credit for finally turning him around, though, it must be Ciara, his missus. 'One of my biggest regrets is not being there for her when I was locked up,' he says.

'Obviously I'm saying this looking back. At the time I was out of my tree. But it was that which eventually clicked a switch in my brain and let me see the benefits of the straight and narrow.'

Marv and Ciara have been together a long time and she has stuck by him. 'While on the out, I used to go on benders, missing for two or three days at a time. Having got myself in a bad place, I'd phone her up, "Come and get me," and she would.'

One time, Ciara got caught breaking into a crack den where Marv had been shacked up for two days. As she smashed a little window by the door, Manchester Police pulled up in a car. They knew who she was and asked what she was doing. 'What does it look like? I'm breaking into this house,' she told them. 'Marvin's in here and I need to bring him home.' The coppers just drove off.

On top of that, it was a health thing. Imagine how your body must feel after twenty years on crack and the rest of it, what it must do to your lungs and other vital parts. It fucks you right up. There's a danger of chronic obstructive pulmonary disease, COPD, for a start, and that's before you get to the impact of all those shootings and stabbings and dog bites . . .

'I know it's a cliché but you start getting old and realizing, don't you? Well, I did and made the missus a vow. On top of that, criminality around the drug industry has got even more violent. People are being run off of roads, they're going in houses and shooting folk . . . getting popped off. It's not an old man's game.'

Marv is no skinny kid any more. How is he even here?

'I've been through the mill and back. I've even got a frontal lobe brain tumour that I get checked out every year – and four slipped discs in my back and PTSD caused by childhood trauma. Abused, raped, all the drugs and the rest of it – I could've killed myself several times over . . .'

So where is Marv now? Well, studying Greek history for a start. 'I've got my brain switched on and found my birth family in London, lovely people who received me well. When you've got family, Greek Cypriots stick together. My cousins have a good relationship with my missus. They message her, have a laugh and stuff.'

He's not yet working for a living – as a result of those health issues we spoke about. And nor for that matter is Ciara, who has had nightmare issues of her own. You can hear more about her story on an episode of my podcast, *Real Porridge*. The main thing is they have both moved away – I won't say where, for obvious reasons – to somewhere new, made a fresh start. Still in touch with their families, all their energy goes into Thalon, the baby, and bringing him up right.

They deserve that much at least. Space to put Strangeways, gangs and terrible times behind them and get on with their lives.

Marv's first cousin has a beautiful mixed-race five-year-old boy of her own, so it turns out there's no problem on any racist front either.

'Back in the day, my auntie was seeing a black guy called Marvin and my birth mum's head flipped. "I don't want you seeing him." "Why?" "I had to give a son up called Marvin," she said. Sadly, my mum committed suicide in 2003, the same year my adoptive mum died, and I never got to know her. But before she went I do know that she made my aunt promise to treat me like a son. So when the family found me and my name was still Marvin they was all gobsmacked.

'I went to her grave, which was sad, as my mum's buried with another sister of hers who also had a bad time and killed herself. But the good news is Thalon and Ciara. I've never really harmed anyone, not badly, just myself. I've got no enemies. Our circle is very small and quiet and we keep ourselves to ourselves these days.

'I live in peace.'

5. Men in Black

So far we've met some of the kinds of people who end up in jail and heard their stories of how they got there. We'll meet more before we're done. But for a brief change of perspective, here are a few tales of my own, to show how it can look from an officer's side of the bars.

Kevin Stone was a classic Scouse blagger: a Liverpool 'crime boss' and importer of illegal drugs. A right royal pain in the arse. At Strangeways, we had him on the high-security Cat A wing, where he mithered us morning till night. However, he did have one use to society. He inspired one of the most entertaining videos I've ever seen – which came in handy, because this was early on in my career as a prison officer and I hadn't done Tornado training yet. Tornado teams being those boiler-suited units of supposedly elite officers who are brought into jails when riots and other such disturbances break out.

Back then, I worked a lot of overtime and got sent on court escorts, which I liked. You'd bring remand prisoners out of jail, take them to trial and make sure they behaved. Depending on what they were accused of, days could be fascinating, sometimes harrowing, but very often dull. The Stone case came during my first year, 2005.

He had already been convicted of money laundering a couple

of years before. Five years prior to that he'd been part of a plot to trade amphetamines and cannabis in Holland. This, though, was the big one. Now he was accused of masterminding a plan to traffic 593kg of cocaine from South America to Europe, the blow in question having been discovered on a yacht moored off the coast of Venezuela.

Thing is, he was sure he was going to get off this time because, when they found this stash, the only evidence that led anywhere near him was a single inky thumb- or fingerprint – the gear was wrapped in newspaper. That wouldn't be enough to nail him, he was certain.

In January, his missus, Olivia, had pleaded guilty to possessing criminal property herself – and had around five grand confiscated. As this latest trial went on, she and other Stone family members were in court every day and, by the look of it, had either not realized the true extent of his crimes or felt cocky about his chances themselves. As it all got worse, you could see Olivia's mood sag, especially when it was revealed that Mr Stone had a mistress. He'd splashed the cash on a seven-bedroom mansion, posh Spanish villa and items of jewellery. Despite his arrogance, eventually the verdict arrived: guilty, Mr Stone.

There was nothing luxurious about Strangeways' E Wing, but back he came, this time to get stuck into a twenty-eight-year sentence.

Boy, did he give us headaches. There were a lot of suggestible young 'uns on there at the time. I knew three who had been at Forest Bank and escalated into armed robbers. Stone stirred the shit. One minute he was demanding to speak to an SO, the next he wanted to see a governor, carrying on like Jimmy fucking Hoffa. *We want this. We want that.* It got so bad that he persuaded the entire wing to stand out – refuse to get behind their door. On Cat A that can mean thirty people.

Usually, situations like this develop into Mexican stand-offs. No one wants to make a decision; it's all about higher-ups minding their own back. The staff stayed on the wing throughout, which must have been a bit hairy. I wasn't there, so don't know what the grievance was exactly – a new toaster, most likely – but a call went out for the number one. Sadly for them, it was his day off. Tracked down, he wasn't best pleased. 'I'm shooting,' he said. 'Deal with it.' Everyone knew what he meant. *Fuck off. I'm not negotiating with them.*

It looked like a riot might be brewing, and normally in such circumstances that would be the signal for Tornado teams, not just from the host prison but others too, to ensure no conflicts of interest – the sort of jaunt I myself went on later, where you are trained to deal decisively with anything. This time, though, the governor said, 'Use our staff.' That's unusual. Other jails sent us their Tornado crews as usual, but it was HMP Manchester's who went on the landing to clean its own house.

In went our lot, marching forward like the Roman soldiers in *Ben-Hur*. Also like *Ben-Hur*, the whole thing would be immortalized on video, and was used for ages in training, before some enlightened fucker decided it was too near the knuckle and withdrew it.

On the screen, you saw one end of the wing, all the different levels, and the Tornado staff coming onto the landings with shields. Cat A prisoners were jigging about in front of them, jumping around and acting clever, playing the hard man, have a go if you're hard enough . . . Before long, one of them standing there giving it the gob gets twatted. He's on the floor and they march over the top of him, no messing. And where is Stone? Hiding in a cell, that's where. Shat himself. These other idiots that he's put up to it could take the hit instead. At least ten packed into a cell no bigger than a standard bathroom, barricaded with whatever they could find.

Now, for rucks like this, the national Tornado teams have an *A-Team*-style van full of a wonderful variety of toys we will never know fully about. Among them are 'pyros' – explosive fireworks, flash-bang grenades like the army use against terrorists. Throw one in and there's a blinding flash, a loud *boom*, people get disorientated, job's a good 'un. These days every officer has a PAVA pepper or 'mace' spray on their belt too, to go with the usual bodycam, radio and baton. It came in very quietly, did that, and there is now a move to kit officers out in safety vests too, as with the police. Anyway, in went the pyros, and the place went up like Bonfire Night without the treacle toffee.

In a space like that, those things go off big-style, ricocheting off walls. Absolute carnage. The Tornado team surged in and, before you knew it, all these lads were getting ragged out. Several were burned and a couple, by the look of it, were unconscious. When I came on the morning after the dust-up, the C&R – control and restraint – team was still there, strip-searching culprits, decanting them into vans, shipping them to HMP Frankland in Durham or south, maybe, sending a few to our seg' unit and scattering them to the winds.

Thanks to Stone, this tension had been building for weeks,

but now it had been sorted and the rabble-rouser-in-chief was nowhere to be seen.

Quite often as a Tornado officer, as I was to find out myself, once I'd done my training, you are mostly sat around eating pizza, waiting for those in charge to get their shit together or for someone to surrender. Well, not that time. And if jails were run so decisively more often, it would be better all round because everyone – staff and inmates included – would know where they stood.

Talk about a morale boost. The news went right around the high-security estate; everyone who worked in the jail was buzzing off it for days. The prison drums were beating.

They said: You do not fuck about with Strangeways.

And here – after another success story – is how *not* to do it.

But first, let me introduce you to Noah.

He was another I met at Forest Bank. Like Marv, he had lived on the street. Unlike Marv, he was an actual gang member, and a very odd one at that. He didn't fit in. He got his nickname on account of his love of animals or, to put it another way, having fucked a dog to death, so it was said. You might have him in your gang – he was a big tough bastard, hard as nails – but he wasn't someone you'd want at your parties.

Bestiality or not, he was an absolute horror show of a human being, twitchy and unpredictable in manner, capable of anything.

Anyway, like me, he was upgraded to Strangeways in the days when we had thirty-six gangbangers on K Wing, him being a member of one crew. Aside from looking over his shoulder on that front, he had another problem. Ongoing rape allegations put another target on his back. Gang power has influence – people don't want to talk, and there is witness intimidation – so that dragged his situation out a bit.

Given his reputation, we berthed Noah in a single cell as a high-risk prisoner. You wouldn't want anyone in with him, anyway. It wasn't long before he'd put his glass observation panel through, right in my face.

Fact is, he wanted off the wing. Kicking off was a cynical act. Sure, some gang members were 'on his side', but he wasn't liked, and the other lot might well have got a free pass. For survival, he fancied a move to the seg', but needed a face-saving way to get there. Hence that broken glass and the threat to my movie star good looks.

I wasn't badly hurt, and when our SO, Bertie Bassett, suggested a planned removal I was first in line, quite literally. As so often with Bertie, it was a smart and spontaneous decision, just how I liked it. In full gear, we'd go straight in, win the scrap and haul him off. We also had a second team on standby for back-up. There were three of us in the first party, experienced by then and of a similar age. Teams weren't necessarily made up of K Wing's hardest or biggest, but our sergeant major, Bertie, knew the strengths of his troops: 'You. You. And you.'

The lads with me were the type it's good to have at your side in an emergency; characters both. One was an ex-workshop instructor and a bit of a scratch golfer. Let's call him Bubba. For a while he gave lessons to our number one governor. One day, having turned down Bubba's day off request due to staff shortages, Bertie took a call from the head honcho, pulling rank, so a day off it was. Maybe that's why he got picked to go up against Noah. The other lad was known as Smithy Two Sausages, and you want to know why, don't you?

One of the jobs on K Wing was moves officer, which took three of us at a time: one in the office, running the ship – booking folk off and booking them on, an important role on the biggest wing in the jail – while the other two, on radios, moved prisoners back and forth all over the place . . . education . . . lads going to the bottom jail replaced by new ones from G Wing . . . new receptions destined for the top jail . . . all were escorted by that pair.

One day, though, the moves officers in question went AWOL, and, what's more, turned the radios off so no one could contact them. The officer in charge got quite worried – what the hell had happened to them? The answer didn't take long in coming.

At this time Strangeways had a little canteen, where officers from every wing could go with their butty lists. You could sit down for a meal too. Our governor, Campbell, has popped in for a sarnie and who should be doing exactly that but our two runaways, tucking into their breakfast. At first, he's thought nothing of it, not knowing they'd gone missing, until back on the wing the moves officer in charge asks if he'd seen the two of them on his travels.

'I have, yeah. They're having a full English.'

By the time I came back on duty, they'd got new nicknames courtesy of my mate Nobby Nobbler, an officer and expert in these matters. One, surname Day, became All-Day Breakfast, and took it on the chin. Smithy Two Sausages, though, got the hump. Not happy.

But back to Noah: I would go into the cell first, as shield

man, while Smithy Two Sausages and Bubba followed up the rear.

Now, as I say, this was a scary guy. No stranger to the seg', he'd also kicked off down there at some point, battering a couple of staff. One of the lads on there was way bigger than I am – six foot two and twenty-one stone – and he had been whacking Noah with batons trying to get him to the floor. It got caught on camera; a right scrap.

But we'd got our team together and I told Bertie Bassett to fuck everyone else off – you had your usual hangers-on, rubbernecking. He told me to take the briefing. By this point the nerves have kicked in. 'Listen,' I said, 'this lad has hurt people before. I'm not going in there to get hammered by him, so get your mind on it.' He's been given a chance to surrender; now we're coming in. Smithy Two Sausages is switched on. Bubba is switched on. I'm switched on. Like in a rugby scrum: crouch, set . . .

Here's how it goes. Slam the shield against the door and look through the 'obs panel' to locate him in the cell. We're ready now.

Bam!

The shield crashes down, and I shout, '*Back of the fucking cell!*' – I'm straining at the leash.

But then Noah starts shouting, 'I'm coming out!'

The governor behind us says, 'Whoah,' and we've withdrawn.

Noah is not for fighting today.

Procedure: he faces the back wall. We walk in, shield up, two guys at the rear come round and put the cuffs on him. This time he's gone compliant. Okay, so he's saved face and got off the wing, just as he wanted, but he also knew that we wouldn't put up with any messing, so there was none.

It hadn't always gone that way.

Someone on my training course, young in service, was involved in a similar incident. Noah wasn't good among people. This time he was barricaded on A Wing. Three inexperienced officers got the job this time; whoever was in charge was out of order. Like ours, it was a planned removal job with officers in riot gear.

Now, normal people in such situations throw their hands up and surrender. Why wouldn't you? You are in a cell when suddenly blokes in big helmets are shouting and rushing in . . . Plenty of prisoners see their arse, and understandably so. It's some scary shit.

But Noah was not normal people. This three-officer team has charged into the cell as ordered and gone for him with the shield but, before it's got any hotter he's said, 'I give up. I surrender!' just as he did with us.

Well, that stopped them in their tracks. But rather than see it through properly, like we did, cuffs on and the rest of it, the front man took him at his word and put his shield down.

Terrible move. Noah spun around and was on them before they realized. More staff piled in, and he ragged every last one of them. Due to piss-poor decision-making, officers got hurt. They'd not been briefed properly.

In the end he got nuttered off, did Noah, to Strangeways' CSU, close supervision unit, as a dangerous personality. He had a special psychological report done in which he recorded the highest psycho rating ever: off the chart. But while he was a serious badass freak, don't be thinking this was a one-off event.

I did read of an incident recently where the authorities got it spot on – the French authorities, that is! It was at Condé-sur-Sarthe Penitentiary Centre in France, which holds a variety of dodgy fuckers, radicalized more often than not. One mealtime an inmate improvised a weapon and took a male guard and female trainee hostage. He had convictions for rape, robbery and murdering a cellmate, and it looked desperate until elite police units arrived in helicopters and got them released with no one harmed. Indecision can be deadly.

This is one big reason why the job can be so challenging mentally on prison officers: a widespread lack of leadership, and organization that, instead of getting better, is actually getting worse.

Quite often you can wind up fearing for your life.

During a lockdown window I nipped over the Pennines to see a fellow officer who wishes to be known as George. The reason for that is he is still battling on in the job, although no longer at Strangeways, as part of what we used to call the Men in Black, or the Dedicated Search Team, as they are properly known. George knows his stuff.

Whilst at Strangeways, George originally trained for the Men in Black because he didn't like 'sitting in the office doing jack shit'. He fancied something different, attracted by the secrecy of it. The Dedicated Search Team, or DST, was mainly about dealing with Cat A types, so had a buzz. 'If high-risk, you searched their cell every couple of weeks. Standard Cat As got looked over every four weeks, which was also when Cat As moved cells.' When a prisoner went to court, that also meant trips out of jail. 'We'd set off early in the morning and search everywhere the prisoner would be going, right down to the toilets. We'd put seals on cisterns, doors and what have you – nobody else would be allowed in. Sniffer dogs would search it all too, looking for drugs, weapons . . .'

Another important aspect of DST work is CHIS – Covert Human Intelligence Sources. It's information gathering, basically – you'll have seen it in *Line of Duty*. It was an integral, if shady, part of prison life.

These regulated investigatory powers are shared by all jails, which, the official description states, 'may use CHIS where it is necessary and proportionate to do so for the purposes of preventing or detecting crime, preventing disorder, or on the grounds of public safety'. On successful searches, most finds came via these sources. 'All prisons will have trained staff in the key roles,' the CHIS outline goes on, 'to ensure that a CHIS is managed safely, to ensure appropriate decisions are taken regarding the information provided by the CHIS and that due consideration is given to the CHIS's welfare'. Regular prison officers like yours truly were never told who among us was trained to do this stuff and who wasn't, but we could guess. It was all very dark, hence 'Men in Black'. (Though the name also came from their uniform, the black polo shirt and cargo pants.) I wondered if these CHIS prisoners would have been reporting on prison staff too.

George sidestepped the question by saying, 'I've actually worked on false cell searches. That happens a lot. It gives us an excuse to go and see a con, while they give a member of staff loads of information.' As I say, shady.

It gets complicated, too, when certain gangbangers might grass up rival gang members so people will buy their stuff for more money. George nodded. 'They are not telling us out of the goodness of their heart, are they? If they can get rid of a rival drug dealer . . .'

Late one night, George and his team were searching an ex-IRA terrorist, a Cat A prisoner obviously. 'The kid was off to hospital two days later – we were making sure he'd no mobile on him. I walked on the wing with two others – we'd had info – and the officer in charge suddenly shouted, "They're here for you." That's the first and only time I've put in an incident report against a fellow member of staff.' Two days later, when George went back, the staff on the wing were no longer speaking to him. That's the prison service for you. 'Our DST boss was seen as a threat because he knew more about what was going on in jail than anybody – a real shame, because he was the ultimate professional. He had a handle on everything.'

But back to the IRA guy. 'We did a hospital escort with him. I think he had cancer, and they had to shut half of Manchester General Hospital. There were loads of us and thirty-odd armed police as well – must have cost a fortune. They'd had info that gangs were offering money to take one of us out. From then on, our phone calls went straight through to the police.'

One of George's team had a panic alarm fitted at his home. 'He let a decorator in one Friday morning and went off to work. When this officer came home, the decorator said he'd trodden on something under his bed, and it had made a bleeping sound then stopped. This kid thought, *Shit, it's the panic alarm*, but that was in the morning and this was evening, so he assumed it couldn't have been working properly as no one had come. On Sunday, he was on nights and got a phone call off a neighbour. The police had just smashed his front door in – two days late. That's the story he told us anyway. We didn't feel very secure after hearing it. If the IRA could've got one of us, they'd have loved it.'

Along with talking over old times George and I spoke about recruitment, and he confirmed that dynamic security is all but extinct across the prison estate. Very little in the way of staff–prisoner relationships at all. He has seen no one taken on with a mature head on his or her shoulders in two years. The majority are kids who don't know how to talk to dodgy people. In such a stressful job it's a recipe for disaster.

'One prisoner assaulted a member of staff,' said George. 'He grabbed them around the throat. We took it to court and he was sentenced to four weeks concurrent with his ongoing sentence. Where's the deterrent in that? He won't serve any extra time. The lad laughed. Only last week, he battered a doctor . . .'

As well as the physical dangers, staff can be left with mental trauma. It ain't just cons. Stories abound of officers self-harming. 'This one day I was checking one of my self-harmers,' George said, 'and he had blocked his observation panel. Something was not right, I thought. Your experience tells you.' There are supposed to be at least two officers present in such cases, but George was sure the kid couldn't overpower him so went in. 'He was hanging, unconscious, blue in the face. So I runs in and goes to get him, but he'd put shower gel on the floor and I went arse over tit. As I hit the deck I grabbed him, snapped the noose and we more or less landed on the floor at the same time. There was this deep suck of air and I got him round. I saved his life.'

During my own first night shift at Strangeways in 2005, I must have heard one emergency cell bell all week. Nowadays you get twenty to thirty an hour, all wanting daft things. 'You can't sit down on dinner patrol, either,' George said. 'You just go from bell to bell. It's endless.' He did admit, though, that life in the prison service has never been perfect, as this early memory of his about a run-in with a well-known Bolton gangster at Forest Bank shows.

One night when he was opening doors on the wing, smoke suddenly billowed from one cell. 'I couldn't breathe, so put my oxygen tank on – which we had back then – and went in on my own.' One of the two officers with him had run off, saying he couldn't do it. George found the lad inside sparko on the cell floor, pulled him out and nearly fell over this third officer, who was slumped by the door due to smoke inhalation. 'I had to drag her away too as she didn't have any safety gear on, but next thing I know this con has jumped to his feet and punched me in my face mask.'

Well, if anything was going to be a red rag to George, it was going to be that. Before long they were battling for supremacy. 'At the same time, my oxygen ran out because it had not been filled up from the last time it was used, so there I was, sucking on nothing. I do remember a feeling of relief, though, that he'd come up swinging, as that meant he was alive. Fortunately, the firemen soon arrived, put it out, and we got the fucker out of there.'

Unsurprisingly, feeling so isolated, George left Forest Bank not long after, but not before the governor had bollocked him for not following proper procedures. And to add insult to injury, 'when the fire brigade came they were unable to find any contingency procedures for fire at night – because the jail didn't have any. It turned out that before the three of us came back into work, the bosses knocked some up so they could say we hadn't followed them.' What they hadn't realized, however, was that the printer left a date on the paper – and that showed they had been printed out *after* the fire . . .

When George and I spoke, some of the managers at his prison had only been in the job for around eighteen months. 'There are a lot like them, young, clever and bright. But as for practical experience, common sense, physical presence and the rest, those things no longer seem to count.'

When he joined up, George had in-person tests in Leyland. 'They don't do it that way now,' he said. 'The first hurdle is an online test and, obviously, if you've got a mate who is sharp and you are not, well, they could do it for you, couldn't they?'

And yet Strangeways and other jails are still short of staff. 'We are always short-staffed. We have graduates now who are taking master's degrees, but being paid by the jail at the same time – working and learning. After two years, having got their degree, they can bugger off or stay in the service. Two years ago, our place took twelve on, and is now thinking, *Oh shit. They are coming to the end of their contract. We could lose every one of them overnight . . .*'

No graduate with any sense will want to stay on landings, will they? It's a stressful and hostile environment. If they are going to stop in the service, they'll go into management. Loads will find better-paid work in the police, border patrol or on the trains. Graduates will *not* become regular prison officers, make no mistake about that.

'Everything we get is second-hand from the police: our batons, radios, cameras – which only run for an hour at a time anyway,' said George. 'The only thing we have new is the PAVA, the pepper spray. They are on about getting us vests due to the weight on your belt – you've got your fish knife, radio, baton, PAVA and handcuffs as well.'

Ought everyone to have pepper spray? I wondered. I've known a few numbnuts in my time, and I'm not sure I'd want them anywhere near the stuff. George, though, reckoned they should. 'Well, numbnuts shouldn't be in the job in the first place, should they? Once they are deemed fit to do the job and be on the landings, then logically they should be fit to carry PAVA.'

Fair dos.

So, *are* brutality and corruption on the rise? I get a lot of people emailing me to say so. Paperwork is heavily vetted from control-and-restraint incidents for a start – in fact, that's a big part of George's job these days – so ought it to come as a big surprise if more suspicious types worry they might be censored or doctored? Not that *I'd* subscribe to any such conspiracy theory, of course.

'All the C&R paperwork has to be vetted,' said George. 'And if some wording needs to be changed, or whatever, it gets sent back and staff are advised to do that.'

He shares an example from a couple of years ago, when he was a senior officer. 'A governor told us to take a telly off a prisoner on basic, which is the privilege level those who misbehave fall to when they can only have what the law insists as opposed to standard or enhanced, no extras. Now, this was a big cell. We went in but I was a bit apart from the others. Next thing, this con is running at me with a brush handle. So, fearing for my safety, I did a pre-emptive strike, took him down before the others restrained him. That was how *I* wrote it up. One new member of staff, though, wrote, 'Went in. Prisoner ran towards Mr— and Mr—wombombed him, knocked him out,' and put his paperwork in to that effect. That is the mentality of some of these newer officers.'

Another time, two cons started brawling on their way to work. 'I runs down and, as I get there, they had him, two members of staff. But they lost their grip and up he sits, trying to crack his mate. I sat astride him from the front, got his arms and pinned them back so the officers could get hold of him again. When they did that, I goes to let go and step off, when one loses her grip again and he's straight up and under – grabbed me by the bollocks. Then he started pulling on them, really hard. So what did I do? Fearing for my safety, I smacked him – a pre-emptive strike to the face, because that was the only thing I could reach. I was feeling it – he was really tugging.'

The incident went to investigation, as they always do, and George got asked what he could have done differently. 'I said, "Hit him harder. My bollocks have been sore for two or three weeks now – I've been in real agony." "You can't say that!" they said. That's how it is. They're just trying to stitch you up all the time.'

The problem, as George sees it – and I agree with him – is that kids coming in don't see the job as a career any more, just a bit of life experience. If we saw stuff being passed on a visit, for instance, we would intervene. They've worked out that they don't need the hassle.

It had started to get like that when I left – I was the thirtieth officer to an alarm bell once, and the only one going in – but it's worse now. 'I just want to do the job,' said George. 'I think the prison service is aping how it used to be in the private sector, not that they'd admit it. They don't want people there for years earning top whack, and do not want to pay out pensions. The pension age has increased from sixty to sixty-eight for one thing, which is another deterrent to joining the service. They are happy for people to do a couple of years, ideally, and bugger off.'

All on the lowest wage, of course. And what sort of age is sixty-eight for a prison officer anyway, for fuck's sake? Can you imagine running up and down those stairs and prison landings nearing seventy?

Your eyesight has to be sharp too, again not helped by being too old – or too young and naive. Cons and their outside contacts are canny. 'One lad's mother hid a phone up her flute, took it out, gave him it, and he shoved it straight up his arse,' said George. 'Experience helps you to spot stuff like that.'

But only if you haven't got cataracts.

There is also the chance of unseasoned officers having their head turned by a celebrity, to which Strangeways is no stranger. If you follow football, you'll have heard of Joey Barton – and maybe how, in 2008, he was sentenced to six months for common assault after an incident in Liverpool in which he broke a teenager's teeth.

'I was there when Barton was in the jail,' said George. 'We had intel he was getting loads of Mars bars, so we had to go to his cell to remove any excess. He was in the gym, so we went there instead. He had twenty cons around him, kissing his backside, Joey this, Joey that. "Which one's Barton?" I said.

"I'm Joey Barton," he said. "Do you not know who I am?" I shook my head, playing dumb.'

That's prison for you. The great leveller. Or at least it should be. But meanwhile in the here and now, as we were rounding up our conversation, I wondered about the extent to which the coronavirus had covered a lot of these issues up. There, too, George put the carryings-on into interesting perspective.

'Before Covid, the service was in dire straits. Staffing levels, assault on staff, suicides, self-harm – all rocketing. The violence, the fighting, was horrendous. Since Covid, they are not in association, and only one in four is let out at any one time. So with the same amount of staff on the wings, assaults – on prisoners, too – dropped drastically. So have instances of self-harm and suicide.'

I wondered if he thought this very restrictive regime would become the new normal, even with the virus under control.

'Well, they are saying, "Look what happened!" It was predicted that suicide and self-harm would go through the roof – they haven't. It's had the opposite effect. Most prisoners don't want to go to work anyway – the majority are quite happy. Unless we are short-staffed, ours get out for forty-five minutes in a morning, shower, clean their cell, exercise, and then same thing, if they want it, in the afternoon.'

'When Covid is over, the do-gooders will be pushing for prisoners to come out again,' said George. 'And when that happens, bullying will come back in and your self-harming and worse will go up again. We don't have the staff to cope with it.'

But it does put the government's plans to build new prisons in perspective. The idea's fine, of course, but how will they run them? Every nick that opens will face the same problems. Troublesome cons will be dumped among green staff, and that is a clusterfuck waiting to happen.

Mike was a lad on Strangeways' K Wing. He's dead now, but back then there wasn't anybody who didn't know or talk about him. He was of large build and unpredictable with it, although, unknown to us at the time, he had a tumour in his head that would kill him. Have you seen *Phenomenon*? It's got John Travolta in it as a bloke who begins to learn things very quickly. They discover he has telekinetic powers, but don't realize something is growing inside.

Helped by his physical size, Mike could be aggressive. Double trouble. I'd been on the wing two days and was on the servery doling out the cleaning officers' jobs. Mike – who had been on there a week – walked up to me: 'Give me a mop.'

'Beg your pardon?'

'Give me a mop.'

I told him to fuck off.

That was our first meeting.

Later, I was at one end of the servery while he was talking to a cleaner, a handy lad himself. Mike was giving him lip. This kid glanced at me. I could tell he was pissed off so I stepped in to defuse it. Our SO, Bertie Bassett, and his two move staff ought to have noticed too, but they were sitting chatting.

'What's your problem?' I enquired.

There was no reply, unless you count throwing his tray at me, missing and plastering the orderlies in grub, and then taking a swing.

Now one of two things would happen. Either I'd sit him on

his arse or the cleaners would be coming over the top. I took option one. A cleaner pressed the bell and Bertie rushed in, super observant. 'Thanks for helping,' I grinned, and it was off to the seg' with Mike.

While he was in there it became obvious he knew my name. How, I don't know, since as I say, I'd only been on the wing a couple of days. He told them all, 'I'm going to kill that Samworth.' And kept saying it over and over again. I must have punctured his pride.

Anyway, it escalated to the point where he was constantly being restrained, moved from this wing to that, taken back to seg', police liaison involved. It became the norm that, wherever I went, I had to ask every morning where he was located. There wasn't a part of the jail that he didn't kick off in; no one wanted him on their hands. In the end they put him on the smaller Cat A unit and made him a cleaner so he'd calm down. How he never got battered I don't know.

But I was not allowed to go on any wing where he was. People were taking the piss, but the prison took threats to kill very seriously. Then the hospital appointments started, and it wasn't long before he was off to the great servery in the sky. I can't remember why he was sent to Strangeways in the first place; I'd lay money on it being something behavioural. There were many like him, inappropriately sent to jail.

But on K Wing, I soon found, we'd get death threats pretty much every day.

It wasn't till much later on that I actually got to know our next ex-customer, when he landed in healthcare with a gammy police dog bite. But the real story took place on K Wing. The officer we called Two Pens, who almost caused a riot when he ordered fish curry for the wing's Christmas dinner once and liked filling in reports, was doing locks, bolts and bars. You go in, check the cell door, give the bars a thump, flush the bog, make sure everything's working, cast your eye over the joint, look for phones and fuck off.

When Two Pens went in, this lad had a towel laid out like a tablecloth. They aren't allowed them, so our colleague, fresh out of charm school, ripped it clear off the table. What he hadn't seen was an ashtray, and the ash, of course, went everywhere, including on this guy's bed. It looked like fucking Chernobyl. It all kicked off, and the kid got locked behind his door and nicked. Understandably, he felt persecuted, and probably was, as that was Two Pens' MO, although he was too dim to realize he was doing it. Once he was fired up, he'd never let it go.

A few days later I was watching workshop four and this lad says, 'Can I have a word, Mr Samworth?'

I said he could.

'What is it with this Two Pens? Why's he on my case?'

I told him I'd no idea.

'Well, I feel like he's picking on me, and you might not know, Mr Samworth, but I've got a brother who is pretty well known. If this carries on, I feel that I might have to do something about it. I know you are going to do an SIR [security information report],' he goes on, 'and I'm happy for you to do it. But I'm telling you, Mr Samworth, he needs to stop doing what he's doing.'

Now, this sounded serious, so I had a word with Bertie Bassett. Practical as ever, he moved the lad to D Wing so it didn't become an issue, but when the lad arrived he was put on 'basic privileges' because Two Pens had stuck his neb in. Before long, the lad told me, 'Right, I've warned him, but I'm on basic now and things are going to happen . . .'

I asked what that might involve, and he passed me Two Pens' car registration number.

Now, the car park at Strangeways is full of vehicles, hundreds of them. If you knew which one mine was, you'd still struggle to find it, so this was a turn-up for the books. I went straight to Two Pens, showed him this bit of paper and asked, 'Is this your car reg?'

'Yeah. How did . . . ?'

'Never mind.' So as not to worry him I went off to tell security.

A couple of days passed, and I've come out of jail and gone to another K Wing officer's house for a brew, and then driven on to one of them late-night Tesco Express-type supermarkets. There was no one in the car park, but when I come out there's a lad standing next to my motor.

'Am I in trouble?' I says, walking towards him.

'No.'

'Then why are you stood there?'

'You need to warn your mate,' he says, and uses Two Pens' real name. 'His behaviour is not acceptable. We know where he lives.'

The old noggin was whirring. I've left work, gone home, been on a visit and gone shopping for oven chips . . . how the fucking hell?

Since I left Strangeways I know from people still there that more staff are getting threatened all the time. Officers' personal addresses are given out and travel around the wing. The online world doesn't help either. It's incredibly easy to find anyone online in this day and age – we are all so interconnected. Dodgy times we are living in. Last I heard, Two Pens'd left to be a postman; he's probably known as Two Envelopes nowadays.

6. Stir Crazy

Having struggled with mental health issues, I try not to judge. But some ex-customers did not make it easy to keep an open mind.

Hugh Pinkman came into healthcare around 2010. We got a phone call from reception. 'Got this lad for you. He can't use his legs.' Disabled, then, or so we assumed.

Well, we got him in his cell and he kicked off straight away, with a gob you wouldn't believe. 'Fucking can't walk, me . . .' – but far, far worse. I'm fluent in fruity language, but he made me blush.

'It says on this form you've threatened to kill yourself, Hugh?'

No response.

We squeezed out that he'd been employed in a desk job for twenty years, but that was it. Width-wise he was huge but short in stature.

We wheeled him into a safer custody cell, and from morning till night it was endless tirades in a high-pitched twang.

He'd become quite famous locally. Usual scenario: an ambulance is called to a guy in the road. 'Can you get on a stretcher?'

'Get to fuck. Can't walk, me.'

So they'd haul him up and cart him off to the nearest A&E, where again he'd get abusive and the bobbies would be called.

He'd have no wheelchair, so there was a flaw in his story right there. How had he got into the road then? Medical staff, coppers, benefits people, none of them had any time for him. He'd used up all his cards. He came to Strangeways after refusing to leave A&E, slagging the nurses off and throwing stuff at them. 'Here you go, guys. You sort him out!'

Our reception staff just took him at his word – couldn't walk – which is why they called us. He stayed in that cell three days before going to court. From the first meeting, though, it was obvious that, whatever he said, he was no danger to himself. The prison genned up and it turned out he *could* walk, so we asked him to leave his cell for meals. But he'd just lie there, and we ended up as a delivery service.

Could we get this bloke out of his pit? We could not. He refused showers, wouldn't let anyone clean the cell, but this was just the start of it. He'd insult the nursing staff too. They learned to brush it off.

This particular day, I was on an early start and got a call. 'Hugh Pinkman must go to reception. He's going to court.' There were four of us on duty: me, a bloke we called Dad, Dog's Knob and Martin, a mental health nurse. We looked into Pinkman's cell and he was on his belly, hadn't moved for ages. It looked like a farmyard shed in there – bits of half-eaten scran scattered around. And there, in the middle of his back, plumb centre, was what looked like a caked-on cowpat.

As they cracked the door, I stood a couple of metres away. I'd already opened every available window, plus a couple of doors to the exercise yard meant to be locked. I'd even spread joss sticks around. Wow! It was as if someone had taken the grill off a blast furnace – but instead of heat hitting you, there was this godawful stench. I've got a strong stomach, me, but you just had to lurch away. Fu. King. Hell.

Martin was a good four metres away, but instantly he threw up. Dad and Dog's Knob steadied themselves before delivering the news to Hugh that he needed to leave the cell.

'Go fuck yourselves!' That's one of the milder responses. No offence to sufferers, but he was like Tourette's on steroids.

Anyway, eventually they got him in a wheelchair, half-naked, though, and there was no lack of duty of care. He had a T-shirt on that had ridden up his back, displaying this huge pancake of dung in all its glory. They tried to wrap a sheet around his lower portions, but he wouldn't co-operate, so they gave it up as a big bad job.

We knew by now that this guy was not physically disabled. He was a fully functioning human being who'd worked for two decades and then, for reasons known only to himself, clocked off. In healthcare we had a bath with a back-lift to get people in, so we wheeled him off to that. At this stage of his stay there was no chance of him going down the plughole. We had to manhandle him a bit, but he wasn't fighting, just unco-operative. Nor would the back-lift work. His tonnage burned the motor out. Reception came on. 'Where is he? You need to get him here.' So we wrestled him into the showers.

There were four of those, and they were opposite the office. We wheeled him in, chair and all, but it still took ages to hose him down. They dressed him as best they could – it was like dealing with a wriggling twenty-stone baby. His T-shirt looked like a crop top – we'd nothing bigger – and the largest trackie bottoms we had wouldn't fit. Improvising like good 'uns, we finally got him as decent as possible.

But if we thought that would be our last sighting of Hugh Pinkman, we soon had to think again.

An hour or so later, back he came! GEOAmey, the prison escort and custody transport service, couldn't fit him on the bus.

In healthcare, we decided he didn't need safer custody; this guy was not going to kill himself. We had three cells where we put older people or lads with disabilities, roomier so nurses could get around. It wasn't long before he had them doing everything for him. He never stopped insisting he couldn't walk, and went from pest to nightmare. You'd put his meal in at the side of his cell, as he ligged on his bed. Pop back thirty seconds later and there he would be, propped up and shovelling it in. Yet he supposedly couldn't walk.

Over his spell with us he lost a lot of weight, but to begin with there were sores under his flab where he wouldn't clean himself. I'd never leave him alone with his nurses, so I'd stand by the showers to keep an eye on him. I remember one of them holding up that gut of his and scraping off at least an inch of cream cheese.

'Hugh,' we'd say, 'why can't you wash yourself?'

Downstairs, in outpatients, I'd seen drug addicts with gangrene having legs dressed, getting compression treatment and the like. This looked and smelled as bad as that – if not actually worse.

It wasn't that he had no physiotherapy either. A physio was involved with Pinkman throughout his healthcare career. Like us, she seemed sure his legs would work perfectly well given half a chance. He was afforded as much care as anyone – he had it all.

When he finally got to Salford Magistrates' Court it was in

a box van with a lift. Reception didn't want him around for obvious reasons, and we were glad to see the back of him. At that time, the court had no wheelchair access, believe it or not, so we couldn't wait for people to report back with the verdict. We thought he'd be away at last – he was a public nuisance, after all, not a hardened criminal.

We should be so lucky.

As they put our boy back on the van, the magistrate came out to speak to him and Hugh called him a cunt. He got another six months for that alone. He did similar next time, an immovable feast.

Every night you got home it was kit off, straight in the shower. Disgusting.

One nurse, Sara, was on her own once, and asked me to come to the showers while she scrubbed him. As he was wheeled in he let his bowels go. What is it Peppa Pig says? 'Everyone likes jumping in muddy puddles?' Well, she'd have given this one a swerve.

It did have its comical aspect. Strangeways' rice pudding must have been the cheapest ever: plain rice in starchy boiled water, no milk or sugar and quite definitely no cream. Delicious! Served from a flask, it stayed hot. Red hot! On this particular day, Hugh kicked off with a vertically challenged nurse named Caroline because he'd no rice pud. So we put it by his cell door while he lay on the bed, as per.

As we walked off, he pressed his bell. I swung around and dropped the flap, to peer through the hatch. Sure enough, he wanged a bowlful right in my face. It burned like hell. In that instant I was after throttling the fat fuck. The shock of it! But as I scraped it off and turned round, I saw it running down

Caroline's mush too. We looked like Laurel and Hardy. I don't know how it got past me to her, since the hatch was twelve by six inches at most. Luckily for him, the pair of us couldn't help but laugh, and so he lived to shite another day.

Hugh went to court three times while he was with us, until his release. Fuck knows where he is nowadays. Wherever he is, I wish him the best.

We had a lad called Sammy in healthcare, doing time for maternal abuse. He came in under the Mental Health Act – which covers the reception, care and treatment of the mentally disordered, management of their property and other such stuff – and didn't have full capacity.

His mother sent us a letter. He'd had violent outbursts, she wrote, might just explode, though personally I never felt threatened by him. Otherwise, it was heart-wrenching stuff, telling us about his childhood and thanking us for looking after her son, doing the best we could. It fair brought a tear to your eye.

He was certainly a strange one. He didn't come with a psychiatric report, for example, wouldn't co-operate with the shrink. Sometimes he'd recognize you, almost like some dementia sufferers know a loved one very briefly and then it's gone. Otherwise, he sat on the floor in an uncomfortable position all night, rocking. A normal person couldn't manage to hold that position for an hour. He wouldn't accept drinks, just mumble, but there was an occasional glimpse of who he really was.

He was chuntering away once, as he did, and I looked through the hatch to ask him about a shower. He looked straight at me and then, clear as rain, said, 'Listen, Samworth, you prick, I'm not talking to you.' And boom! Off he went, chuntering again. It was bizarre.

And as with Pinkman, his body odour was terrible. You'd have to take food to his cell, couldn't get him out. He was so unruly. He would make staff jump with sudden movements. Startle them.

I'd two cleaners with me and suggested we give him a shower; he was on a three-officer unlock – i.e. there must be at least that many with him to let him out. He'd likely get naked, so we'd drape him in a sheet, take him down, shut the door and leave him for quarter of an hour. He might get washed, might not; we'd encourage him with clean clobber. Again, might put it on, might not. While he was there, nurses or orderlies cleaned his cell. He was on the same landing as the office.

This particular time, he wouldn't get dressed, so the three of us walked him back. I held the towel round his waist so he was decent, and guided him in, but before we knew it – wham! Behind the door, his wet feet had gone from under him.

Ouch – the dull thud of scalp on concrete! I looked through the hatch. 'All right, Sammy?'

He was chuntering summat about Samworth, had a bit of an egg on his head.

So I went to tell Sandy, aka 'Matron'.

'Is his head bleeding?'

'No, it's not.'

'All right, I'll document it.' And then off she went to the hatch. 'Sammy? Sammy? There you are. Are you all right?'

From the second knuckle, his middle finger was at 90 degrees, dislocated. If he held his hand flat, it pointed to heaven. 'Does it hurt, Sammy?' she asked.

'*Euuggh . . . Samworth . . .*' Chunter, chunter.

We got a doctor up from downstairs, did the paperwork, incident report and all the stuff that goes with it. The doc took a look and said he needed to put it back. It would be extremely painful. Best give him diazepam.

So off Sandy went to get some, and when she opened the cell he took it, no mither – which was unusual. No chance normally. It must have been hurting. He had a lot, so it wasn't long before he was out cold. The doc said we'd have to come and hold him, because when he put the finger back it would be painful and he might well react. 'You are going to have to hang on tight,' he said.

Fuck me.

One of the lads who went in was a C&R instructor, so had seen his fair share of stuff but, whoah, this finger knocked him sick. 'Do I have to come in?' I was laughing this time, through shock.

The doc didn't mess about – walked in, got the lad's hand and yanked the finger – crack! We were pinning Sammy down, but suddenly he sat bolt upright. Everybody shat their pants – doctor included.

'*Fucking Samworth . . .*' Chunter, chunter – and we were out of there.

I couldn't make my mind up about him. He was continually assessed while with us and we'd fill in our forms as usual. There would be those fleeting moments of sanity, but no one, while he was in Strangeways at least, could fully put their finger on what was going on with him. Was he blagging? If he were, he'd have made a great actor or Hollywood super villain. I came to the conclusion that he can't have been. No one could sit on the floor like that all night if they were trying it on. You just couldn't. The incident had its funny side, but I did feel sorry for his mum and, on reflection, Sammy himself. He had a debilitating personality disorder, even if he had been convicted of a criminal offence.

Another incident started with an alarm bell on H Wing.

H Wing is where prisoners go to from I Wing, the detox unit, so they are next door to each other. The lads are still on meds – methadone and that sort of thing. One kid came from there over to us, restrained.

The first we knew of him, though, was when two officers came into outpatients. One had a wound on his head. The other was in shock from seeing his mate twatted and had them worried about his heart and blood pressure.

KK was the nurse manager when this prisoner was brought to us. 'Why is he here? If he's assaulted staff, then he needs to be on the segregation unit, not healthcare.' So off they went in a proper troop, as many as twenty of them. The culprit had a bit of claret on him, be it from himself or the officer we didn't know.

I listened on the radio as they took him to the seg'. He said he was going to kill himself, so there would be ACCT (Assessment, Care in Custody and Teamwork) forms to fill in and all that. 'Whoah! That's not for us,' they said. 'Take him back to healthcare.'

When he came back, it was strapped into an Evac chair, and he was still fighting the staff.

There are appropriate ways to move prisoners, and most of

the time an Evac chair is not one of them. Human rights issue or what? If he wasn't walking, he should have been cuffed and carried back. That's what we were taught. When someone kicks off, there are ways to deal with it. But they wheeled this kid in like Hannibal Lecter. He went in the gated cell, claret all over him, on constant watch.

KK was trying to get things sorted, but staff were kicking off: he'd twatted their mate, who'd gone off in an ambulance – plenty of emotion, even though now they could only glare through plastic. Within sixty seconds the entire entourage – governors, officers, SOs, you name it – had fucked off, and he was ours to deal with.

And when I say 'ours', I mean two officers and a few nurses. It had taken twenty of them to get him here in an Evac chair, fighting all the way, but apparently we were now enough. Glad to be of service! With us, he went on to act like a child now and then and threatened to harm himself. So we'd just take everything out of his cell for a couple of hours, which usually calmed him down.

At Strangeways, it was as if everyone thought healthcare was staffed by superheroes, yet it was talked about and treated like the prison dustbin.

Strangeways, high-profile, was always full of the sort of evildoers that could – and quite definitely did – give headline writers a hard-on.

Murderers sell papers, don't they?

In terms of quality of inmate, though, the healthcare unit in 2013 was an absolute chamber of horrors. We couldn't predict who – or what – might be coming our way next.

As a rule, even the worst creatures didn't put us off our stride, because we were used to dealing with the mentally deranged, where applicable, and had some very cruel customers. As professionals, we treated everyone the same, whatever their backstory.

Take David Minto, jailed for the shocking murder of sixteen-year-old Sasha Marsden, after falsely offering the lass a part-time job at the Grafton House Hotel in Blackpool. He was sentenced in July 2013, and then we had him on healthcare in the year to end all years there.

We knew the details of Minto's crime, although it was only recently I saw the pictures – splashed across one of them true crime TV channels – but the facts were awful enough. After meeting Sasha on a night out in Blackpool the year before, he'd stalked her on social media and offered her the job before sexually assaulting and stabbing her fifty-eight times in the head and neck, injuries so severe the poor girl could only be identified from DNA on her toothbrush. And then, having killed her, he wrapped her in carpet underlay and dumped her in a bin bag in a nearby alley, like he'd just put it outside his front door. Twisted beyond belief. He was given a minimum thirty-five-year sentence.

You never get used to working with people like that, especially when you have children of your own. Carrying such stuff around with you day and night is bound to mess with your head in the end; all the more reason for ensuring that prison officers and nursing staff have quality psychological support.

When we got him, although he was twenty-three years old, he acted like a child. You would never guess he was in for such a brutal murder and had been caught bang to rights. It was as if he didn't appreciate what he'd done, which was disturbing in itself. Minto was one of the world's dumbest criminals; a vacuous fucker obsessed by trivia. He even spooked his fellow inmates – and there were some real hard cases among them. 'Do you want all them chips?' he'd say, carefree as you like. It was of no consequence to him that he'd taken the life of a lass, who'd only been looking to fund her route through college, and wrecked her grief-stricken family.

Like another of our inmates, Mark Bridger, who I've written about before, jailed for the abduction and murder of five-year-old April Jones in 2012, Minto was a high-profile case some folk were keen to be in the orbit of, gathering tall tales for dinner parties. There, however, the similarities ended. Bridger – who was also on healthcare during 2013 – was cunning beyond belief, playing up to the Independent Monitoring Board (IMB), whose representatives were all over him like a rash.

But those two were far from the only twisted individuals to enjoy our hospitality in a year that I and several others are mentally still working our way through.

There was Jamie Reynolds, a sadomasochistic type who strangled a seventeen-year-old neighbour to death. Our cleaner Lucas, who you'll meet soon, brought him onto the wing as a Cat A prisoner.

In his early twenties, it came out that Reynolds had been into asphyxiation for a while, and had actually been given 'a final warning' by police after trying to strangle a sixteen-year-old girl five years before. He was finally caught and arrested after killing Georgia Williams in her own home in Telford, dumping her body in woods near Wrexham and doing a bunk to Scotland in 2013. They found all sorts on his computer – images of bondage, torture . . . over 16,000 of them.

I believe he came to Strangeways healthcare for his own safety, to get him 'out of area'. Also high-profile, and on his way to a whole-life sentence, he was one extremely disturbed dude. A former classmate – the best friend of Georgia's sister – learned that he'd doctored an old school photo of her with a noose, bulging eyes and bright red lipstick. As a kid, he'd torture neighbours' pets, and had been obsessed with hanging and necrophilia since the age of fifteen.

At some point Reynolds ended up on E Wing outer, the VP – vulnerable prisoner – unit. He was another who just seemed so calm about what he'd done, so laid-back around nursing staff and while interacting with fellow prisoners. Psychologists would ask him, 'Do you realize the consequences of what you've done, Jamie?'

'Course I do,' he'd reply, very matter-of-fact.

The conveyor belt that year – it was endless. One on their own would have been bad; together they were super fucking dangerous. Sometimes I lie in bed at night and their faces and stories come back to me. I don't invite them in – they are always there, swirling around.

Amir Ali came to Manchester from Bracknell. He'd been hearing voices, and they told him, in a Manc accent, that someone on Stretford Road was going to kill him. His response was to drive north and stab the first 'suitable victim' he found. That just happened to be an eighteen-year-old gap year student called Elijah Roberts. Ali casually walked up to him and, in broad daylight, stabbed him four times in the chest, before driving back to his Shropshire flat and going on as normal. A few days later police used his registration number to track him down and arrest him. Only twelve days before the murder, it turned out, he'd punched another innocent pedestrian in Nottingham.

Ali got a minimum of thirty-five years for killing Elijah, who was described as a quiet and unassuming kid. I remember doing an AAC (administrative appeals court) report with KK, my friend and nursing colleague, looking for triggers. 'Amir,' our nurse manager Bradders would ask, 'did anything happen to you?' Got nothing back.

Often, people can start hearing voices after a traumatic event – the death of a parent, maybe – and something snaps. Mother dies, and they go on a killing spree. Classic pattern. Ali, a mature student of engineering in Coventry, came from a well-off family, and prior to then was said to have been a model citizen with no history of mental health issues, until those voices suddenly piped up around Christmas 2012.

The prosecution claimed all that was bollocks, only not in so many words, rejecting a manslaughter plea by reason of diminished responsibility. They said he'd dreamed it all up as a last resort, once it became obvious he had done the deed. Either way, his real reasons didn't matter to Elijah, did they? He had been due to study history at Sheffield Hallam University that autumn but, witnesses said, was left dead or dying on the pavement as his killer ran back to his car sniggering. Those 'threatening and abusive voices' went silent. The jury reckoned he'd just wanted to see what it was like to kill.

It was obvious, though, that he wasn't all there. There was no emotion. Bradders would say, 'Do you remember doing it?'

'Yeah, I do, Miss Bradbury . . . The voices . . .'

'What did you do when you got home?'

'Oh, I washed me car, got some tea . . .'

He was on no medication, no drugs in his system, but he acted like he was heavily medicated, and wasn't with us long. He was assessed fairly quickly and they shipped him off to Ashworth, the high-security psychiatric hospital a few miles north of Liverpool that housed the likes of Charles Bronson and Moors murderer Ian Brady back in the day. I only mention Ali because he was another of those, like Jamie Reynolds, who'd be there on the news just as you were trying to wind down after another trying day. I've driven home from work, cracked a can after locking him up for the night and here he is again on the telly. It was almost surreal. There was no escaping it.

While researching this book I went to see Holly, who was a Strangeways governor at the time I was there, but who has since left. She admitted to having been a huge fan of the film *The Silence of the Lambs* as a young 'un – indeed, so obsessed with Jodie Foster's criminal profiler that she went on to get a BSc in Applied Psychology and joined the service herself. 'I've always been interested in dark things,' she said, 'horror, the paranormal, serial killers, true crime . . .'

Among other things, we spoke about safer custody and, when we got on to Mark Bridger, she told me how he'd got inside her head. As with all high-profile cases, governors knew everything about Bridger because the police liaised with the prison throughout. 'We knew what he'd done to that poor girl,' she said, 'yet had no counselling to cope with that information, or support. Nobody asked us how we felt.'

Point taken, but Bradders, KK and the rest of us on healthcare knew everything the governors knew and had to deal with the creature every day. We wrote his AACT reviews. We had to stomach him crying because he wouldn't see his dog again – or when spaghetti hoops on the menu upset him. It put you in a bad place.

It's around a decade ago now, all of this, but the images don't go away. I can't tell you how many times a week I think about Scott Mantle, for example, a lad who had the particular talent of bleeding himself dry, by the pint, until he was on the verge of passing out. He had very few scars; just tiny holes where he knew the right veins were . . .

He came to us after being caught on the run from Highpoint Prison in Suffolk, where he'd been serving an indefinite sentence for beating a motorist with a claw hammer and baseball bat. They found him on the lam in Scotland and he was sent to Belmarsh, then off for another trial at the Old Bailey that he refused to attend at first, before ending up with an extra six years – in our company – at the end of July.

To escape in Suffolk, he'd slashed a nine-inch gash across his own shoulder, and then outside the hospital he'd held up his prison escort with a replica handgun. You just knew he was one of those who'd go on to develop a prison career. Start with a bit of disruption, dirty protest, self-harm, until eventually showing others how to destroy the healthcare unit.

Mantle was so manipulative he meant constant hassle, day after day, hour after hour, minute by ticking minute.

Adam Downworth, a serial rapist, was with us then too and, very unusually, he was made Cat A *after* his sentence, not before it. He was a proper evil bastard him, battered his victims, facial fractures, the lot. His *modus operandi* was to hide behind bushes in parks and then leap out and overpower women as they walked home late at night, using tips he'd picked up from books about ninjas and self-defence. We had him in healthcare for months.

Up to his trial he seemed like a normal lad. But once he'd been sentenced, something snapped. One day, he got a bit demanding with Bradders, so I stood in front of her and gave him a few verbals back.

Wow, did he bite.

I remember saying, 'Oh, *there* you are,' as his true self came into view.

We had a lass come to education who started doing art classes for these guys, which the prisoners loved. Downworth was on that course, as was Michael Cope who, after murdering his ex-girlfriend, lived in woods near Manchester for a month before they tracked him down. David Minto was 'into art' too, as was Scott Mantle.

Cope had a record of domestic violence, in and out of jail, and as 2013 moved towards 2014 ended up on healthcare as he'd asked for protection. It was reported in the media that he had a 'paranoid and controlling mind' and had been abusive to Linzi Ashton, his twenty-five-year-old partner before battering, raping and murdering her that summer, only weeks after she'd warned the police she was in danger. She had one hundred and eight injuries. All of which meant Cope was well known not only outside the jail but also within it, which limited the number of wings on which he would be safe. The seg' didn't want an AACT case like him on their hands, so he gravitated to our landing.

Together, him and Scott Mantle basically taught this lot and two or three others how to wreck the joint. So at one point in 2013, not only was it wall-to-wall with highly dangerous Cat A prisoners, but Mantle, Cope and co. also put loads of cells out of service – no power, pulled sockets, smashed lights, blown fuses, you name it. Once a cell no longer has a working bell, you can't put anyone in it. If they died, the prison would be fucked. We had an entire row in that condition. Yet they were on intermittent watches at best, because you still had to keep an eye on them; and all of it with just two officers on duty. It gives me a migraine just thinking about it. That was a long and intense few months, all right.

Anyroad, back to that art class. Obviously with dodgy fuckers like Michael Cope and Adam Downworth in there, us officers would leave the door open and pop in now and then to make sure they were playing nicely.

One time they were making Christmas decorations. It was still gloomy for the time of year, and the lass who ran the classes asked why we didn't have a Christmas tree up? Copey, earwigging, nodded towards Downworth and said, 'Because he'd hide behind it, miss, and when we turned us backs, he'd batter you . . .'

That passed as humour to that lot. Healthcare could be a very sinister and dark environment.

Safe to say we had our hands full then, but the biggest name to come our way in 2013 was Dale Cregan. I decided not to talk about him in book one because I didn't want to give him the kudos. To be honest, it was still a bit raw too, after hearing all sorts of stories about him partying at Ashworth Hospital.

Recently, though, I heard the father of one of two police

officers he murdered speaking out about it, talking about how it has affected the family, and felt a surge of sympathy. Well, why wouldn't you? Their names were Nicola Hughes and Fiona Bone, and they were killed in a gun and grenade ambush orchestrated by Cregan after responding to a report of a house burglary in Mottram in Longdendale, Greater Manchester, in September 2012.

At the time, our then Prime Minister David Cameron called it 'a despicable act of pure evil'. Spot on. Cregan rang 999, posing as a member of the public, and told them he'd seen someone throw a concrete slab through the rear window of a house in a cul-de-sac in the village of Mottram and run away. He'd seen the direction they went off in, he said, and would point it out to any attending officer. The women, on a routine patrol, walked into his trap.

When they arrived and walked up the garden path, unarmed apart from Nicola's taser, Cregan opened the door and began to fire a pistol, hitting both officers in the chest. Body armour meant the bullets didn't get through at first and they were able to beat a fast retreat. But Nicola, running up the path, was then paralysed by a shot in the back. Laid on the floor, she was then shot three more times before Cregan turned his attentions to Fiona, left with eight gunshot injuries, the fatal one a wound to the upper side of her chest. Cregan then returned to Nicola and shot her six more times in the back and side of her head. As if that wasn't enough, before tearing off in his BMW he then left his 'calling card', an M57 hand grenade, which, of course, caused further injuries, Nicola dying not long afterwards in hospital.

An hour later, Cregan walked into Hyde police station and

gave himself up, knowing he was already wanted in connection with a pair of gangland murders earlier that year, having only five weeks before avoided an unsuccessful attempt to arrest him on that count. The first victim there was twenty-three-year-old Mark Short, shot dead in a pub in Droylsden in May, a crime for which Cregan had already been brought in and then released on bail. The second was Mark's father, David, who had also been killed by a gun and grenade attack, this time at his home in Clayton in August.

Cregan, on the run, had felt the net tightening, calmly telling the arresting officer in Hyde, 'I dropped the gun at the scene and I've murdered two police officers. You were hounding my family so I took it out on yours.' Even so, it took him until February to plead guilty to murder in Preston Crown Court and that, combined with the other killings and three separate counts of attempted murder, earned him a whole-life sentence. One theory went that he shot the officers so he'd quite definitely be made Cat A. I don't know about that, but had he gone to any other part of the prison estate, I am in no doubt that he would have been got at and killed as part of the gangland feud.

Not long ago, I went on James English's podcast. He asked me to talk about my experiences with Cregan, so I did, for the first time in public. I wanted to put across what a pathetic bully he was.

It wasn't just about him. I remember two members of the crew he knocked about with really well – they spent time with us at Strangeways, awaiting trial. The Manc constabulary went after anyone who'd had anything to do with him, and rightly so. They'd lost two of their own, so left no stone unturned. He ended up with nine associates in the dock alongside him.

One was Damian Gorman, who took part in the first murder at the Cotton Tree pub in Droylsden where Mark Short was killed as part of that family feud with another crew, the Atkinsons, who Cregan was pally with. Matthew James was the other I remember: the police alleged he was planted in the pub as a spotter to let Cregan know Short's whereabouts inside.

When Cregan's gang came into Strangeways, at first they were all playing the big man – jigging around, high fives, bigging it up, usual Manc strutting – but soon they started to get naughty. Being Cat A, most of them were on E Wing or down the seg' or got sent to us on healthcare. Cregan split most of his time between the first two, but we had him once or twice. Gorman and James we housed for months; they came to us because things had started to get tasty between the lot of them. It looked like it was all going to kick off.

Let's start with Cregan.

We certainly knew he was coming – there was this massive media circus. There were lots of security issues around this guy: he'd been chucking grenades around and wielding firearms, hadn't he? It was believed arms were still knocking about, so when he came to the jail it went off OTT. Roads were shut amid shitloads of armed response. He'd often make his court appearances by video link.

The prison opened an ACCT form on him as soon as he arrived because he was very high-profile – among the highest, in fact. Our healthcare manager, KK, was part of his review. She asked me to escort her there. I couldn't sit in, wasn't invited, but she told me he'd been matter-of-fact, very cold, and had absolutely loved the situation and himself.

Like Mark Bridger, Cregan was one of those prisoners the service considers high-risk – everyone wants their day in court with them. They do not want any issues arising. They wanted this guy found guilty – didn't want him harming himself, for example, so he might get out of facing the music. Anything like that and, you name it, it would have gone right to the top, with even MPs sticking their oar in.

Cregan's first port of call was the segregation unit, which is pretty much twenty-three-hour lock-up in normal times: an hour's exercise by application, shower a day if you want one, a phone call on request, and usually you're let out to collect your meal. That's it. You are not associating with anyone, other than occasionally on the exercise yard.

I went down to the seg' with KK. It has special cells where they put the real bad boys – just a plinth to lie down or sit on, no toilet or any other mod con. The unit does, though, have bits of gym equipment – exercise bikes and things. Cregan was pedalling away, grinning and laughing, taking the piss, happy as Larry. I recognized his face. He'd been in the papers, and who forgets a mugshot like his?

Back in healthcare KK was upset. His behaviour in the review had shaken her up. They'd had a plan for looking after him, but he'd turned cold, off-hand, not engaging with their questions. 'No point crying over spilled milk,' he'd said.

This was one heartless fucker.

There was always this stars-in-their-eyes shit around him, though, with hangers-on acting like groupies. I worked in healthcare outpatients now, and there was loads of bollocks around him being one-eyed. Cregan always told people he'd lost his eye abroad, in Thailand, scrapping with drug lords or something. But one of our lads, Mason, who later became an orderly, who was in the jail at the same time as Cregan, eventually got out of him what had really happened.

Mason was a good kid. I liked him a lot. He didn't run with anyone; he was a businessman who'd seen an opportunity to grow weed and sell it at a high return. Cregan, on the other hand, was a drug dealer who would rob anyone – even fellow dealers – of drugs and money, adding to their debts. Scrag-end behaviour. The vast majority of the criminal fraternity had absolutely no regard for him at all.

Mason owned genuine businesses too – paintball, car lot – so made some money legit, but like most folk inside, he also moved in darker circles, and Mason had had dealings with Cregan, bumped heads if you like. Cregan was threatening him, so Mason filled him in good and proper. It was an aspect of Cregan that never got mentioned. He couldn't fight; got others to do it for him. He kept a couple of lads round him who were proper scrappers: not top-rank hard nuts, but super fit and loyal.

So there'd been this beef between Cregan and Mason, and Cregan had gone over to Mason's house. And here's the sort of guy he was: Mason was out, so Cregan gave his nine-year-old son a crack! Mason resolved to have him for that. Eventually he did, and he smashed a plant pot on Cregan's head. This was before Cregan killed the PCs, so Mason was always sorry he hadn't completed the job, and then none of that would have happened.

It was Mason who told me how Cregan had lost the old

mince pie, and it wasn't at all like he boasted. On his first trip to Thailand, him and his crew joined in a stag do at a beach bar and got hammered. Another gang of UK lads asked if he'd take a group picture of them, paddling. Cregan said he would, took the shot, and then chucked the camera in the sea. Well, it all kicked off, and he and his mates got thrown out of the bar.

Fast-forward to his second Thailand trip. Cregan, being Cregan, goes to the same bar. The owner clocks him, gets the local gangsters round, and bingo: half as many eyes in his head, carved out by a knife or knocked out by a knuckleduster, depending who you believe. It's said they tried to cut his throat too.

So here he was in Strangeways, where at first it were Dale this, Dale that. He loved himself, loved the hype. One day we took him to the dental clinic in outpatients. HMP Manchester is designed so they can get to healthcare from the Cat A unit without leaving the building. As we saw with Johnny Mo, its most dangerous prisoners aren't allowed outside unless they are double-cuffed in Chubbs, with dogs on hand. So you'd take them up and over the top, inside all the way. Added to which, before these trips you'd do a full strip search – and on the way back too. We'd borrowed a couple of extra officers for that.

Wouldn't you know it, though, as we were getting ready to take him off, Cregan told us the SO had said he didn't need to remove his boxers. Normally, we'd do the top half first, then the bottom half with T-shirt back on. So that led to a bit of a ding-dong. I said if he refused to strip, we'd take him back to the unit and he would not be off to the dentist.

'You can't fucking do that.'

'I can if you're not following procedure.'

Anyway, we got him there eventually, at first in a holding cell for normal location prisoners. One or two waiting with him were ingratiating themselves as per 'Y'all right, Dale?' and he was bigging himself up in return. The idea is: wand him down, get him in the surgery, wand him down again, strip-search and back to the unit.

The dentist asked if I would be coming in too. Usually with Cat A prisoners we would step inside if asked.

'Do you want us in?'

Aye, he did. This was a normal civilian dentist faced with Dale Cregan. You couldn't blame him for being frightened.

'Right, in we go,' I said, but Cregan stopped in the doorway.

'What are you doing? I don't want you in here.'

'Well, you might not, but he does.' I cocked a thumb at my colleagues. 'And he wants them two in here as well.'

'Why's that?'

'Because the dentist requested it.'

So he started questioning the dentist, and that's how it was with him. He turned everything into hassle. Loved to challenge authority. But in that holding room there were also some proper hard lads who didn't acknowledge him. Huge tough bastards like Gareth Holland, a real big hitter in Salford, a well-known drug-dealing gangster, but with us a complete gent. His nickname was 'Knuckles', and he could deliver punches with either hand. Deffo somebody you would not want to mess with.

Knuckles and Mason – in fact, the vast majority of prisoners

– had no time for Cregan. They thought he was a dog for what he'd done. Not so much sympathy for the dad and lad he killed, mind. 'In our circles,' they reckoned, 'if you mess around, then this will possibly happen.' The two lasses, however, were another matter. In the real hard bastards' view it made Cregan a coward, not a lad to be admired.

Cregan's laid-back attitude didn't last long. His own crew began to fall out among themselves, which led to Damian Gorman and Matthew James heading our way.

Gorman I got on well with straight away. He was in his early thirties, maybe, with a young girlfriend and child. James, however, was an arse at first: very demanding and treated people like shit. Because he'd come from Cat A he was, 'I want this . . . I want that . . .'

I was having none of that. 'You're not on Cat A now,' I said. 'You're on fucking healthcare. You'll get what you are entitled to, when we can give it you.'

Up until the last two weeks of the trial, it looked like Gorman might walk, while James was looking at a thirty-plus stretch. Then suddenly their fortunes switched. Gorman eventually got thirty-three years, while James was one of four Cregan co-defendants who were found not guilty and subsequently offered police protection.

Once the verdict was in, Cregan was rushed into the seg' among reports that the head of a crime family down south, sympathetic to the Shorts, had put a price on one particular bit of his head. Pluck out the good eye and you could earn yourself twenty grand.

In his defence had been psychiatrists who'd claimed it was

losing the first eye that had caused brain damage which had led to his murderous actions. To which I reply . . . Well, you can probably guess . . .

Basically, there was nothing wrong with Cregan, as anyone who worked with him knew. He was only on an ACCT form because the authorities wanted him out of harm's way. Soon he came to us on healthcare owing to 'feeling a bit low' – in other words, the governor had said we had to take him. We didn't want him. We had plenty already.

There is simply no percentage in having someone like him around who is going to disrupt the unit, but we had no option. We put him in a cell outside the office. The security train came with him: George's lot, the Men in Black, with their dogs, cuffs, kitchen sink. And in he went with his bit of property. The governor came into the office and made the usual sort of speech you roll your eyes at – 'We need to make sure this guy stays fit and healthy . . .' Like we're all thick as fuck.

Anyway, just as the speech is getting into full flow, Cregan rings his cell bell, and so the governor toddles off to see what he wants. When he comes back he says, 'Cregan hasn't got a television.'

'That's right,' I says. 'Everyone who comes on healthcare – Dale Cregan, Mark Bridger, Father Christmas – none of them gets a TV on their first night. We're assessing them. Tomorrow, if we feel it's safe, he can have a telly.'

'Well, what if I override that?'

'Tell you what, Guv, you want to do that, you can. However, I won't be getting him a TV. KK here won't be getting him a TV. Karen Bradders won't be getting him a TV. You want to get one and install it yourself, we will happily make notes to that effect.'

He spat his dummy and fucked off.

Not that Cregan gave up so easily. His bell went again.

'Where's me telly?'

You can imagine. We were having none of this. He rang again. 'Right . . .' I said, and had the same chat with him I'd just had with the governor. Cregan got no kudos in healthcare; fucking hated us from start to finish.

Next news, he starts on about the gym. 'There'll be no gym on here, lad,' I said, and put him on a three-officer unlock straight away.

'What am I on an unlock for?'

One, he was a dangerous prisoner. Two, he had already made threats to kill a nurse in front of segregation staff (none of whom challenged him, by the way, or did anything about it).

As soon as he clocks I'd be taking none of his shit, his bottom lip is out and off he skulks to sit on his bed with a proper cob on. He did not want to be among us. But why would you not put Dale Cregan on an unlock? Are you going to take a risk with a lot of female staff about?

Cregan's first stay was short. He wanted off, so off he went.

The second time was to prepare for an operation.

If you don't have an eyeball in the socket, the socket shrinks. He made a big deal of it, demanding a glass eye, and the prison agreed he should go out to have it sorted. This too would have gone right up to government, with massive costs attached. When he went, there were armed coppers everywhere, helicopters, folk on top of buildings with rifles . . . His hand grenades might still be at large, so it made sense.

It was arranged that the hospital would close the entire floor on which he was going to be treated – and while he was waiting to leave healthcare here, no one could know. It had to be hush-hush.

One Friday evening, Bradders comes to see me. 'Mr Samworth,' she says, polite as ever. 'I've been to security. Dale Cregan is coming in tonight because he is off to hospital tomorrow.'

'Why are we getting him?'

'We are in the middle of the jail, so he won't be able to signal anybody and no one will know he's here. From health-care, he'll go on the van with the posse. However, I haven't told you this. I'd imagine he'll either just turn up or someone will phone you. Act surprised.'

And off she popped.

We were shutting shop at teatime, everyone locked up from half five, and I was the only officer on evening duty. I had a couple of nurses with me, as that's where they tended to base themselves of an evening – to feel safer, I suppose. As predicted, the phone rang and it was a Man in Black. Not George; another member of the dedicated prison search team (DST) who are also part security.

'Who's that?'

'Sam.'

'Sam, have you got a cell?'

'What for?'

'To put someone in.'

'What they coming for?'

'Can't tell you.'

'Okay. I need to know what they are coming for. They might need a safer custody cell. Are they at risk of harming themselves or can I put them in a normal cell?'

'I can't tell you.'

'Who is it who's coming?'

'I can't tell you.'

'Okay,' I said, having had my fun. 'I've got a cell.'

They appeared at the end of the landing: three Men in Black, dressed in polo shirts, baggy combats and boots. Dale Cregan was with them, carting his belongings. One MIB walked down the landing and ushered me into the office, grave as fuck.

'Right, we've got Cregan for you,' he said. I'm thinking, *No shit. I can see him.* 'But,' our friend added conspiratorially, 'he is NOT here.'

'How do you mean, "He's not here"?'

'Don't put him on your roll.'

This would make no sense to anyone reading it. If I had twenty-two on the unit, did a roll count and put twenty-three, there'd be questions, wouldn't there? Nor did I use names anyway; just gave them a number. How would that have let anyone else know Cregan was with us?

I'm thinking, *This is fucking bizarre*, but let them put him in a cell anyway with his kit, a bit of grub and the rest of his shit. He still got no TV, by the way. And then I got a call from the duty governor.

Not long afterwards, in 2015, this individual would be behind a lot of the 'modernization' that was going to fuck Strangeways up. Once, after he'd been having a go at Bradders over something trivial, she asked me to get rid of him, so I went, 'Taxi for the governor!' Steam jetted out of his ears.

He stomped off the unit, slamming the gate after him, to general hilarity.

Anyway, here was Buster Bloodvessel again and *I hadn't got Dale Cregan in a cell*, even though I had.

'Who are you, again?' he said, knowing damn well who I was.

'I'm Sam.'

'Well, Sam, you've got Dale Cregan in a cell.'

I'm smiling just thinking about it. Was it a test?

'No, I haven't, Guv.'

'No, listen. You need to know a few things.'

'I haven't got Dale Cregan here,' I repeated.

He said I was getting uppity – no sense of humour – so I went through it all with him. I *hadn't* got him here, *hadn't* got him on the roll, he *wasn't* on the board that told us which cell prisoners were in, whether they were dangerous or on an unlock or whatever. He told me not to be stupid. I was thinking, *It's not me who's stupid, chum*.

They brought Cregan on at about 8 p.m., and as soon as they did so he went in a cell next to someone who was mentally ill. When the Men in Black put Cregan in, Buster says to me at the top of his voice, 'Mr Samworth – is that Dale Cregan?'

I've gone, 'No. Dale Cregan's not on here, mate.'

One of the Men in Black, just doing their job I know, looked at me as if to say, 'Give us a break, Sam.' His two mates glared at me like I was a cunt. But it was Friday night, and before I went off shift I did the roll call and updated the night officer. 'We've got Dale Cregan with us, or rather we haven't,' I told him. *Nudge nudge, wink wink, say no more*. 'The roll says twenty-two, not twenty-three, so if the Oscars query it, just show them the handover book.' I'd written it all up in there, even though security said I shouldn't, just to make sure that the night officer and me were covered.

Before I fucked off home, I went to Cregan's cell, where he was sat drinking pop and eating chocolate. Ever been for an operation? It's usually nil by mouth for twenty-four hours. So I rang my mate Buster Bloodvessel, the duty governor: 'Dale Cregan, who we *haven't* got on healthcare, is eating chocolate and pop.' He went bananas. *He's having an operation . . . blah blah* . . . 'Whoah! Your lads have brought him on, put him in his cell, given him all this stuff, that's nothing to do with us. I'm going off shift now.' That was how I left it. Crack on!

Cregan never got to hospital next morning. Someone in the hospital environment, a porter, nurse or whoever, had put on social media that they were 'getting a strange one in from Strangeways'.

Operation cancelled. I bet they were popular!

We had Cregan on healthcare again around August 2013, just before he was shipped off to HM Prison Full Sutton, near Pontefract. Lucky them. While he was there, he went on hunger strike. No more pop and chocolate – for a week or two anyway.

That September he was shipped over to Ashworth, where he stayed until March 2018, before returning to HMP Manchester about eighteen months after I left. Excellent timing for us both, I'd say.

Parasites like him are never going to be turned around, will be a threat while ever they draw breath and, lived with every day, drain the human spirit.

*

If you become aware a prisoner isn't eating, after three days you start paperwork on them, to make people aware of it. In the office, there's a clipboard and sheet you write on every day. If you saw them take fluids or have a cheeky brew, you'd make a note of it.

By the time of Cregan's third visit we had a new manager, who was above Bradders and KK. Again, Cregan was not happy about joining us, and was also having visitors check up on his mental health.

When a prisoner properly stops eating, loses a lot of weight, they might go to a mental health forensic unit. If they still refuse to eat – like Ian Brady – you end up feeding them. High-profile cases like Cregan are likely to end up at one of England's three high-security psychiatric hospitals – Broadmoor, Rampton or the one nearest Strangeways, Ashworth. It was the staff there that came to see him.

If Cregan was playing at it, we had one healthcare customer who went eighty-four days without eating. Let's call him Barry, quite baby-faced, no five o'clock shadow or anything like that. Were it not for his 1980s mullet, he'd have slotted into a crowd. Very innocent-looking, he had nevertheless been in segregation, a classic psycho in the making; future serial killer if you ask me. As a kid, he'd done the bizarre stuff you see in films: microwaved cats, frogs in the blender . . . He'd tried to kill his sister by setting her car on fire with her in it. A stamp collector he was not. He'd been down the seg' for years, went on a food refusal and came to us.

About five foot eight and chunky when he came into the jail, he wound up losing about four stone. Weirdly, I got on well with the lad. He liked me and he liked Bradders. Didn't much care for the rest of our staff, though, threatened to stick a pen in their eyes: officers, doctors or nurses. As for psychiatrists and psychologists, he said they lied to him, and to be honest, often they did. Us pair were honest with him, as far as was appropriate.

'Miss Bradbury, will I be going to Broadmoor?'

'Quite possibly, yes.'

'Do you know when I'm going?'

'I can't tell you that, Barry.'

Although he originally went on 'hunger strike' after a falling-out with the seg' manager, that was his real reason – he hoped to be moved to hospital. Even so, over those eighty-four days, all documented, he did agree to orange squash and such, so took regular fluids. As I went past his cell I'd say, 'Want a cup of tea?' I'd get him hot water and he'd make a brew. Didn't want anything else. Barry was well behaved, lucid, could hold a decent conversation, wasn't weak or wobbly and still had capacity.

So why did he hate psychologists and the like?

He showed me a report signed by six of them, not one of whom he'd ever met. He'd had no interview; it was copied and pasted from other sources. Yet they had 'written' a report that might keep him in jail forever. No wonder he had a deep mistrust and dislike of the profession.

This was, however, a highly dangerous individual. He was ice-cold. I was under no illusions about that, although couldn't help but enjoy his company. He was on a permanent three-officer unlock and had no desire to come off it. One of the seg' staff came to see him one day, and he'd always want to know who was arriving before I took them up to his cell. If it was someone he didn't want to see, he'd kick off big time. When I told him who it was this time he said, 'Nah. Tell him to go away.'

As it happened, he did end up at Broadmoor, and while he was there he watched a Strangeways TV documentary I was in. Three years later, the healthcare manager and a nurse went to see him, as he was mithering to return. Get back into the prison system and you'll finish the sentence and eventually be freed. With Broadmoor, he'd come to realize, you aren't getting out.

Anyway, he didn't get his way, but he did send a message. I found it strange that he was allowed to, but there it was, a little envelope the nurse must have slipped into her pocket.

Mr Samworth, it read. *Really enjoyed the Strangeways documentary. It was nice to see your happy smiling face. Like they always say, the camera adds forty pounds to you.* Cheeky get.

The most memorable shrink was the one who came to see Dale Cregan. She'd waddle into a high-security jail in stilettos, rara skirt, bare legs, tight top, push-up bra . . . Normally none of my business – what a woman wears is her own affair – but come on! That would be crazy in any prison, and doesn't show a lot of awareness for someone trying to get inside a criminal mind. But what do I know? I'm just an officer . . .

Anyway, when she came to assess him – with plenty of staff about, thank goodness – he was still on an unlock. We knew that although he was allegedly on food refusal he was still eating, but she didn't. After assessing him, she was giddy as a kipper. 'I think we are going to be taking Dale to Ashworth – he's not got capacity.' Capacity means the ability to make your own decisions.

Well, I'm telling you now: Cregan was no different from when he first came in. Maybe there were a few pounds less of him, no more. He might even have put weight on, due to his medication. Another thing – Ashworth was competing with Broadmoor and Rampton, as it had been rumoured that one of them was to be closed. Politics again.

I don't know the cost now, but back then over thirty grand a year was needed to house a normal prisoner, a quarter of a million-plus for a Cat A case. Imagine the kudos for Ashworth, getting Dale Cregan. The press. The profile. Why wouldn't they want him? Anyway, she duly got her way, and the papers ran stories on his mental health.

In my opinion, he didn't need Ashworth then; at some point in the future, maybe. But off he went, and then came the tales of how he was living it up. People were understandably upset but, for balance, you do have to realize that reports of prisoners being on PlayStations all day, when they're not swimming in the pool or eating pizzas, can be far-fetched. And actually, although Ashworth is highly secure and full of dangerous people, you have to remember it's not a prison.

High-security hospitals, like Strangeways' healthcare unit, are about trying to make people better, and are therefore set up for patients rather than prisoners. Friday night might be pizza night, but they're not sending out to Domino's for it; it's made in the hospital's own kitchen. If you are well behaved, you might get to use the pool. They had a TV room to keep them occupied.

Cregan would have liked that, for a couple of weeks anyway. 'Slice of margherita?' ''Aving it!' But guess what else a mental hospital is full of? Mentally ill people – and Cregan will *not* have enjoyed that. His day-to-day existence would soon be depressing as hell.

I have no doubt he will be in and out of high-security mental hospitals for the entirety of his prison career. When he fancies pizza, gets fed up or is feeling low, which everyone does in jail, he is always going to be Dale Cregan, isn't he?

There will be no escaping himself.

7. Criminal Intent

Let's get back to the age-old question that I asked upfront: what is prison for?

Punishment? Obviously. Revenge? There must be some of that to it. Victims' families and society at large expect their pound of flesh. That's human nature. Jails should quite definitely be a deterrent, scary enough to put folk off a life of crime – in theory. They also keep murderous people such as the villains we met in the last chapter off the streets. Prisons should make the jungle a bit more civilized.

And then there's rehabilitation. The idea that, with enlightened thinking and improving activities, you can turn these bad boys and girls around, transform them into law-abiding citizens. Well, let's test that theory, shall we?

Meet Frank, my one-time neighbour in Manchester – when he was on the out, anyway. Within the prison system, we never had a wrong word. I've seen him in bad places, kicking off, and found I had a calming effect. We get on. I never talked to him like shit; treated him with respect. Our relationship started in the seg' at Forest Bank, where we met.

Frank describes himself as 'a career criminal'. He's been bent up loads of times, but he's around fifty now, getting old like the rest of us. He ought to slow down, but I can't see it happening. I doubt he'll ever give up, whatever it costs. In the two or so years we've been in Wakefield he's been locked up three times. He has more fingers in more pies than a government minister – only he gets punished for his antics. Yet still, he's always on the lookout for the next opportunity; the threat of prison is no deterrent to Frank.

Once, he was telling me of how he hoped to do one last 'dream job' worth millions of pounds – nothing specific. I told him, 'You start doing things like that and you are looking at big time: ten years-plus for armed robbery.'

The reply he fired back didn't surprise me. 'Yeah, Mr Samworth, but just think if I didn't get caught . . . !' There'd be kudos with the lads – who he'd see right – top job! 'You had a go – well done, Frank. Cracking!' Pats on the back, all that sort of shit. It's another universe for most of us, isn't it?

It hadn't taken him long to find out where I lived, and once he was out he'd go out of his way to pop over for a chat while he was jibbing about, up to no good. I had no worries with him, like a lot of people might. I didn't hide where I lived. He knew where my garage was, that I had a motorbike in there. I actually felt safer in the knowledge that he knew that I knew.

When we bought our camper from Amy's dad I had to park it by the roadside at first. One day Frank spotted me and bobbed over. 'I've just seen a camper van,' he said, sounding a bit like Mark E. Smith from The Fall. 'Tidy motor, very tasty.'

'Please don't tell me you're after that,' I said.

He started cackling. 'Is it yours?'

I nodded.

'It's safe, Mr Samworth, don't worry. We *were* getting kitted up to take it, like . . .'

You might have gathered by now that he's a character; I guess you could call him a cheeky chappie.

Prison officers either love or hate lads like him. He's done a lot of seg' time; the whole nine yards: smashed cell, dirty protest, you name it. I remember a cracking SO at Forest Bank called Steve, who went on to be a driving instructor, so a glutton for punishment. He told me that Frank was his first 'bend-up', i.e. his first restraint, while working at Salford Magistrates' Court. Frank would resist to the max.

There's not much to him. He's classic 'Don't judge a book by its cover'; a real tough fucker. His body shows the sort of life he's had. Hard. Facial scars galore. He's not the sort of guy you'd want to interrupt while he was cracking a safe. I don't know if he's had a really violent past, but I'm assuming that as a criminal he is probably very ruthless and cunning.

It was in 2002 that he came down the block in the seg', there for a short stay as I recall, and I was on overtime. I dealt with him when he was angry, wound up and feeling anti-Establishment, which all prisoners are at some time. Yet we managed to get through it all without serious personal conflict.

Believe it or not, he is also very generous. If I'd needed money and such – which I didn't – he'd have doled it out with no hesitation, I'm certain. He likes to spread his ill-gotten gains around. In many ways he's the perfect husband: married to the same girl for over twenty years and a good earner, a busy lad.

His missus, meanwhile, is 'sweet', i.e. well looked after. It must be hard being with somebody who, at an estimate, has spent well over half of a twenty-five-year marriage either properly locked up or held in custody on remand. Perhaps it becomes normal. I know he expects to go to prison from time to time; I wonder if she accepts it too. It's a mindset difficult for the likes of thee and me to fathom.

As I write, he's inside again, but we met up before he got sent down for the umpteenth time. He could be back prowling the streets by the time you read this.

Like I said, Frank isn't his real name. I agreed not to divulge anything that would reveal his identity in return for a really honest interview. Frank by name; Frank by nature.

When we got together, after he got my number and dropped me a text, it was in my camper van in a car park outside a Costa coffee drive-through. I got the coffees – he likes his milky – and off we went, to begin with him talking about his own impression of prison officers.

'You've got officers who are there to get a wage and pay their bills at the end of the month,' he said. 'It's a job. Then there's those whose lives haven't gone the way they wanted. Bullied at school, maybe, or had other bad experiences. They want to exert authority. Some couldn't get into the police force so went for second best. That lot are dicks, and try to run your life. Then there are officers who are easy-going. You can talk to them, they stick to regulations; you know where you stand. Everybody knows where the line is and when you have crossed it.'

What sort of prison officer were I then, Frank?

'If anything, the last type, but I don't see you as an officer now. If I see you on the road, I'll stop and talk, friendly, like. I saw a screw the other week, won't name him, who I drove up alongside, pulled the window down. "Not so big and tough now, are you?" I says. "Benson and Hedges come in tens and twenties now, pal. I'm here. You're here. If you've anything to say, say it now." D'ya know what I mean?'

How about bent officers, I wondered? A lad at Forest Bank once told me they are hated, seen as weak. Frank, on the other hand, finds that corruption has its uses.

'They are in every walk of life, aren't they, bent people? It's not just officers. Same as there's legit people everywhere; them who are straight down the line. Here's how it is. You're an officer new to the job. I'll come over to talk to you, get to know you, be Mr Nice, know what I mean? I'll chat about general stuff – my life, perhaps – get a conversation going. At the end of it I want you to think, *Not a bad lad, him*. Then at some point I'll approach you with an offer of five ton to bring in a phone. Once you've done it, you know how easy it is. Then I say, "Listen, mate, there's more work like that just as easy . . ." That's how you start them. But if I've got a bent screw, I might tell the lads, "Yeah, I've got one bringing it in" – but that's all they are getting out of me, because that's my little cash cow. I'm not naming anyone. That's my golden egg, mate.'

Drops of rain began to pitter-patter on the camper van roof.

'Saying that, a couple will know who the officer is. The mate I'm padded up with might. Whoever's sorted the parcel – someone I can trust on the out – will be in on it too, but it can't be common knowledge or it's over. Another thing: if the screw gets done, he's off to prison and will want to reduce his sentence. They look for conspiracies, so where are you going from there? He'll be sticking you and all your mates in it.'

I asked Frank why he never asked me to bring in a parcel.

'Because you're a straight arrow.'

How did he know?

'Because of the way you are. I'm a good judge of character; my gut doesn't lead me wrong. Fuck the dumb shit, boss. I'll go straight when I want to go straight. Until then I'm a flat-out criminal.'

The other thing is that prisoners have twenty-four hours a day to work this stuff out, seven days a week. And a lot of them are bright. How did Frank feel about the idea that blokes like him must be daft?

'Not educated? Let me tell you, I've got qualifications. I'm an intelligent lad. You could not do my job if you weren't. I'm a different intelligent to you: I've got street smarts. You take me to any building you want – and I mean *anywhere* you want – you roll up on it now, yeah? You and me go and have a look at it, and I'm telling you, we're in there. I don't give a fuck what's in it, or on it, yeah? I'm getting us in. That's my career. It's what I do. I put locksmiths to shame, me.'

Shitloads of officers, even ones who have been in a long time, are so naive about this sort of stuff. They are absolutely clueless.

'Well,' said Frank, 'I don't know about that. You judge people individually. Certain officers who'd been there a while, you could not pull the wool over their eyes. You could not get up early enough to do it. But then you get others like the ginger cunt on C Wing who was with me in the hospital when I got stabbed up. He's one of them dickhead screws who try to exert authority but have none, know what I mean?

'Here's one for you. We're at Forest Bank, me and Fred, a mate doing fourteen years, and the wing's on lockdown. I'm number one on servery and he does the board outside cells, letting officers know who not to disturb before they get up for work and dinner, or else there could be trouble. Fred was crazy; know what I mean? Go in his pad, he's chasing you out. Fuck me, I've seen him chase officers down the wing half-naked, just because they've come in to do bolts and bars. But we had the wing on "lockers", kept it running cool. Any issues, we sorted it. Know what I mean? Leave it to the boys.

'At the end of the day it's our house. This is *my* fucking home. We live there. You officers only come to work there. All right, you do long shifts, some big hours, but first and foremost you're visitors. If there's an issue, I suffer the backlash. If things aren't running good, I can't do what I need to, because the heat's on me. So, rather than let that happen, the shit gets sorted from inside.

'Do you know how many times I've had to talk people round when they've gone over the bars, nooses around their neck? "*Come near me, I'll fucking jump* . . ." I tell the screws, "Just fuck off in the office and give me two minutes. I promise he won't jump." I go over. "Here you are, go in your pad, sort your head out and I'll get you some fish." Sorted. No big deal.'

Fish, for those who are unaware, is the nickname for spice, aka 'the new smack'. I took the opportunity to ask Frank if he'd ever done it. He admitted he had, which surprised me. As long as I'd known him, he never touched drugs, apart from the odd spliff maybe.

As Marv explained earlier, spice is a so-called 'zombie drug': one of those synthetic cannabinoids you read about that have taken over in the prison system. They cause pretty unpredictable behaviour, and if the mix ain't right – whoah! Spice is quite definitely the Devil's work.

Peddling drugs, from tobacco upwards, has long been a prison industry, and Frank explained how it had grown into even bigger business. But there are other ways to make brass too, mind. 'I'm a smart lad, me. When I go in, I don't ask my people out here to send postal orders; I live off the jail system. I'm good with my hands. See something once and I can do it. I put them talents to use.' Give Frank a loaf of bread and water-based glue and he'll give you a doll with flowers in it. He also does plant pots. 'They dry up nice. I make displays; sell them on as ornaments. I do model Land Rovers too. The lads bring me PVA glue and matchboxes from the workshop, bits of plastic and CD cases that I cut up and use to put little windows in.'

He's proud of that detail. 'You look in the interior and it's got a steering wheel, dash . . . It'll take me a week to do that and I'll get two and half hundred quid for it. Don't need any workshop. I just tell 'em, look. I'm not fucking stable. Put me behind my door, stick your telly up your arse, I've got my fucking stereo, and I'll sit behind me door "matching". I make scrolls as well – you'll get a hundred and fifty for them . . . carousels made from bread . . . there's dough in it.' Must make cells more homely, I suppose.

But when he's not making his models, that's when the drugs kick in. 'What else am I gonna do? You can only kip so much. Sleep all day and you wake up more tired than you were to begin with.'

Of course, selling drugs is also an option, which used to put a lot of the people who bought them in debt. When I came into Strangeways on K Wing, maybe a fifth of the wing was on drugs at the most, while lads like Frank jibbed about on the landings, doing their own thing, when they weren't behind their doors.

At heart, Frank is a free marketeer, believes in the power of profit. 'Debt? Let me tell you this. On my last tour at Risley, we was on a wing, yeah, and it was canteen day, which is when you get paid and can buy stuff. Well, for some of them their future canteen money was gone three weeks before they could fucking use it. That's how far in debt they were.'

Some would have already spent what was coming to them even further ahead, which is a problem because they only get ten to fifteen quid from the jail and the rest is topped up with private funds – to a limit of another fifteen or twenty quid if they've got it, and been behaving. At Risley, Frank said some were behind by as much as £40 or £50 or more a week.

Here's how the official canteen system works. Back in the day, it used to be done on paper – a sheet would come round and the inmates would have to tick the item or items required. It would also tell them how much private cash they had in the prison 'bank', the prices of those items, and the most they were allowed or able to spend on them. Every week, some of their money would be moved into that 'spends' account.

Nowadays it is done by computer, but the principle is the same. They tick what they want and that order is processed by the couriers, DHL, and gets delivered on Fridays.

You can think of it as an online grocery store, the prison's corner shop, selling food and drink mainly but also useful items like shaving razors, toothbrushes and prayer mats. How some of those things are packaged depends on the level of security; we had no tinned goods in Strangeways for a while, for instance.

Some jails do fresh food and in dispersal prisons I've heard you can even buy prepacked chickens to cook. There's no alcohol, obviously, or tobacco since it got banned. They even used to sell joss sticks, incense, but stopped that because they were being used to mask the smell of other illicit substances!

'One day,' Frank went on, 'a kid comes round and he's trying to buy a pack of eights, which is three vapes. They cost four or five quid on the canteen. This lad is paying £20, with interest, because he hasn't got the money to do it legit, so is in need of our credit services. Inside, we set the economy. I've no patience with them bitching that the wing is on its arse because they can't afford a pack, when it's them that got themselves debted up.'

But how, you might ask, does this work given that there is no actual physical money in prisons? How can that debt be handed over, especially as there are no electronic cash transfers available either – and who would want them anyway, as that would point directly to the drug supplier? There are five ways at least.

One, your funds become their funds to the amount owed. You end up shopping for your supplier, not yourself. This also enables them to build up stocks of goods that can then be shifted – for profit or use as bribes maybe – as they wish, thereby further strengthening their power and influence in the jail.

Two, cold hard cash can be handed over by proxy on the out. Or three, money might be paid into their prison account on your behalf. Four, maybe drugs or phones are smuggled in as payment and, five, a debt could also be fully or partly paid off by an agreement to assault another prisoner. It's a merry-go-round.

At Strangeways, during my early days as an officer, I

remember one lad getting leathered. He was an all-right prisoner who just happened to be in a pad with a kid who owed money and was then released. The lad left behind inherited the debt from his ex-pad-mate, couldn't or wouldn't pay it and got filled in.

That sounded terrible to me, but Frank reckoned it wasn't so clear-cut. 'It's like this: if you're padded up with another guy and come to me for drugs, your mate is going to smoke them too, isn't he? You won't just sit there on your own; it's a partnership. I guarantee it, pound to a pinch of shit. In cells, it makes jail time a bit easier when you act as a team. Thing is, if you don't smoke fish and your pad-mate does, you're not staying with him, are you? You wouldn't bunk with someone stoned, stinking the place out and rotting away, personal hygiene gone out the window . . . when all the fucker lives for is his fish. You'd be saying, "He's a scruffy fish head, get him out of my cell." So to me, if you're in with a fish head, you are smoking it too.'

It's common knowledge that the most nervous time for a bent screw bringing stuff in is when he or she arrives for work. Having got through reception and onto the wing, once the parcel is passed on it's not a danger to them any more. They might even feel euphoric.

It can go wrong, though. I interviewed a kid for my podcast – Chris, his name was – who'd been on course to play professional football for Preston North End. But he got injured and the dream was over, so he became a voluntary fireman and also a prison officer at HMP Lancaster Farms instead, both jobs part-time. There were loads of gangbangers from Manchester and Liverpool, and in no time they had him bringing stuff in. He did it for the Scousers at first, but when the Mancs found out his workload doubled. He said it was a huge relief to get caught. He'd made a mistake, hadn't been able to see a way out of it and, from doing two jobs that made him a pillar of society, when it all did come out and he was bailed it brought shame upon his family.

Luckily for him, he wasn't sent to Strangeways. As he'd been a prison officer they sent him to Shrewsbury, which was then a Cat C, where he was among loads of ex-drug police officers and one other prison guard. You could sense the weight had lifted from his shoulders.

I asked Frank, 'If I'm a bent screw, bringing you stuff in for two years, then say I can't do it any more – are you going to grass me up?'

'Am I fuck. I'm just going to send my boys around to see you on the out. Not me personally, you understand. That's not my way.'

For a while at Strangeways, as you know, we had a thing with people finding out officers' addresses. Maybe they were bringing stuff in, or maybe just coming on too strong. Let's say Frank and an officer like that had a bad day: would he find out where they lived and threaten them?

'No, not because we've had a falling-out. I'm a realist me, a proper guy. We all have bad days. I might go after screws that think they are untouchable, king of the wing, just to show them they're not. Maybe somebody can drive up in the car park, wind the window down: "My mate says you need to back off, pal. Heed his advice and off you pop." The types who aren't doing their job right think they are ten men.'

If you think this is far-fetched, it really isn't.

As Frank says: 'You can jump on the prison car park at six in the morning, sit for an hour, see who's coming in and driving what, on their way to work. I don't have to wait until you finish your shift.

'Once you've gone inside, I'm walking over to stick a tracker on your car – the one I've got cost £500, the dog's bollocks. I'll charge it to 100 per cent, put it in its little magnetic case and slap it where you can't see it. They are very strong, won't fall off. After an hour, they go into sleep mode. But the second the car moves, it wakes back up and you get a location on your mobile phone – Trackserver app. It's meant to be a security device. I can turn it on and off from anywhere in the country. I could follow you in your camper. I've got one for my bike.'

And finding any address online is a piece of piss nowadays.

'I could find out where every screw lives, but I don't want to. I don't want to threaten you all. I'm not that kind of guy. At the end of the day it's just a job, and some of you don't deserve threatening. Why am I going to apply pressure, mate? Because that just makes for an awkward situation inside. It makes things tense. I want an easy life. As long as I'm a nice guy and not getting in your way, you're going to leave me to it. Shit runs downhill.'

Frank told me it's got to the stage where lads like him have stopped 'giving tick' because it's not worth the hassle of beating people up. 'If you keep coming to me and are good for it, well fair enough. But I'm sick to death of being bounced. We call it Fuck Off Friday, canteen day. Or Black Eye Friday, because you are either fucking off or getting a black eye for not paying what you owe.'

It's no coincidence then that canteen day is also when more cons get moved from the wing than usual. "If we are going to move you off here, mate, you're going to have to tell us who your tumble is with and what it's about." That's jail policy. It's obvious they are grassing. CHIS (Covert Human Intelligence Source) jobs, most likely.'

What's the current status regarding violence against staff?

'Listen, no one gets smacked in jail for nothing. You don't just smack 'em for the sake of it, same as out here. They bring it on themselves. I've taken a few beatings myself in my time. Shit happens. The screws' attitude is a factor and so is spice.'

Picture this: someone has been on the stuff, collapsed and started fitting. The officers and maybe healthcare staff rush in, nurses around them as the prisoner twitches on the floor. He's probably unconscious. On goes the oxygen mask and they try to revive him.

'Yeah, and he doesn't have a clue what's going on. But the minute I open my eyes and I've got ten people grabbing at me I'm flipping – *Whooaahhh!* It happened to me once. I've smoked some fish on the landing and my mates have seen I'm about to go. They've walked over and said, "Come on, mate. Let's get you to your pad, put you on your bed and you'll be right." One gets hold of an arm, starts pulling me in this direction, another gets hold of the other. I'm yelling, "Hey, how about you both let me go!" and a screw comes over. Normally I'd be fine with him. He's an SO now, I believe, used to be Strangeways, fucking safe as houses, old school. He puts an arm on my shoulder. And in the moment I believed he was there to do me wrong. Mental psychological shit, isn't it? I've bobbed down, picked him up like a rugby tackle, took him off his legs and tried to flip him over the balcony. He's a big lad like you. Next thing, three or four lads have come over, dragged me off to my pad. I got nicked for it. About a week later, I seen him again and felt a bit of a cunt. I told him, "Sorry, mate. It wasn't me. I was fished in."'

I mentioned to Frank that tobacco had caused similar issues before smoking was banned in prisons. As expected, he found that second bit, about the ban, hilarious. Fair near cackled his cock off.

'Nah, nah, nah, ha ha. Don't get it twisted. You can still smoke in Cat Ds. Here's the scam we had. Every week, at Risley, guys come in from Cat Ds for piss tests and whatnot. I rang my mate to see if he knew of anyone doing that. He said a lad's on his way from Thorne Cross [an open prison in Cheshire]. He knew he'd test positive, which meant he would be moved back to closed conditions and up for it.

'So I says to my mate, right, get a soap powder box and fucking fill it with phones and ounce packets of tobacco. Give it to the kid at Thorne Cross and tell him when he gets here I'll have somebody take it off him. Well, he's also come in with two hundred sheets of spice. It's all paper now. We don't use the green matter you'll have seen.

'There are ways and means of getting stuff in. If he's here for two weeks, he can make a couple of grand, and why not? Good money. It's only like going off to work on an oil rig or something, timewise.

'With fish, what I'd do is print a load of depositions off, or a few sheets of A4 that look like depositions, and spray or dip them in the gear. Depositions are classed as legal documents, so I would go into reception and throw them on the side. "What's that?" "It's me deps – got me name on the front. Frank versus Elizabeth Regina." It's a load of bullshit basically, but let's say I take two hundred pages in. Each A4 sheet is worth

£150 or, if you're selling it to your boys, £50. It's fucking cost me pennies, man. I can take you to Bury New Road, yeah, and we can buy pre-sprayed sheets, fiver apiece. That's £145 profit, just from walking through reception with my deps. You make thousands, and without serious risk. "Any phones or drugs on you?" "Nah, mate."'

What do the customers do with that paper? Smoke it, of course. But lighters are banned in prison, so how do they get around that?

'You can buy vape devices. They have capsules in them: twist the top off the cap and take out the stuffing, fibres and an element at the bottom. You then get your paper, roll it into a ball, put it on the element and stick that on the bottom bit of your vape. Press it and the element glows red, the paper starts burning and smoke rises, which you inhale. You only need about two centimetres' worth, half a centimetre wide, and it will flop you. Lights out.

'But you know what? If I smoke a bit of fish in the morning, I've got the full day ahead of me and I'm behind my door until five o'clock at least, longer in lockdown. I'll get out for my dinner, but that's just a five-minute walk to the servery and back. So, if at nine o'clock I can have a brew, a pipe and wake at noon, fished in and not remembering a bit of it, well, it's not like I've been asleep, just unconscious.'

So you wake up and you've killed time. Although, as with any drug, how fast its effects wear off depends on how much you take.

Frank had his pipe one day and woke in a pool of blood.

'I'd split my head open. It was thick and black, congealing down my fucking face. I must have caught it on the corner of a unit, then hit the floor. I'd done it eight o'clock at night, the screw had already looked in and it was now eleven o'clock. He wasn't due to check again until two in the morning. I wasn't on hourlies. My face was out here . . . Fuck me.'

He got on the bell and people came running, a nurse deciding he ought to go to hospital. But when she nipped out for dressings, an officer whispered, 'Frank, you don't want to go, do you, mate?'

'"Well, the nurse said I need to, Mr Green. But if you're telling me I don't need it" – in other words you'll be fucked because you don't have enough staff for night patrol as it is – "then no, I don't need to go. But you owe me one, know what I mean?" He never delivered on the debt, the piece of shit, but that's how I am. Glue it up. Clean it up. What else are they going to do to me?'

I was still interested in tobacco. How much does that cost?

'You're looking at about seven quid for one roll-up these days. It used to be phonecards and snout, but now it's toiletries, munch [crack] and vapes mainly. That's the currency. If you've money, you can get smoke. Every week we had Daz-boxfuls of tobacco coming in. It doesn't look big, a Daz box, but every pouch has one or two ounces and you've got sixteen in the box. An eighth of tobacco gets you £70, £140 for a quarter . . . so that's £280 for half an ounce – more expensive than drugs, pretty much. Drugs go cheap, so they keep buying them.'

Cigarette papers are now rare an' all.

'If you bought an ounce of tobacco, I'd throw in Rizlas with it. Special offer. No lighters, as I say. You just buy vapes off the canteen.

'But here's the best bit. It used to be a bastard to charge your phone inside. Now you get a USB cable to charge your vape device, three or four inches long. What you do is cut off the charger bit the vape screws into, which just leaves your plus and minus wires. Join your phone to them two wires – charger sorted! Plug in wall. Cool!'

To promote family ties and stop the smuggling of mobiles, some prisons have begun putting phones in cells, but Frank reckoned they are too expensive to use. 'If I'm on standard prisoner privileges, I'm only getting £15 a week in my prison account. On basic, it's only £2.50. Out of that, if I smoke, I can't afford a pack of vapes and I also need toiletries, as you have to keep yourself clean, don't you? Prison issue's no good for anyone; I wouldn't let my dog use it. If I write to people, I've got to get writing materials. So all of that and I've also got to buy phone credit? Fuck off. But if I can get a mobile for £200 . . .

'Fair enough, it's an outlier, and some people can't afford that. Some jails you go to, mobiles cost five, six or seven hundred quid, depending on the one you want. There are shitloads of phones in Strangeways. You are never going to stop them, are you? After prostitution, prison is the oldest profession in the world.'

For Frank, crime really is a business, in and out of jail. And it's a matter of honour to him that he isn't seen as sponging off his family. 'When I'm out, I'm grafting for them, not just putting dough in my pocket,' he said. 'I'm making sure they live nice. I'm not bragging or owt, but we do. There's times when things are bad, but my missus works has a job, as straight as they come. We're like chalk and fucking cheese, us two. Been together forever. How she puts up with it, I don't fucking know.

I'm away a lot. But she knows that when I get out she will live like a fucking queen.'

Given which, what I ask next might be a daft question. We don't have time machines, but if we did and he could go back to before the first time he was locked up and could pick a different path, would he?

'Nah.' (I knew he was going to say that.) 'And let me tell you why. If I hadn't lived the life I've lived, I wouldn't be who I am. I might be a flat-out thieving bastard, and if it ain't nailed down, I'll rob it, it's true. Actually, even if it *is* nailed down, I'll still come and take it, but that's my life. It's what I do, and I class it as a job. But that's not me as a person. As a man, I've a good heart on me, a decent set of morals. Some might say I can be a bit ruthless here and there, but I do what needs doing when it needs doing. It doesn't make me a bad person.'

Like a lot of people in prison, he's been stabbed, macheted . . .

'Oh, yeah, but that's just an occupational hazard. I don't go out armed to do what I do. I don't need to.'

There is a lot of gangland business in the area where Frank lives, the place he was born and raised. He said he doesn't do any of that. He has, however, always been known as a car man.

'I can get cars for anyone who's got money for cars. I make sure I'm friendly with them all. I don't give a fuck if you are warring with him: that's between him and you. But I'm not going to give you something so-and-so can't have, or something that'll give you the drop on him, because he's my mate, and you are too. I stay out of it.'

A bit like Marv, then, and also like Marv, Frank has led a violent life.

'Well, if you look at me, I'm scarred up to fuck, aren't I? But I don't see that as a bad thing. I see it as experience.'

How far would he be prepared to go?

'If anyone hurts anyone in my inner circle, I'd do life for them.'

How about robberies – let's say with a security guard? Would he knock them out? Tie them up? What?

'Half the time you just run at them, don't need to do anything. If they want to get brave, that's their problem. I tell them beforehand, I'm not here for you; I am here for that. I won't be killing anybody. People have hid in offices until I've gone – fair enough. They don't get paid to grapple with me, do they? Most of the time, doing what I do, I wait for people to leave first. Unless it's a situation where you need someone to get certain things done, d'ya know what I mean?'

'I'm interested in how people cope with life after prison,' I told Frank. 'But, for you it never ends, does it? You've had quite a tour: Forest Bank in the private sector, Risley, Liverpool, Strangeways . . . So here we are at the start of the 2020s. You should be able to tell us the state of play?'

'Oh my God,' said Frank. 'It has changed for the worse. Back in the day, it were kind of constructive. You had stuff to do. Before 2015, you had officers who'd been there ages. Couldn't believe Strangeways on my last tour. It had always been what lads call a "screws' jail". That's not a bad thing. If I go and ask a screw for something, I'd get told to put an application in. I tell you this much – if you put an app' in, your shit got done, it got answered. You knew where you was.'

So a screws' jail isn't one where six-foot-four officers leather prisoners, then?

'Nah. It's *your* jail, man. *You* run it. As a prisoner, you got fuck all and plenty of it, but you knew that; happy with it. Nowadays you go to officers, "Any chance you can sort out this or that or the other?" "Yeah, yeah, I'll sort it." You've asked them first thing in the morning, but when your door's unlocked at eight and you come out at dinner it's, "Boss, did you manage to . . ." "Oh, no, no, no . . . I'll do it in a bit . . . I'll do it before tea." Teatime comes, you see him again. "Gov, did you sort that out for me?" "No, I'm going home now, I'll sort it out tomorrow . . ." We call them yes-men. It's fucking frustrating.

'See, when new staff come in, there's two ways it can go, right? A lot depends on which officers they've been tailing. Tailed a prick, they will be a prick. They get taught dickhead ways. It's not what you want, that. If you're a dickhead to me, I'll make your life hard every day. If you are all right with me, I'll make it as easy as I can for you.'

And then there is the age issue. Too much greenery about.

'Are you fucking mad? They are straight out of school, mate! Nineteen-year-old kids with keys . . . Six weeks' training,' Frank said, 'and they are on the wing, knowing nothing about the system.'

Every jail in the country, private or government-run, has PSIs and PSOs – prison service instructions and orders, all written down in a handbook. In jail, these are law. The rules of the outside world still apply, but prisons also have their own, and if you break them, you are punished, either by losing days or with time down the block in seg'. For inmates, they also tell you your rights, set out what you are entitled to, no matter what any prison officer might think. 'Is it in the PSIs or PSOs?' End of story.

Frank used to ask for that handbook a lot. What's in there could have been his specialist subject on *Mastermind*.

'I did, aye. It tells you how the governor should deal with things, and gives you guidelines on how severe punishments should be, what they need to prove to find you guilty, what they don't need. Nothing worse than an inexperienced screw saying, "You can't walk down the landing in shorts and flip-flops and dressing gown." "Well, actually, if you want to check your wing rules, you'll see I can, to and from the showers . . ." At least, that's how it is in the private sector. In the public sector you can only wear shorts in your cell. Female officers may get offended if you've got your legs out. I know this stuff. They don't.'

No surprise, then, that since 2015 the levels of violence in prison have risen. They're employing younger staff mainly because they're the only people they can attract. But there are other issues too.

'It's also to do with how you are locked down for so long,' said Frank. 'I have an hour to get on the phone, get me shower, clean me cell, so ain't got time to come over and speak to you. "All right, Mr S, how you doing?" There's no relationship-building. If I'm not talking to you, there are certain things you're not getting to know either.'

It's true. When officers and prisoners chat on a friendly basis, important stuff gets passed on – it's your dynamic security in action.

'I might say something as a friend that I wouldn't otherwise,' said Frank, 'just to keep conversation going. The way I treat prison officers is as key-turning gatherers of information. If they don't get the info, they can't keep the jail secure. If I'm not speaking to you, you don't know if he's getting whatever off whoever and wherever, times and dates. You don't know he's got a phone, pulls it out at certain times, yeah? But if you're speaking to lads, you can get to know that without anyone having to grass anyone up. "Oh, you should have seen what happened the other day in there . . ." A lot of lads are dumb enough not to know. Then off the screw goes, in the loop, to write it all down in the office. That world's gone now.'

I'm guessing some readers will be surprised at that, but I'm not. It rings true with my own day-to-day experience.

'Fuck the fact you're staff, yeah? If I've got respect for you as a person, I respect you as a person. We built enough of a relationship for me to be here now, doing this. There's certain other officers who, even if they only tried speaking to me, would get splatted. You earned that respect as a prison officer even if you're not one any more. But even if you were, I'd still speak to you because I like you as a person.

'Fuck the job; it's work. And to you it was always a job. It's like what I do: to me it's just a job. I put a lot of hours in, but I see it as work. It's not legitimate work, but it's work, and that doesn't define who I am as a person or change the way I am with people.'

So, come on then, Frank, I asked, how would you make prisons better? Turns out he's also a fan of dynamic security and would like a return to proper prisoner–officer interaction, where everybody knew where they were and just cracked on with it.

'Strangeways in the old days . . . if I jumped on the netting, they'd lock the fucking wing down, jump on after me and drag me off. You weren't allowed on there, so that's how it went. Now, they hit the panic alarms. What's the point? Staff rush in from everywhere – for what? They won't go on the netting – just lock a few doors until the Tornado team arrives. They make a big thing out of fuck all.' Result: chaos for all concerned.

At Strangeways, Frank worked as a qualified industrial and biohazard cleaner. Rather than have a cell out of action for two weeks and pay an outside firm £500 to come in and do it, we'd use him. He was also my top painter on K Wing: two cells a day. Smashed it.

'Whatever job I do, I fucking apply myself. It used to get me out. With some lads it's, "Boss, if you don't get me some tobacco, I'll cut myself." Certain jails you can hold to ransom like that; they pussy about. Back in the day, if I'd said that, the officer would have said, "Wait a minute, I'll go get you a fresh blade so you don't infect it."

'You could still get phones and so on, but it was tighter. If I wanted to get on my phone, I'd only use it on association, because you'd get sneaky bastards with detectors at night. They'd put a box outside your cell if they thought you had one – make a call and the light on that box changed colour. Then early morning they'd come and raid me. Now I use it any time, they don't give a fuck.'

Prisons still have George's dedicated search teams, the Men in Black, trained to search for phones and such. These days they are often co-opted to reception, though, because jails are short-staffed.

'When I come in from court, there they are,' said Frank. 'They've only just got X-ray machines in HMP Manchester, yet they've had them at Forest Bank for a bit. But here's the kicker: if I come in on remand, I'm not getting body-scanned. Cool.'

And once inside, prisoners need organized activities.

'Here's an odd one, right? If I go to places like Risley, a Cat C jail, I'm allowed to buy modelling matches, glue and sandpaper off the canteen. Nothing wrong with making or having models, yeah? They don't let you post them out, though, or keep them in your cell. What you have to do is box them up and put them in reception. However, at Strangeways I can only have matches and glue and do my models if I'm a lifer. What, if I want to get creative, I need a life sentence? What about everyone else? There's fuck all to do there but fish and tobacco.

'Oh, and books! I like reading. A lot of the lads can't fucking read, but plenty like me can. I'll read this! What are you supposed to do with your time? You can't sit in your cell all day vegging on telly, can you?'

Most prisons have a library. At Strangeways it was on F Wing, in the bottom jail; the officer there had been in the job years. He'd go around the wings on a rota system, take eight prisoners down at a time, bring them and their books back, take some more and so on. In some prisons, depending on security categories, they can buy new books too, like they can magazines and newspapers, or have them sent in, another opportunity for the sort of spice-smuggling shenanigans Marv described.

At Strangeways, dead pigeons might be slung over the fence – or rats, there are a lot in Manchester – packed with drugs. On the way back from visits in the bottom jail, prisoners are made to stay strictly on the road, but Frank recalled a day when one con kicked off in the line, knowing officers wouldn't bawl him out in front of everyone. Once they got back to the top jail, they pulled him to one side, asked him to wait on the grass. Smart boy, not-so-smart officers. 'Alls he needed then was an excuse to kneel down and pick it up, didn't he? Took it back to his pad, opened it up, took out what was sewn in there and disposed of the rest. It was very naive of them.'

Lesson one: never underestimate the ingenuity of prisoners.

'Shoving stuff up your arse is not a problem. Listen, that's my fucking safe, isn't it? Only I've got a key to that. And anything inside is mine. You want it? Try and fucking get it. It's the most secure location you've got in prison.'

One day, Frank got himself caught with a parcel up there, as shown on the scanner. 'What can they do but send you to the block and wait? I'm not handing it over. Fuck you, mate, it's mine. What I used to do was pull out enough for a little joint, and then put it back away, long before I even got my joint on. I'd make my joint and stand behind me door about two minutes before they came round with the scran. I'd absolutely stink the fucking place out with the peng. Screws looking in. "How much more of that you got?" What can they do? If it's up your arse, it's staying there. You try pulling it out of my arse cheeks, mate, and prepare yourself for a rape case. Indecent assault.'

Of course, strip searches come with rules and regulations that must be observed, and must be carried out by two members of staff. At HMP Manchester we'd position a mirror behind them and tell them to drop and squat. Look with our eyes. That was how DST used to do it too.

'An officer once told me to lift my testicles up,' said Frank. 'What? "Lift your balls up." You come and do it, you stupid bastard. Don't tell me what to do with my nuts when they are *my* fucking nuts. Want me to drop and squat? I'll drop and squat, but really and truly I shouldn't as I've got disabilities. That's as far as I go with a mirror, you fucking nonce. I'm the sort where if you strip-search me and I'm pissed off and have nothing, I'm going to make you uncomfortable.'

Frank reckoned he had a certain officer kicked off the wings in Strangeways. 'Get this, right. Some kid's gone awry, so I'm making his life hard, next thing I'm on bully basic. Grassed me right up. Next day, two officers come in and one was fucking new. I didn't like him and told him as much. It was his attitude: young in the head, thought he was the big man with the keys – type who thinks he's a Marine. Anyway, he's come in my pad with my property card after I've gone on basic. "Strip search," he says. We'd have a cell search too.'

This was a double cell, full metal jacket, so a toilet at the end of the bed, en suite. Table and chair bolted to the wall, not very wide.

'The officers were stood in my doorway, one behind the other, door shut. The one in front was the dickhead, in the job six months, but the one at the back was also green, didn't know the score. About two months in the job. Let's call him Officer B. Officer A says to pass him my T-shirt, so I did. He's searched it, given it me back. "Pants." He's searched them too, put them on the bed. "Socks." He passed them to Officer B, who searched them – same with my boxers.

'Now, I've thought straight away, this is fucking wrong, and what's more he's also done it to my pad-mate, a Brummie kid who was due off in six weeks, moving a bit closer to home. Didn't like it in Manchester, not got the easiest life. Anyway, he was on basic too, having it hard, and found himself involved due to my bully basic and cell search. So as soon as the search was done and they'd put us in a room while they rifled the cell, I said to him, "When you got strip-searched, was the officers side by side as they should've been, not one behind the other?"

'Officer A had called me a bully and I'm not. I can be a bastard, but never a bully. It kills too many people. So I told this Brummie kid, "Here's what we do. I'm trained to listen to suicidal prisoners, so at three in the morning get on the cell bell and when they ask what you want, say the Samaritans. They'll get Oscar One. On the phone, say you've had a bad experience. Tell the truth about the search, but then how when he passed your duds behind him he looked you in the eye and cupped your nuts. You froze, through shock or disbelief. It brought back memories from when you was a kid, you didn't know what to do . . . You're feeling suicidal over it, can't speak to other officers because you worry they are in the same pot."

'Next day, come dinner time, the door cracked open. "Frank, you're wanted." Okay. Walks down to the SO's office: two Manchester CID in there, governor, PO and an SO. Want to ask me about the strip-search incident. I did my best to assist. "I thought it was dodgy at the time, but what can you say? They are officers," I said. "When I've got back to my pad, my pad-mate says he wanted to smack the officer; I can only tell you what the lad's told me." Next thing it's, "Right, lads, pack your bags." Pointing at us one after the other, they said, "You are going to Risley . . . and *you* are going back to Birmingham."'

Eighteen months later, Frank returned to Strangeways. 'A certain officer still wasn't allowed on wings to work with inmates on an individual level; could just escort them back and forth on visits.'

Why they don't quote lads like Frank in prison officer training is beyond me. And he had more insight in his locker.

'Another time, I got an officer sacked, again a ploy with a pad-mate. This prick had been on my case for weeks, a young idiot with a stupid attitude. So I said, "Here's how we do this cunt. You tell him you've got mail but you're dyslexic – can't read or write. You expect it'll be bad news but don't want the other lads to know what's going on – any chance he could read it for you? Lead him to the cell, and as he walks in I'll smack you on your nose, bust it. Then you fly out the cell, holding your face, and run down the landing. On camera all they'll see is this officer come into the cell and you rush out covered in blood. They'll question him and when he says that it was his pad-mate who smacked him, you turn around and say, "Did he fuck." He'll have a bit of explaining to do. Sure enough, that's how it played out.'

Prison is a brutal, dog-eat-dog environment. You need to be quick on your feet and even swifter between the ears to survive it.

'He was a dickhead, trying to make life hard for us. Well, don't make life hard for me in my fucking house. He was definitely bullied at school.'

On remand, Franks makes his regular visits home, every week without fail. But once he's been sentenced, he cuts his missus off a bit.

'I do speak to her on the phone now and then, so it doesn't get awkward when I come out. But I miss her and she misses me. That's life. We've been together a long time and just crack on with it.'

Going home must be fun, though?

That throaty cackle again. 'One time, I'd done two and a half years of a five-year sentence. So out I gets, has a drink and it's upstairs to the bedroom. We're just about to get passionate, me on top ready to do the deed, when I roll off. I says, I can't do it.

"'How d'you mean?"

"'Can't do it, babe. Feel like I'm unfaithful.'"

"'Who to?' she says.

"'Pam,' I tells her, holding up my hand. "And her five ugly sisters.'"

Frank was thoughtful for a moment. 'In cells, you get a lot of silence. You might get an hour to yourself when your mate has a visitor, although one or two twisted individuals do sit there having wank races. Mostly you just tug one off in bed, and that's fine, because the bunks are bolted to the wall.'

Thank you for that image, Frank.

'Fucking hell, then there are panic wanks. I'm in my cell, single occupancy, and bored. There's a female night officer on and she's a bitch. If I'm feeling a bit horny, I might get a bit of blood in it, yeah, ready to do the deed, and then get on the buzzer for bog roll. Now, I estimate that gets me two to two and a half minutes before she rocks up outside. I'm at it, no time to waste. She's coming and so am I! The idea is to reach the peak before the officer looks through the hatch . . .'

Prison really is another world.

8. Inside Out

The plight of IPP prisoners is an issue I feel really strongly about – and at last a few barristers seem to have woken up to it.

IPP: Imprisonment for Public Protection. These sentences, created by the Criminal Justice Act 2003 and in use from April 2005, were officially abolished in 2012, but their draconian effects are still being felt, by prisoners and their families, collateral damage from what was quite definitely an assault on natural justice. If you ask me, half the time the judges didn't understand the sentence they were passing themselves. It was, and still is, a ball of confusion.

Here's how the Ministry of Justice itself describes IPPs in its own factsheet, freely available online.

> They were designed to protect the public from serious offenders whose crimes did not merit a life sentence. Offenders sentenced to an IPP [were] set a minimum term (tariff) which they must spend in prison.

Once the tariff is completed, they can apply to the parole board for release. But:

> The parole board will release an offender only if it is satisfied that it is no longer necessary for the protection of the public for the offender to be confined. If offenders are refused parole, they

214

will be on supervised licence for at least ten years. If offenders are refused parole, they can only apply again after one year.

Trouble is, they didn't work so were scrapped. But for those handed an IPP sentence originally, the ramifications are still being felt. Again, in the Ministry of Justice's own words: '. . . they have been used far more widely than intended', for example, for those whose crimes were so low-level they had a tariff of two years. This factsheet was written following a prime minister's review of the issue in July 2011, shortly before IPPs got the boot in favour of 'a range of consistent tough sentences with fixed lengths, which will see more dangerous criminals given life sentences and give victims a clear understanding of how long defenders will be imprisoned.'

At the time, the MoJ revealed that they had been 'handed down at a rate of more than 800 a year and as a result more than 6,500 offenders are currently serving IPP sentences.' The changes, though, would not be retrospective. 'Current IPP prisoners will continue to serve their sentences, and will only be released when the parole board assesses them as suitable.'

In the here and now, that's the crux of the problem right there. The parole board and prison service still employ human beings with as loose and unpredictable a grip on IPPs as ever; folk as prone to jobsworth-style failings, bureaucratic incompetence, individual agendas and personality clashes as the rest of us.

As of November 2019, the Prison Reform Trust reported a figure of 2,223 people in the UK still on IPPs, nine in ten already past their tariff expiry date. Some 1,206 more were back in jail having been recalled from the community.

How would you like it if – as happened to one lad I know

– you get six months for street robbery and then, fifteen years later, are still inside on the same charge with no light at the end of the tunnel? Guys like him end up haunting the seg', self-harming and super disruptive.

Another reader contacted me whose partner was involved in a hit and run. He was driving, fucked off and someone died. It got him ten years. This was a while ago and sentences have shrunk; do that now and it's two years max. He'd been in the wrong, so ten years was right and proper. But in 2020 he'd already been in eighteen years: eight over tariff. Why? you ask. Well, as we've read, at ten years you become eligible for parole, but can get knocked back. When she wrote, there was no sign of his release. I've seen murderers serve less time than that, although I suppose if you kill someone, a car is a lethal weapon, isn't it? I don't know why the parole board said no in this particular case but, unless it was as bad as the original crime, the bottom line is, he was on his way to double the amount of time originally merited by law.

IPPs were supposedly brought in for violent and sexual offences, before some high-up broadened the scope. They were meant to protect the public against those whose crimes didn't deserve life, but who were still too dangerous to release after the original term. Misbehave on parole and back you go, no messing. You're only leaving with a clean slate if the parole board judges it safe. But that can lead to a merry-go-round of reviews in which people are constantly held back and frustrated by bureaucracy.

It's true that some of these IPP prisoners can sign up to programmes that, in theory, might help to persuade a future parole board they will be less likely to reoffend, but they aren't always available, which to me just about sums the whole mess up.

I've touched upon the IPP issue in the *Real Porridge* podcast and other podcasts, because it bugs me big time. Every now and then I get a message on Twitter or wherever from official bods or members of the public who deny it's a problem. 'People don't get locked up for nothing,' they say. 'They must still be a danger in some way.' Well, let me tell you, I know otherwise. They can and *do* either keep IPP prisoners banged up or bring them back in from probation and lock them up again with absolutely jack shit reason. That's my opinion and I'm sticking to it; experience doesn't lie.

So what, specifically, are things that might persuade the parole board not to wipe the slate clean? Good question.

In short, the same things that can get anyone recalled from normal probation, I suppose – committing or being charged with another crime, breaking conditions attached to their licence or (and here's the killer for IPPs) behaving in a way to lead their manager to believe they *might* commit another crime. In other words, it can come down to personal opinion and, for obvious reasons, that can feel very unfair and random, especially when you have worked through the full length of your original tariff.

And prisoners being prisoners, it's not unusual for them to have a row or whatever from time to time, episodes that for any prisoner other than an IPP mean nothing in the bigger picture.

If the subject of IPP sentencing interests you – and after the story that's coming, I expect it will – then have a look at an online blog by someone called Russell Webster, posted in October 2020, a year in which there were more IPP recalls than releases, on the back of an eighteen-month study written with Kimmett Edgar and Mia Harris of the Prison Reform Trust after the parole board renewed its advice to members on how to terminate IPP licences.

Russell, who according to his blog is a full-time consultant specializing in substance misuse and crime, writes, 'The probation officers we interviewed had different understandings of the length of time that people had to wait before they could apply for their licence to be removed. Some believed it to be four years [which is actually the length of time people on IPPs for non-sexual offences must wait to apply to have probation supervision suspended after their initial release].' He continues: 'Furthermore, some probation officers incorrectly assumed that if somebody was recalled to prison, the ten-year period before which they could apply to remove their licence would start again on their re-release.'

As I say, arse, meet elbow.

When the IPP sentence was abolished for new cases, there were over 6,000 old cases still in jail, 'for public protection'. Five years later that number had halved, but hundreds served as much as five times the length of their minimum term. And we are talking about actual people here, with families and real lives, not just a collection of statistics. It's time to stop arguing the toss on this a decade after it was supposedly scrapped and finally get rid.

There have been stories galore in the news. Such as that of Tommy Nicol, thirty-seven, who got an IPP with a four-year tariff for stealing a car and injuring its owner. After serving six years and unable to get therapy, he drew a circle of blood and hanged himself in 2015, leaving his sister to campaign for change.

Shaun Lloyd nicked a mobile phone and got a two-year-and-nine-month tariff. He served nine years – yes, nine years – before being released, despite having a partner and child.

James Ward earned himself a ten-month tariff for actual bodily harm following a fight with his dad. Struggling with his mental health, he then set fire to a prison mattress and wound up serving eleven years before being released following a media campaign by his sister in 2017, who said he'd been 'left to rot'.

It affects women's prisons too, of course. Charlotte Nokes received an IPP sentence for attempted robbery. A talented artist, she was given a fifteen-month tariff but served eight years before being found dead in her cell in 2016.

I struggle to get my head around it all. For me, the people who *should* be on IPP sentences are terrorists. Over the last few years we've seen plenty set free and they've gone and murdered people after.

In the summer of 2020, as the first lockdown was relaxed, a kid from Libya knifed three innocent blokes to death in a park in Reading. It turned out he had a long history of jail time owing to violent offences like assaults on police officers and emergency workers. He'd even spat in an arresting officer's face and called her 'a slave'. But even before this, in February, a guy had stabbed another three bystanders in Streatham High Road in London, before being shot dead by police with a hoax device strapped to him. He'd been released the week before, having served half of a three-year sentence for terror offences. I could reel off plenty more examples, but you get the picture.

Brainwashed terrorists do pose a threat, yet we aren't doing anything to address that in our prisons. There is no GCSE or A-level in how not to be a terrorist. Nor is there any attempt to deradicalize them. While they pose a risk, we should keep them inside. Yet I don't know of any terrorist on an IPP. At some point we return them to society.

When a normal prisoner gets his or her paperwork, it will come with a sentence calculation. They get an EDR: earliest date of release. Got two years? Out in twelve months. Be a complete arsehole inside, peddle drugs, assault people or whatever, as long as your misbehaviour does not go to the police and end up adding time, you will still leave on that date. Your sentence is up.

On IPPs, however, the EDR says ninety-nine years – i.e. no earliest release date. And these were handed out for all sorts.

An orderly with us on healthcare, in for robbery, had been given an eighteen-month IPP. Somebody somewhere deemed he might still be a threat to the security of the nation after then. Why, I don't know. The length of the original sentence doesn't seem to suggest it. This kid volunteered for every single course on offer. He pre-empted his parole board landing him with a 'We want you to do this or that' by attending healthy relationships, drugs and alcohol courses. He did some twice. He was a model prisoner, but wound up serving seven years for a crime that had originally earned him fewer than two. On the out, he breached his licence, something to do with his bail hostel as I recall, a minor thing, very easy to breach, so in he came again.

I'd better explain what a licence is. Let's say you get a two-year sentence and are let out after twelve months, that then puts you on a twelve-month licence. In effect, you are serving the rest of your time outside, so anything naughty and they can bring you back. It could be anything: missed or late appointment with your parole officer, failed drug test – you don't need to commit a crime.

It can get to feel never-ending which is why, as we've seen, these prisoners are quite definitely at high risk of suicide.

What's more, many of them didn't even know they were on an IPP when they came in from court. It was only when they got their paperwork that they saw ninety-nine years. Some passed out or had a mental breakdown – hadn't realized the implications.

There are dangers even while you're inside. One wrong word to an officer goes on your file and that's your parole gone, maybe for two more years. We know how frustrating bureaucracy can be on the out; just imagine how much worse it is behind bars. Your next parole meeting might not happen for weeks. They are in no rush to deal with IPPs. If there is a half per cent chance of problems, they don't sort them out.

I knew about IPPs at Strangeways, but loads of people have been in touch since, which has really brought home how big the issue is. The injustice of it bothers me, but there are practical aspects too. One woman I spoke to had a son who was eighteen when he got an IPP. He'd assaulted someone and got two years, rightly so. But he has now been in for fifteen years – he's thirty-three years old!

Why, I don't know. She didn't tell me, or if she did, I've forgotten. Given his violent past, it's possible he had a ding-dong with someone and maybe an officer made note. That's the sort of thing that can knock them back. Hard as it may be to believe, I've known situations where they weren't even given a reason. I'm not saying these people are angels. If they are prone to fighting, that's what they'll go on doing most likely, but for a non-IPP prisoner that's taken as read. When their time is up, it's up. Not so with him. Can you imagine how his mam must feel about that? Take people like that out of the system and prison numbers would immediately be plenty lower.

But let's get back to my trusty camper van, and this time we're parked on a back street in Stockport.

We were on your typical cobbled northern lane and it was a struggle to park, actually, what with all the double yellows about. I didn't want a ticket. That would be breaking the law.

Lucas is an IPP prisoner who was out on licence when we met during another lull in lockdown. We were near his latest flame's back-to-back terraced house. The man himself resided in one of those big soulless complexes on his Jack Jones. He has to be careful about who he lives with on an IPP.

But now he'd lost his flat. He'd got it through a trust and his rent was in arrears. At the height of the coronavirus all the benefits got cocked up or delayed, so that was him stuffed. When we spoke, he was absolutely terrified of probation now that he was homeless, because they might send him back to jail for who knew how long. If that happened, he expected to be in for at least three or four more years.

When he was in Strangeways, I'd seen Lucas in healthcare before his parole hearing. He was nervous, understandably. There was a chance he was going to get out, but his probation officer had been off long-term sick and not passed his details over until the last minute. 'I can't make a decision,' her proxy had said, 'I don't know him . . .' And that was that for another six months. Is it any wonder lads kick off?

I'd also sat in on two of Lucas's parole meetings, and can confirm they look for anything. If an officer has fallen out with them, feels bitter and writes 'had an altercation' or such, those in judgement can knock them back. How would you take that? Lose all hope, wouldn't you?

Lucas isn't his real name, by the way. If I told you that, then somebody, somewhere, might use what follows to sting him for another stint.

At first when he came out of jail he had another partner and – this is me talking, not him – probation had him over. The lass stood by him, but must have been at her wits' end. Having a loved one in jail on an IPP – it's thankless. You don't know if or when they'll get out. Then Lucas had two paroles end badly in twelve months, and it split them up. His probation officer was hostile. Like all of us, they have good days and bad, but some are bullies, and this one was permanently on his case. 'She was giving it: "Why is your son on the floor, eating toast? That's not hygienic, is it? Does he need his nappy changing?" Interfering with the set-up. Her report went in and social services got involved.'

For Lucas's partner this was what broke the camel's back. 'Lucas,' she said, 'I can't have social services being involved in my life. I don't want the kids at risk.'

Only recently, Lucas told me he and his current partner had had a new baby.

Lucas is from a family with a background in crime and that, coupled with the colour of his skin, landed him in strife well before the IPP. As we sat in my van, him looking like the cool, laid-back kid he is now, a couple of chains around his neck, earring in, he told me his life story, in between puffing on a vape now and then.

Lucas's early years were uprooted, flitting all over the world without properly settling down. Of a Jamaican background born in Surrey, as a toddler he moved with his mum from Chertsey to Germany. Fluent in the language, she'd landed a job, chasing a better life. There she met and married an American serviceman and, from the Wiesbaden airbase, they next took Lucas to El Paso, Texas, his sister later being born in Louisiana. Spending no longer than two years anywhere, Lucas was unable to settle, grew into a bit of a handful and was briefly taken into care before his mother sent him back to live with his dad. That new arrangement only lasted a few months because the pair of them just couldn't get along.

So next up, he went to live with an aunt during the week and his nana at weekends in south London. But by then, aged twelve, he was now under the watchful eye of the British care system, to begin with by way of a voluntary order and then a full care order that lasted until he turned eighteen.

'In America, we'd live in family housing,' he said. 'I'd make friends, start school, but just as I was getting used to it, it would be time to move on again. I don't think it affected my education, but it did affect my sense of belonging.'

It also seems to have sent Lucas off the rails. 'I was naughty, always getting hidings and into trouble. No one could figure it out until one day I went to the doctor's. He had electrodes on me, all sorts. They took sugar out of my diet and put me on Ritalin, the brand of drug used to treat attention deficit hyperactivity disorder, three tablets a day. In class, I started getting good grades in tests and exams, but the damage had been done.'

In England, one last barney with his dad and going back into care put the tin hat on it. 'The moment I walked in that children's home, something hit me. It was a feeling of me against the world.' This was on Christmas Day 1988.

Lucas comes across as bright. He's a likeable guy you warm to. And having worked in a children's care home myself and seen the positive changes in antisocial behaviour that can be achieved just by giving kids your attention, playing cards, going to the park and such (and also how some care/social workers just don't get that, causing huge damage) makes what came next extremely relatable.

'How did I get into criminality? Growing up, playing cops and robbers, I wanted to be a cop, or a soldier, lots of things like that. What turned me was being in that children's home, where you had the example of older lads up to no good – I soon realized life was about survival of the fittest.' Nor did it take him long to work out whose side the police were on.

'I was beaten up by the police very young, racial insults too, to the point where I thought they were going to kill me. I wasn't originally being arrested for anything, just walking past and saw what they were doing to some other people and challenged that. Members of the public told them they were out of order, so they took me away, to Croydon police station. As we walked in, one of them pushed me from behind, clever move. I've lurched forward in the direction of the desk sergeant and they've all jumped me as if I was going for him, got me in a cell and began smashing my head off the floor. I was only thirteen. My eye came up . . .'

I believe him. Lucas, like me, is someone who has got involved in things others might say he shouldn't, due to a sense of justice.

'I went to magistrates' court, told the truth, and basically the magistrate's answer to everything was that he would take the word of these upstanding policemen over my word any day. I felt a huge sense of injustice, heartbroken. I was hurt that I'd told the truth and that's how I'd been treated.

'But it was after that that the pattern started, when I began mixing with the older kids in the home. We used to have a laugh, ringing the police just to get them out to chase us.' There was also another issue any parent will recognize. 'At school, a lot of kids had mums and dads who'd buy them the latest gear, while all we got was clothing grants. It wasn't a lot and the staff wouldn't let me spend it all on one pair of trainers, so I had to get a cheaper brand, plus a couple of T-shirts and so on . . . ending up with all the stuff you daren't wear or everyone would bully you. So that was another thing. I soon learned I had to get my own money.'

The push over the edge involved a girl living in a flat for young mums next to the home. One day her boyfriend, a removal man, was looking for help at work. 'She suggested me so I jumped at the chance. At the end of the first day, he handed me £80. I was thirteen, couldn't believe it. I said, "Is that for me?" "Yeah," and this went on for a couple of weeks, £80 a day. I was coming back and throwing it in a drawer, no sense of money back then. It was mad. On Fridays we experimented with alcohol, cigs, weed . . . like a lot of kids. Suddenly everyone's my friend.'

It was then that Lucas had his first big criminal operation, as he puts it. 'I bought my first spliff and was smoking it in this house nearby and liked it. But when I came out, the air hit me, knocked me for six. I was literally crawling. I got back to the home and there was this guy, really kind member of staff, considerate and caring, and when he spoke to me it was like a slowed-down record . . . He told me to go get some sleep. He must have brought food up because I woke up next day covered in chocolate. But it dawned on me . . . thinking about the woman who sold me this weed . . . bringing all this money out . . . *Hey, I've got a drawer full of cash too, haven't I? Let me see what I can do.*' I ended up buying nine ounces of cannabis resin off her, a "nine bar".'

And once he worked out there was even more money to be made by flogging it himself or, better still, getting others to do that for him, including to a pair of helpful workers in the care home who, among others, were apparently happy to buy weed on the recommendation of a thirteen-year-old – they mightn't necessarily have known they were buying it directly from him – Lucas's criminal antics were well and truly under way. Easy to see now how from that moment a future behind bars was inevitable.

One early stretch was at HMP Onley in Northamptonshire, which back then, having opened as a borstal in 1968, was full of juveniles and had a reputation for aggro. Since 2004, when it was officially the most violent young offenders' institution in England and Wales, it has lost the young 'uns and become a Cat C men's jail.

'I was quite young, and went there in a group. They gave us sandwiches and called us through, one at a time. When my turn came I got up and they said, "You're last." I'd no idea why, thought maybe they recognized my name. When I did go through it felt like they were trying to get a rise out of me. "Whose keys are these?" Mine. "Who lives there?" I do, with my girlfriend. I went along with it for a while but then bit, and I was pulled over the desk. Well, the punches rained in. This was in the 1990s, and they were calling me "black bastard".'

Lucas was bundled off to the wing and refused to eat. 'I was no tough guy, but if I can't trust these people . . . First three or four days I wouldn't come out of my cell, until the governor apologized on their behalf. That got me eating again and joining in with activities. When I finally left it was as if nothing had happened.

'My family's reputation also had a lot to do with it.' At Onley, Lucas told me, they thought he was cut from the same cloth. 'But what they didn't know is that I have never really mixed with them. My own bits of trouble were my own, but because I'd come up from London they expected mayhem.'

At Strangeways, Lucas had seen me before I saw him. He was in on a charge of armed robbery, got six years, but if you spoke to him now, you'd never guess he was capable of that. As I say, he's a calm and likeable bloke, far from your stereotypical meathead.

Armed, by the way, goes wider than guns. It ain't just firearms. It can also mean things like crowbars and baseball bats, anything really. You might be carrying a screwdriver or something. In this case there was a gun, but it turned out to be an imitation.

The raid on a Co-op in Stockport took place at around ten

o'clock at night, in December 2007. Lucas and another lad went in with stockings on their heads and pointed this imitation firearm at a customer, telling him to kneel down and 'be cool'. Meanwhile, the second lad threatened a member of staff and filled a duvet cover with cash from the till. He then tried to force another worker into a back room in his hunt for a safe. This latest staff member, though, found some courage from somewhere, picked up a meat cleaver and threatened Lucas's mate with it. What's that the papers say? A struggle ensued. Meanwhile, a second customer nipped outside and called the police. During the scrap, the imitation firearm hit the deck, along with a display shelf full of wine. Messy. All four of them were brawling by now and ended up outside, where Lucas's mate fucked off. The staff kept hold of Lucas until the police arrived.

'I was the only one caught,' he said. 'The guy I was paired with got greedy – started saying he wanted the safe, wanted cigs. We'd already got money from the till – what was he doing? He got himself in problems and it all kicked off. I went to help. In court you could see me fighting these two have-a-go heroes on CCTV. He ran off and left me.'

They questioned Lucas in Cheadle Hulme police station; had him in a bulletproof cell; reinforced glass so they could see him. Lucas kept shtum.

'By the time the police finished with me I was literally telling the magistrates at Stockport that I wanted to go to prison. In police cells, there are no books or telly, and I'd been held in custody three days. I got sent to Forest Bank first, but then, after an escapade where they decided I should be Cat A, I was moved to Strangeways.' No one else did time for the raid.

At this stage, on B Wing throughout his remand, Lucas had no idea he might end up on an IPP. 'I programmed myself that I'd get life, because I was in trouble for a few other things as well.'

Fearing a verdict is what it is, but sometimes the size of the sentence isn't the only thing to worry about. In court, there is an open gallery. People were watching the proceedings on behalf of other 'interested parties', to hear what came out of Lucas's mouth. The trial was stopped at one point, when someone who claimed to be his mate started laughing. The judge said he should choose his friends better.

In the end Lucas sidestepped the extras by pleading guilty to armed robbery. 'Even that carries two life sentences, because armed robbery is a firearm *and* robbery charge. For the firearm I ought to have got six years and for the robbery six years, run concurrent.' In fact, although he was given the IPP in 2007, his sentence is still not yet over.

'When it hit me was when I came back to the jail and the nurses asked if I was suicidal, which seemed a bit weird. It took a month before I got the paperwork, and that hit me more because it said ninety-nine years . . .' Which for Lucas, of course, meant 198 years, as he had two sentences. 'I thought, *That's me finished . . .*'

The IPP sentence can only have been because the judge still thought Lucas a danger to the public. And the implications of that, rather than a more usual life sentence, must have flown over Lucas's head because, as he says, he didn't grasp them at the time. When it finally dawned, he felt like killing himself.

'I couldn't imagine living like this for the rest of my life. At one stage all the IPPs started kicking off on B Wing – no one had come to see us; we were just dumped. We had an IPP forum in which I asked a member of staff, "Are you telling me I could die here?" Yeah, he was. No one had ever been released on it. You don't want to hear that.

'When I got it, there was no way of proving you were no longer a threat to society. It got political: you were hearing it was inhumane, barbaric, but nothing got done. To this day the original sentences have not been changed. They were giving them out for shoplifting and stuff.'

An IPP sentence could also put a target on your back. 'In prison, you are surrounded by dangerous men. Sometimes you are in a situation where you may have to fight to defend yourself and the system doesn't see it that way. One fight is held against you.

'You're in a culture where, if you go to a member of staff and say, "Guv, he won't leave me alone," then you've put the whole prison on alert – you could get killed for that. All that theory about talking to a member of staff if you have a problem – it can put you in danger.'

While he was still in Forest Bank, he said he came out for his dinner once, and an officer who wanted to clock off started being abusive. 'I tried saying, "Look, there's no need to speak to me like that," but my back went up and I started swearing. I turned around to pour my water, heard footsteps behind me and he punched me straight in my face. Took all my front teeth out, but even then I didn't fight back. I was saying to him, "Are you insane? What are you doing?"'

The subsequent report said that Lucas had threatened to harm him. 'I mean, they made the charges disappear because of the injuries I received, but I had to go in front of a governor who said I'd do well to abide by his officers' orders.

'It's situations like that,' said Lucas, 'that make it hard for an IPP to wind your neck in and stay out of trouble. A small black guy came in once who'd tried to shoot someone. The bullet missed its target, but had hit and killed somebody else instead. He was looking at life.

'So, I've come out of my cell and he has decided this day to be gangsta with me. I told him to leave me alone. He wasn't having it, to the point where I was contemplating getting it on. But a member of staff had seen us arguing across the landing. You've got me: big. This guy: short arse. No one asked what was going on, just dragged me to the SO. "They say you're a bully. Well, you won't be bullying here." I was miffed, as I had enhanced status, no issues, couldn't work out for the life of me where this came from. I'd been arguing with a guy who'd killed someone and thought he was a gangbanger. Yet I'm the one stereotyped!'

It's true that once some people get that prison officer's uniform on they can't help themselves. I knew a few myself. For obvious reasons, Lucas doesn't have a lot of time for prison officers, but he had made time for me. When I asked why, his answer made me blush, but it also gave me an insight into how, as a profession, we are seen by those we are there to guard.

'The reason I am sat in this van is because you are a decent man who I've got a lot of respect for,' he said. 'I don't have respect for a lot of officers, but you are one of the few who stood out.

'You used to try to get to the root of the problem. Some days I wanted to smash the place up, set the wing on fire . . .

but you'd take ten minutes, watching the lads on the yard, and let me vent. I'd feel better. If I had a problem you could help with, you would, and if you couldn't, you'd say so. It was that honesty. Young officers should sit down with you and learn the game, because you say it how it is.'

It was good of Lucas to say that, and I quite definitely agree that being a prison officer ain't just about rattling keys and being brutal.

'There were times when I thought all I was good for was criminality,' Lucas went on. 'You'd discuss that. And that's when I started getting that paradigm shift, began thinking there's more to life. It made me reflect. I left healthcare with no intention of committing more offences, and I'm proud to say the last time I was arrested and convicted of anything was the time I got my IPP sentence in 2007.'

There is a thing called the Personal Officer Scheme, where officers report on prisoners every day and governors or whoever can read what they have written online. The idea is for officers to get to know prisoners better as individuals and thereby, you'd imagine, make the people who'll ultimately take the decisions on things like privileges and parole aware of encouraging or mitigating factors that might otherwise stay unnoticed and unreported. But the thing with IPP is, people rarely put positives down on their reports; the emphasis seems always to be on how they misbehave, people watching their own back maybe. They might even be a handy way to settle an old score or two.

'It's like in the parole meetings,' said Lucas. 'Other people not doing their job right means you are punished more than you would be: get another year away from your family and no one cares. If I went back to the wing, going ballistic at the injustice of what I'd just seen, then at the next parole hearing – in a year or maybe even two – that can be used to keep me there still. I've had it up to here with it.'

Parole hearings should be current, about the last six months, and they're not. They repeatedly bring up things from years back.

The problem is, it's based on personal opinion and not very structured. If you've had an argument with someone months since and that person wants to get you back, they'll write up a report. It's crazy and unprofessional. Imagine being in the army and getting away with that because you've got a personal grudge. Not cool.

Another huge beef – people putting their opinions in reports about prisoners they haven't met. They are just going by an account someone else has written, when that person hasn't met them either!

'It ends up a mess. In my file it says I was sectioned in my twenties. I've been trying to explain for eight years why that's inaccurate. I did spend some time in hospital, but it was only due to burnout. I'd been working in Liverpool – too hard, really – and it caught up with me. I had trouble sleeping, was exhausted. I was in for a week. They gave me a choice of going to hospital to make sure I was all right, be monitored, that's all. I had no problems; stayed there a week and they let me go.' Next thing Lucas knew, somebody somewhere has taken that piece of info and interpreted it as him being a danger to the public.

'That was over twenty years ago. The thing with lifers, they get the sentence for the crime they did. IPPs are not like that.

When I get years, it's punishment for the crime and anything on top is for what they *think* you are capable of, which is an absolute joke.' An IPP sentence weighs heavy; the gun is always at your head.

Even so, Lucas's file was generally excellent. He behaved himself and was made an orderly pretty much everywhere he went, as he did with us on Strangeways healthcare. In 2015, he obtained his release, but was recalled for a year in 2018.

'I thought that was it, I was back inside for life, but fortunately the parole board saw it my way. They went nuts. The guy said, "Why has he been in twelve months? There's nothing here. You've given me all these papers and there is no evidence, no substance behind the reasoning." I'd been stitched up. I was lucky that people on the board sensed it didn't smell right.'

That case, by the way, is still with the police, which is why we can't elaborate further. No compensation yet or other repercussions. 'When I got out this time, the chairman looked around and said, "Why wasn't this prisoner released eighteen months ago?"'

As I write in 2021, if Lucas – now forty-five years old – applies for a job, he still has to say he's an IPP prisoner if anyone asks.

'My crime ain't spent. As it stands, I still have a ninety-nine-year licence. I haven't got a car: all them years inside meant I never had a chance to learn to drive. Now I'm in the straight world, not breaking the law any more, but it still has a massive impact on my existence. I don't drink, I don't go out – it's not worth the risk of getting in trouble.

'There's no point everyone saying IPPs are a dark stain on

the British judicial system if they then keep it going. If somebody's crime deserves a whole-life tariff, well, you've got that sentence. Use it. I'm not saying people shouldn't do time – if they do crime, they deserve it. But give them the maximum for their offence. Keep it simple.'

And what has IPP solved? Last time I checked, everyone is still shooting and stabbing each other out here.

9. Collateral Damage

Prisoners themselves are far from the only ones caught in the crossfire of a jail sentence. As the staff who looked after visits, we got to watch prisoners' children grow. At Strangeways, I myself saw Lucas's go from being three-year-olds swinging on posts to teenagers.

Two years ago, my publisher emailed me to say someone by the name of Kate wanted to send me a letter. It turned out her partner was called Darren Spensley.

'I bought your book for him to take on holiday,' she wrote. 'One day, as he was reading it, he suddenly said, "Fucking hell. I know this guy!" and he has not stopped talking about you since. He says you were a good man. I thought it would be nice if you knew what he thought of you.'

I remembered Daz – of course I did. It would be good to reconnect, so I got Kate to give me his number.

Although the first time he was sent to prison it was for a violent crime, with us Daz was easy-going and polite. And when I say violent, I mean he came off better in a fight. Daz is the type of lad who is not going to back down. When you are brought up in the sort of area he was, you tend not to. Someone comes up to you in a pub and punches you, you hit him back harder, get the better of it – that sort of carry-on. But if you have a scrap and the other bloke ends up with a fractured jaw or broken nose, you are looking at prison time. There are no mitigating circumstances. Daz wasn't proud of his history; it was what it was.

We arranged a meeting at the Trafford Centre – me, Daz, his missus. Hugs all round, and then him and me sat down with a brew while Kate went off shopping. That was the first time. Over the next three or four months we met up five or six more times, our conversations dead easy, not awkward at all. And the second time he brought his kids from the second of two earlier marriages, a lass and a lad, his two youngest of three. We all sat down – kids love a Costa, don't they? – got them a milkshake and chatted away.

Daz said the girl, who was around twelve years old, wanted to ask me a few questions.

'Yeah, no problem,' I said.

Boom! I was welling up already. I could see it coming. 'What do you want to ask?'

'Were my dad good? Why did you have him on healthcare?'

They are the forgotten victims of all this, the children. During prison visits, the kids sit quietly and everyone thinks they're being really well behaved, but that's not how it is in their head. The jail environment is intimidating for adults, so imagine how it must be for children. And there's the fact that it's a parent – theirs, the only one they've got, who they love – is in there. That really hurts.

When Daz and me then met up again back over the Pennines in Bury, I got to meet Megan, his eldest, who was born to his first wife. Megan is in her twenties. That time I hardly spoke to Daz at all, just to his daughter, who is a good kid – a bit of an Instagram influencer. But she too has had a lot of issues. She didn't know me from Adam, but off the bat told me about eating disorders and the like, how it all impacted on self-image, which is vital to young people these days, especially online. We had a very frank and open conversation.

That first meeting, Megan admitted she felt very angry towards her dad, having effectively had to grow up in a single-parent family. Held him responsible. Originally it had left her bitter towards him – didn't like him at all. Yet twelve months later, they were getting on great, to the point where she was on the verge of moving in with Daz and Kate, her dad's latest partner. Their relationship is strong now. There is hope.

Megan's dad left her life when she was four and before then had actually missed her birth, when he first went to jail. Despite that, family photos suggest they had a strong early bond, but his departure did lasting damage. When Megan was sixteen years old it was Kate who reached out to her.

'Kate sent me a massive long paragraph about how she hadn't had her dad in her life, and when he passed away she regretted it. At first I thought, *Nah*. I didn't want to know, because I thought my dad was a knobhead. But then my brother agreed to meet him in Pizza Express and asked if I'd go too.' She went along to support him, but that time didn't say a word.

I know where she's coming from, given how my own dad left my mum and me when I was two. The next time I saw him I was fourteen and he just turned up at the door. I fucked him off. He'd betrayed us, and I wasn't interested in getting to know the man who did that. I am who I am because of how my mum and her family raised me. What he did give me was my name, Neil, but I don't answer to that if I can help it.

Recently one of his sons, my half-brother, got in touch to tell me the guy had gone into a home; he'd had a stroke and lost capacity. I'm not interested. If someone called me tomorrow to say he had died, it would mean nothing.

This shit runs deep.

'That was my mindset at high school,' said Megan. 'I didn't care. I thought, *He's not bothered about staying out of prison for us, so . . .*'

At least Daz kept trying, mind. Although if ever he did turn up at the school gates once he had been released the second time, Megan would be told to go inside. 'I wouldn't be allowed to speak to him. Everyone else's mum and dad would be waiting and they'd run into the playground, while I'd be taken to after-school club because my mum had to work till six. She was bringing us up on her own, so had no choice but to do that. I seemed always to be at school. It left me with a fear of abandonment.'

'My mum always looked after us well, but would go on the odd holiday, and I always worried that she wouldn't come back. She'd go into shops for milk, and as I was waiting in the car I was afraid she'd leave me forever.'

Patching things up with Daz, her dad, is helping her with that.

'He's a completely different person now; I couldn't see him going back. It's just about him being there. My car breaks down: I'll ring my dad. I never had that before. If our house is full of people, I'll go see him and Kate, who I visit even when he's not there. In some ways, it made me mature very early, on my own. Losing him was my biggest-ever heartbreak, but I won't blame him now because there's nothing he can do.

He always says sorry, but there's no point in regrets. You can't change it.'

One of my most recent chats with Daz was at his bungalow in Cheshire, a nice little gaff in a lovely area. It's good to see him and Kate doing well, creating a nice life for themselves.

Daz and me had met in Strangeways after his second alleged offence, when he came in on remand in November 2009. But how many times had he been inside before Strangeways?

'Just the once: Section 18, fighting, in 2000. I was in Forest Bank for a week and then got sent up to Kirkham. I got three years and nine months, my first taste of prison. My brother and me got involved in a fight on a street corner while we were out walking his dog. The guy ended up really poorly: broken cheekbone, arm . . . severe injuries. It was the first time I'd ever been in trouble with the police.'

He spent six or seven months at Strangeways on healthcare before his release in August 2010. He'd been charged with involvement in a 'drugs ring' that was alleged to have been operating as a courier service, bringing coke – class A – from Europe to Manchester, with this particular shipment worth £25 million. It was eighteen months later when he was arrested. By then, he said, 'I'd got myself a job at a paper mill, driving nights, £360 a week. Twelve-hour shifts. That gives you an idea of how much I'd got stashed away with this drugs conspiracy! All I'd done was driven a van for a friend, and naively got involved.

'My solicitor wanted me to go guilty and take a deal,' Daz went on. 'I was looking at over twenty years. He said I should take the minimum they were offering, eighteen, but bollocks. I hadn't known I was importing cocaine, genuinely. I knew they were up to no good and bent as nine-bob notes, but that wasn't me.'

The trial of Daz and his alleged co-conspirators lasted for weeks. Eventually the jury reached a verdict. The first one to stand up: *Guilty*. 'He was standing next to me and just collapsed. I thought, *Shit, here we go. I'm next*.

'"How do you find Darren Spensley?"'

'I only heard the word "Not . . ." and that was it, euphoria.'

'I'm not a religious person, but I did think that if there is a God out there, if he would just help me out this one time, that would be me done with crime forever, not a speeding fine or anything. And apart from these restraining orders with my kids, I've stuck to that.'

He's talking about an initial two-year restraining order his second ex-wife placed on him when they broke up after his release from prison. 'I couldn't speak to her, she couldn't speak to me. But I did used to talk to her and she'd talk to me. We'd get back together for a bit, have a night out . . . and when we fell out again the police would be on, phone records backing her up. Even though she might have initiated it, with a call or text.' Because they lived close by, he ended up making thirty court appearances in two years, and got locked up four or five times.

'My children also came under that umbrella, but as they lived within half a mile of me I'd pass them on their way to school as I went to work.' One such misdemeanour saw him driving his wagon one day, spotting his kids and winding the window down – 'All right, Dad?' 'All right, love?' There you go: restraining order breached. At one point Daz got done for texting his son sixty-two times.

'I gave my daughter £20 for her birthday, which she got

questioned about at home: "Where've you got that from?" "My dad gave it me . . ." Police got involved, another restraining order, twelve weeks in prison.'

Nineteen times in four years they got him. It started with fines, then community service, winding up with four prison sentences.

'The last one they said, "There's no telling you, is there? You've no respect for the law." I explained that I've got every respect for the law, but what I won't do is walk past children I love and care for. The restraining order was coming to an end then, and I told them that if I did still see them after that, I was not going to ignore them.'

Daz said that, mentally, that final three months in jail was the hardest ever. 'Normally in prison it's about routine. You sit down, watch telly, walk twenty yards for your food, another twenty yards back, twenty more yards to the shower, same to the toilet, hundred metres to the gym . . . It's a doddle, really. But I was trying to get contact back with my children.

'One guy on community service made me laugh. A friend of mine had properties and this guy was telling me he's a roofer, said he ran his own company. "I can do this for you, that for you . . ." He offered to come and do repairs. "I've got a van, I've got everything, mate, I've even got me own fucking ladders." Those were the kind of people I had to engage with for eight hours every Sunday when I wanted to be with my kids. Physically, I knuckled down and got it done.'

Jail had been bad enough – 'I'm not there to pay the bills any more, am I?' said Daz. 'To look after the kids, put up with what's being said at school. Other side of it – me, I've seen some picture on Facebook, you were out partying, living the life of Riley . . . That's how you see it behind bars. But they're not, are they? They suffer just the same as you in every way, shape or form. My second wife would visit every week, children with her, on time and looking fantastic, then an hour or two later off they went. You have massive jealousy, even though it was your poor choices that put you there.

'Remember the Stockport lad whose missus wasn't going to stand by him?' said Daz. 'He got out of Forest Bank and cut his ear off. He'd then been going around K Wing in Strangeways saying he was going to kill himself – I used to serve him his dinner. England won 2–1 and he hanged himself that night. Maybe the guards were watching football.'

One lad I still talk about a lot. He was on healthcare, an IPP prisoner who was abused as a kid. His family didn't want anything to do with him, he was way over tariff and I remember him saying, 'I am going to kill myself, Mr Samworth. I like the staff on here so wouldn't do it to you.' About a month after he left healthcare, he hanged himself on C Wing, as promised.

But then Daz found that getting released hadn't drawn a line under things either. 'Coming out, you don't realize how much it has affected you,' he said. 'You think you're all right, but I wasn't the same person, the world wasn't the same place. The man I was wasn't there any more.

'I felt guilty being on the front of the newspaper. *Local man imports half a billion pounds of cocaine.* Six weeks later, not guilty, you get a tiny piece on page seven, but who reads that?'

He went to pick up his son at the school gates and one of the mothers said, 'Here he is, the fucking drug dealer.'

'I couldn't help myself. "Drug importer, I think you'll find," I said. "Not drug dealer." Rebuilding my life from that, negativity on your CV. "What have you done for the last year?" Everybody knew. The boss of the company I used to work for fell off his chair laughing when I asked for my job back.'

It has taken Daz years to get back on track. 'I turned to drink. My wife was never the same. The kids were affected. I came out to a house I no longer fitted into. She had her routine with the kids and I was getting in the way. We were different people; never going to get on again. We tried to stay together for the children, but couldn't and that's when the restraining order came. That was that. We are great parents apart, but together it was finished.'

Daz was telling it true. When someone is nicked, life goes on outside, and the distrust and even hate gain momentum.

I've seen lads who, having got seven or eight years, would act the twat on purpose, to finish the relationship. But some expect their partner to wait forever – unrealistic?

'Yeah,' said Daz. 'My first time in prison, I said, "That's it, we're done. I don't expect you to wait around. Crack on. Be happy. I don't want you here every two weeks." She turned up a fortnight later, next visit. That was her choice.

'We got through it, stayed together, and things worked out for a short while. With my second wife in 2009, the year I met you, Sam, I did the same. "Do your own thing," I said. "Look after the kids, bring them up."

'I didn't want to drag everybody down, but she said I'd be home in no time. Well, I weren't, and it had a massive impact. Bail fails, next one fails . . . Come out looking like a baghead because you've lost so much weight.'

The last time Daz was inside – on a restraining order – he took a course on parenting. Many prisoners are poorly educated; you'd help them to write letters home, tot up how much money they've got, so teaching them to read and understand basic maths is obviously a top idea. Encouraging them to acquire the sort of life skills Daz did is also useful, plus it keeps them occupied.

There's a flip side, mind. I've argued earlier that gyms in prisons, aside from keeping people fit, build absolute monsters that officers can physically struggle with. In terms of thinking skills, every hard-boiled prisoner I ever met said education just made them better criminals. I'm all for occupational stuff, such as plumbing and motor mechanics, but best not show anyone how to build a nuclear reactor.

I'm joking. Education is quite definitely a good thing. Healthy relationships, domestic abuse . . . these were the kinds of things they studied. 'It gave me insight into how the woman feels,' said Daz. 'Prison is a disease. You can either go through it yourself, or pass it on to everybody around you and they get tarnished with it.'

It's hard for prisoners when they come out, then, and even more so when you've only got one eye. I'll finish by introducing you to David, an ex-customer during healthcare's madder-than-usual year – the time when Dale Cregan, Michael Cope, Adam Downworth and their fellow inhabitants of the chamber of horrors were sending us home to nightmares. David's tale shows how, even in Strangeways, prisoners can go on to have a happy ending, although in his case not before some serious grief that changed his life forever.

David is a cheerful lad with a playful personality who finds life amusing, which is probably just as well given what he's gone through. All his offences have been violent but he's not an armed robber or anything. In Moss Side, where he was brought up, arguments turn into fights and this lad can handle himself. Let's say you and me have a fight, we both get broken noses, you go to the coppers and I've got a criminal history, then I'm the one who is going to get locked up. Quite definitely.

He comes from a big Manc family – one nana dropped twenty-plus kids, the other eleven – and he doesn't even know how many stepbrothers and sisters he has. Last time he came out of prison he got a message on Facebook saying, 'I'm your brother', which led to him finding another four.

'I've got uncles too – pretty bad ones among them. One has just gone back inside. Another is an escape artist. He's done four escapes, but they only give him credit for the treble: a sweatbox, a Crown Court and a prison. He tied a screw up, stabbed him and went over the wall. He's slipped from a police station as well.' His uncle hijacked the sweatbox, drove it away. 'Full of YPs it was. He told them, "Anybody who goes, go! Those who don't, stay." He got fifty-nine years for the prison break, served thirty and is out now, driving around without insurance.'

That made David chuckle. If you find that surprising, perhaps you ought not to, given that he admits he committed his first crime as a twelve-year-old. 'I did juveys . . . fifteen was my first time in prison. I walked in and it was full of my mates.' He can remember being driven up in the van. 'I was thinking, *Oh shit, I've got to smash everyone's head in, avoid rape,* and all that. But when I walked on the wing there was a big flower painted on the wall. I thought, *This is a soft touch, this – are we going into nursery?*' He's lived in Moss Side three or four times, and single-handedly destroyed one of his first family homes in Fallowfield. 'I was only young and set fire to it for some reason,' he told me. His nana also lived next door to the infamous Noonan clan.

Nowadays, David seems like a changed man – but it took a fair old while to get there. 'My last sentence scared me,' he says, 'and then there was that business with my eye – but you can never say never, can you?'

Now you need to know about the incident that left him half-blind, a story that, to David's credit, he is very open to speaking about. We won't use his attacker's name.

David first came on healthcare in 2010, then had another pop in 2013, with a job as an orderly both times before the incident took place in March 2014. 'I'd just got my head in my fitness, me,' he says. 'Didn't mix with the nutters. I couldn't deal with them, because you knew they were monsters.' But then an officer warned him to watch one particular pair of prisoners because they'd tried to get him fired as a cleaner a few times. 'Somehow, this kid got it into his head that I was bullying him and his mate, which I wasn't. I'd done nothing to them, didn't care about them. They weren't even on my radar.'

One day David was mopping the landing when the kid passed. The two of them hadn't been getting on great but there wasn't any real beef between them. Even so, at this moment, the kid snapped.

How David came to lose control of that mop he couldn't tell you. 'I just felt a sort of a blow – bang – straight in the face. I seen the handle move and that was that . . . I wouldn't say it's given me nightmares but obviously I've thought about it a lot since. From what I remember, I give him a good run considering he got the first hit. I punched him and know he felt my presence. If he hadn't been so sneaky, one on one I'd have knocked him out. I remember going weak. He was trying to smash my head on the wall but couldn't physically do it, and then staff arrived. I'd lost a lot of blood. But it weren't till I went in my pad and looked in a mirror that I saw it and thought, *Fucking hell . . .*'

David was sent for surgery on his eye, but the doctor said there was no way he could save his sight, even though they left the eyeball in. The damage was done two days before David's birthday. What a present!

Make no mistake, a mop or broom handle in your eye socket will inflict major trauma. 'They told me it went into my frontal lobe, and I had a neurologist and an opthalmologist on the case. One is for the brain, the other for your eyes. It's serious potatoes, innit?'

David's eye attack never went to court. Neither him nor me knew why, although there was a rumour the bloke who attacked him was a grass, a CHIS job. Maybe he went QE or something – Queen's evidence – and got immunity from prosecution. I remember the lad who did it becoming a cleaner on K Wing later.

So now there's David and me meeting up again seven years on. He looks settled enough now, even if the new him has come following a bit of a struggle. An injury like that, from which you'll never physically recover, must have affected him in all sorts of ways, although he's held down a few jobs on the out. I know how dark my own thoughts are: what is it like to lose sight in an eye?

'It can be dodgy. The damaged eye follows my good one, so when I look at people I might have told them thirty times I'm half-blind, they still think I'm staring them out. I worked in a couple of restaurants, but then couldn't do it any more because I felt at risk. People come at you with hotplates and stuff. I also felt woozy to begin with. Just walking or stepping off kerbs was weird.'

Has he lost his anger over the incident?

'I wouldn't say that, no. Someone cracked him for it, I think, but there's been no retribution from me. The day I landed back in the 'Ways, I had his address put under my door that day. I'm not arsed.'

There was also the time he ran into the officer who had been on bed watch with him at the hospital one night, an awkward fucker who'd refused even to let him go for a piss and a shower. 'It were in Bargain Booze. "You remember when you wouldn't let me take the cuffs off?" I said to him. "I ought to smash your head in." He fucking shat himself. What was I going to do, jump out the hospital window with a brain injury and one eye?'

'When I first come home without sight in that eye,' David went on, 'it sort of made me relax a lot. I felt more vulnerable, if you know what I mean, and it made we want to turn away from all of that. I felt isolated. But when I went back to Manchester I felt, hang on, I'm sort of the victim here.'

So there was one last time he got sent down. 'It can be difficult out here, because you've got that past. I'd been working in a kitchen, doing well. A taxi driver parked in front of my drive and I asked him to move, that's all. He came at my mate first. There was no reason for him to do what he did. I happened to have my knives from work on me and stabbed the guy, but not before he hit me with a tyre iron. There were cameras everywhere around where we lived and it must have been shown on film how the guy attacked me first, but I doubt they even looked. They did look at my history of violence, though, and then it didn't matter, did it? He got away with it, I got eight years, and that was my last sentence.'

On probation, he spent five months in a hostel of the sort he'd been in and out of from being young; his ma would never let him use their home address on bail. This hostel, though, was full of nonces, a bit like Mr Subtle's in chapter three. 'I complained about it, which got me out. Why do they not have separate hostels? You don't want to be in with sex offenders, do you?'

You do not, and especially when you've spent so much time around them on Strangeways healthcare.

But let's look to the future. How does David, a lifelong criminal who has experienced Strangeways from the other side of the door to myself, see that panning out – assuming he really has left it all behind? What's next on the agenda?

'Get married and have children, hopefully this year – the missus is pregnant,' he said. Recently, I was pleased to hear that the baby has since arrived and after a health scare early on is now doing well and thriving. I wish him all the best. A proper family man, he has also now finally moved from Moss Side.

'It is difficult for you, as officers,' he said, before I got back on my bike and headed home to Yorkshire, God's side of the

Pennines. 'It's all right going to work with someone normal like me, but you also have to deal with the rest of it.

'Remember that guy who eventually hanged himself, the one who was found just sitting there, smiling, with his throat slit, ear to ear? A grown man doing that: six inches by two . . . He looked content, didn't he, happy to have done it? You don't forget things like that. I know I haven't, and I only saw that once. You saw stuff all the time.'

It's true enough. Staff on normal wings might not witness anything so extreme throughout their careers. In healthcare, we had no option but to engage with people. It was a big part of what we were there to provide. Empathy.

Here's my sleep pattern even now. Go to bed at 11.30 p.m.: no trouble falling asleep. At 1 a.m. look at clock. Get up and go downstairs at 3.30. Get our lass up for work at 5.30 a.m. Take Stephen, my dog, out for a walk. Think.

10. **Back to the Future**

Here we are coming to the end of *Strangeways Unlocked*, then: another book finished, with the prison service in as unruly a state as it was at the end of the last one, if not more. Meanwhile, yours truly is still dealing with the after-effects. You might leave the prison service, but the service won't leave you. When I'm shopping in the Trafford Centre and the personal alarm on the staff radio goes off, my immediate instinct is to run for the cells.

So if you're in a similar boat – not just from prison; PTSD and illnesses like it can affect anyone in all sorts of jobs, police, armed forces, paramedics, the NHS – never underestimate how useful it can be to talk to someone else who battles demons like that. Remember: you are not alone. I thought it'd be a good idea to hear from one last witness, a female prison officer.

After I left HMP Manchester in 2016 with PTSD, officers like Amelia remained on the front line. Three weeks before Christmas 2020 I biked through snow, sleet and fog across the Pennines to see her.

Back in the day, Amelia was an ACCT form assessor, which means trying to support those who aren't coping with prison life. The form itself, as I said earlier, is an A4 pad used basically as care planning for prisoners, usually self-harmers, who are thought to be suicide risks. Brought in around 2005, it was part of the jail's strategy of creating a multidisciplinary team so the responsibility for such prisoners didn't rest just with day-to-day staff.

'You would also assess those who came through reception the night before,' said Amelia, as she served up my drug of choice, a bacon sarnie, in her cosy conservatory. 'It was a pit of despair. One guy, teacher or social worker, was in for interfering with children – his own and his neighbours'. Job and support bubble gone, he had nothing to live for. How, as an assessor, do you try to keep someone like that alive when in the back of your mind you think he doesn't deserve it? I was a victim of child abuse myself, and yet I still had to persuade this guy to think positively: "You *can* carry on living . . ."'

Wow.

'I told them feeling bad showed they'd emotional intelligence. Everyone has an emotional piggybank, full to busting sometimes, and at others running low,' Amelia said. 'Those around you dictate whether or not it's topped up with compliments.'

I used to find that when people were cut down in cells and asked if they were glad or gutted to be saved, most would say glad. The ones who were gutted needed moving off normal location to healthcare.

But ACCT forms are devalued if you can't trust them. The feeling we had was that some officers opened them willy-nilly – 'I can't have my tobacco so I'm going to kill myself.' At other times staff were just being a cock to get someone off their wing.

I asked Amelia how she dealt with the blaggers. 'You could have ten ACCT forms on K Wing and three were blaggers,' she said, 'which takes time away from the ones who are genuine. It also made closing them a headache. I'd go home worried about whether or not I'd done the right thing – what if something then happened?'

Once, she was on G Wing when the phone rang. 'Amelia, we've got a guy coming up on an ACCT, transferred from Liverpool Prison.' His document turned out to be not the usual twenty pages but as thick as an Oxford dictionary. He was a prolific self-harmer.

'I interviewed him, and he said he didn't know why he'd been moved. He told me his self-harming was minor, but assured me he was happy to be here, so I told him we'd put him on the ones, which always had loads going on. I didn't have any concerns.

'His last entry was that morning, while he was still in Liverpool. When we spoke, it was two o'clock in the afternoon. The next time someone saw him was an hour later, and this officer opened the flap, looked in and the lad was lying on the bottom bunk. You couldn't see the floor for blood; it was horrific. It was, "*Staff! Staff!*" Bedlam. We cracked the door and there he was, fully conscious, one arm hanging with a little nick in a vein. I asked him why he'd done it. "Oh, this is what I do."' Turned out, the reason he'd been sent from Liverpool was because he'd bled the blood banks of Merseyside dry. So whenever he went to hospital there, the medicos would refuse to treat him.

'Prison has never been a quiet place to work,' said Amelia, but these days, she told me, there was more trouble. 'You'd hate your eyes for some of the things you saw,' she said. When officers went into work they didn't know whether they would go home in their own car or the back of an ambulance.

Spice was indeed a huge issue. 'I must have spent more time at Manchester General Hospital than anywhere else,' she said. 'You'd take one lad from the jail, come back and get another. Most were aggressive; some needed cuffing to the bed. It was a horrendous.'

At the same time, said Amelia, in the induction unit, 'We got people who had never been in prison, so a big part of it was not terrifying them.' G Wing therefore needed appropriate staff. Not Billy Big Bollocks or some lazy bastard in for an easy gig. Amelia wanted to be able to interview applicants so they would get the right sort. 'I needed to know that the people working for me on the landings were looking after these people, not treating them like crap. I didn't want meatheads. Discipline, yeah, but a bit of understanding.'

Bottom line is, her requests to grill recruits fell on deaf ears. Instead, she said, the prison sent her officers who used to call these first-time prisoners 'bed wetters'. 'I'd say, "Hang on, this person, his family might be on holiday – he's not got any-one . . ." We got called "fluffy officers" – I was always the peacemaker. Us and some other staff got together to rewrite the induction process, but it was never put into practice due to the amount of bang-up prisoners had to do.'

There were two reasons why a prison officer like her was co-opted into the role – staffing shortages and the latest prison thinking. 'I went into the offender management unit, and we used to get redeployed – everyone did. No continuity any more on the wings. It literally became about trying to run a regime: keeping wherever you happened to be that day afloat. I often didn't know my colleagues.'

According to Amelia, Strangeways was the first UK prison

to get a gold award from Investors in People, the lot that in 2015 had advised the jail to move its staff around. That might be okay on the out – say, in engineering or your average office – but in prison it's not. What you need, top to bottom, is familiarity. No wonder it went pear-shaped. Amelia saw it slightly differently: 'It was a good thing and a bad thing.' But while we must agree to disagree on that, we were definitely on the same page re the general chaos.

Everything happening at once was what really knackered it. For instance, you might get away with moving experienced staff around, but when you are throwing raw recruits into the lions' den . . .

Consequently, as time went on, the short staffing was increasingly down to people leaving. 'We had lots of young staff. One was the daughter of an officer. She had to cut someone down. I was on the care staff, so had to talk to her about it. She was traumatized, and had to leave like you did, with PTSD.'

'It started going wrong when they began treating the prison service like a business,' Amelia went on. 'They gave everyone their own budget and the camaraderie ended, no helping each other out.'

One officer used to hide in the office frying sausages rather than go on the landing. He ought to have been good at that because the prison had sent him on a fully paid for nine-month catering course. Eventually word came back that he hadn't been going – basically just took an extra day off every week. In any other line of business, you'd be sacked. Not so in the prison service. They let the wrong 'uns slide.

Amelia would tell the staff: if you are doing a cell count and see someone in their cell crying, have a look in and see what it's all about. Don't just carry on counting. Needless to say, many ignored her.

By the time I left Strangeways, the jail had got so desperate it ran a bonus scheme for officers. On top of the usual overtime, if you worked even more hours, a bonus kicked in, and it was quite a lot of money. They needed a real incentive, because officers already worked enough. It was exhausting. Even so, by the time Amelia had finally left in 2018, bang-up was already twenty-two hours a day. Had Covid not happened, I'm convinced that prisons would have been burning by now. And even though there isn't much difference between twenty-two-hour and twenty-three-hour lockdown, there'd still have been another Strangeways riot, quite definitely.

Before Strangeways Amelia had worked in a women's prison. She told me one last story, which can stand as a kind of Aesop's fable that sums up everything I've been saying in this book.

It was about one girl she'd had on the wing there, a survivor of family abuse. 'She began to self-harm and got into petty crime, nothing too serious – throwing a brick through Threshers' window, nicking the odd bottle of vodka.' She'd felt safer in prison, which is why she was reoffending.

One week, though, Amelia and her team had had to cut her down three times. She kept trying to hang herself. 'The last time we nearly lost her. We were doing CPR, and she started breathing again, thank goodness.'

Amelia was due a week's leave, and the night before she was scheduled to go, she was worried about whether this kid, who she had grown to like, would still be alive when she got back. So she came up with a plan.

Now, this was when Tamagotchis were all the rage. Remember

them? Handheld digital pets from Japan, huge in the late 1990s and early 2000s? You could get a cat or dog, horse or whatever, and the thing was, you had to look after it, give it exercise.

Amelia brought one in on a keyring. 'Here's Billy,' she told the girl. 'I've had him three hundred days, and I'm going to leave him with you now because I'm off for a week. I want you to make sure he's alive when I come back.'

'All right,' said the girl – she seemed very keen. 'I will, miss. I will.'

'I told her not to tell anyone about Billy,' Amelia said, 'as I'd get into trouble. Then I spent my week off worrying over whether she would be all right, and if I'd get caught! A Tamagotchi would be looked on as an unauthorized item.'

Sure enough, as soon as Amelia got back, a union official in reception told her she had to come see the governor. 'The Tamagotchi was in an evidence bag on her desk. My stomach lurched. Oh, I needed a poo!'

'We found this in a prisoner's cell,' the governor said. 'Is it yours?'

'Yes,' Amelia replied, and explained how she'd thought the toy would give the lass something to do, keep her occupied and ward off any thoughts of self-harm.

'They knew I was telling the truth, remembered the terrible nights we'd had, but they said they would have to conduct an investigation. So I told her to look at the girl's medical record, and compare how many incidents she'd had in her week with the toy and how many before.'

Three days later, Amelia told me, they called her back into the office. 'I thought they were going to dismiss me. But instead they just said, "Where did you get them from, and how much do they cost?"'

She was given a tenner from petty cash, and sent to buy some more.

Like a fair proportion of the British public, as the Covid pandemic worsened I gave the daily news reports and briefings a wide berth. As if being locked down for months on end wasn't bad enough, the drip, drip, drip of tragedy, misinformation and fearmongering screwed with the heads of everyone I know. And it was quite definitely worst for folk living in care homes or on their own.

Amy works in a dementia home now, still in the care industry. She works really hard, three days on, three off. My fear was not so much about *us* catching it – which we did eventually, at the back end of 2020, and recovered fairly quickly – but Amy then taking it to work, as the residents there are very vulnerable people. Most are seventy-plus; a lot are eighty- or ninety-plus. Thankfully, that didn't happen. As a front-line worker in the care sector, Amy was in the first group vaccinated. I got my first jab with all the other middle-aged types. The only thing I felt was hope – a chink of light under the door. We couldn't get the second and third doses in us quickly enough. Vaccinations allegedly mean freedom, and that will do for me.

But if mentally healthy people found Covid a trial, just imagine what it has been like for us with psychological issues. As I say, the number of messages I got after book one was humbling. But it came as a shock that so many who got in touch are still unwell, with the isolation of lockdown a major exacerbating factor. 'Keep doing what you are doing,' they tell me. 'Keep fighting for mental health.' It has become my driving force.

Of course, when you have experience of the prison service – either side of the door – being locked up, or down, is nothing new. But for the vast majority of us lockdown has been a new experience, and very restrictive. You haven't been able to go out and do exactly what you want, where you want to do it. You've had a glimpse of life as a guest of Her Majesty.

However, on the out you've had the freedom to break the rules, haven't you? No mixing, they say, but people did. Some had garden parties and family get-togethers, sat in the garden blowing bubbles! I hear one bloke took his wife and kid on a drive to Barnard Castle just to test his eyesight.

Then again, even in jail there is a society of sorts. Prisoners mix – in association, workshops, the servery, on the yard and elsewhere throughout the day. Or at least, they used to.

It was getting bad enough before the coronavirus hit, but even as we look like beginning to get on top of it, our prisons are quite definitely in the region of twenty-three-hour bang-ups. I'm speaking to people now who tell me they are virtually in their cells for seventy-two hours with just one shower and a phone call every three days. And that has come about mainly due to the horrendous turnover in staff.

Robert Buckland who, until a recent government reshuffle, spent seven years as Solicitor General, then Minister of State for Prisons and then Lord Chancellor and Secretary of State for Justice, has called for no 'mass association' at all, a view backed by the head of the Prison Officers' Association (POA), unless there is 'purposeful activity'. But how do you define purposeful?

And when we look outside jails, what with the pandemic, worker shortages, the fallout from Brexit and what have you, the country as a whole feels like it's going to shit. As society crumbles future prisoner numbers are bound to rise. In other words, we'll have even more going inside than we do now and far fewer staff to look after them. The time bomb is still ticking, isn't it?

I realize that some – like George in chapter five – reckon a lot of prisoners have enjoyed being in their cells all day. They say there has been a fall in bullying. But I still think it would be better for them to be out and about. The past wasn't perfect, but it was better than this current shitshow. Nor do I think the prison estate will completely open up in tandem with the rest of society. They haven't got the manpower or management skills to do it.

Before the pandemic, bang-up issues escalated, due to staffing shortages and the retreat from dynamic security, so of course, having fewer incidents will have been welcome. Any officer would be glad of a quieter life. But as we've seen throughout this book, the pandemic has covered up the sorts of issues I pointed out in *Strangeways: A Prison Officer's Story*. Surely, in a civilized society, the only way to run a jail properly is to give prisoners a proper disciplined regime and sense of purpose.

These days digital education is currently being pushed as the best way of turning lives around, but with no thought to the consequences. I was talking to one former officer the other day and he told me that nowadays everyone inside has an iPad. I've got nothing against technology – iPads, phones and such can have their uses, but they should not be the only game in town. Letting people use those behind a prison door is no substitute for giving them a taste of freedom, with the usual necessary restrictions.

I read somewhere about these 'sobriety ankle tags' they are now using on ex-customers they reckon might breach court-ordered drinking bans. Apparently, they monitor the wearer's sweat levels every half-hour, and alert probation when alcohol is detected. Great, but it will never replace dynamic security, experience and common sense. When you are dealing with damaged people you also need the human touch, don't you?

Getting some sort of morning till night routine going again would also reduce drug use. As we saw with my old neighbour Frank, people often turn to drugs through boredom, and there are some very bored prisoners right now – bouncing off the walls, I expect.

Will the service listen? No. It hasn't the numbers or quality of staff to make it work. Folk are leaving in droves. The future will be behind the door – a very restrictive regime.

But don't just take my word for it. Back in March 2020, when I was still reading the media coverage and lockdown was getting under way, BBC News reported that the prison watchdog had revealed inmates were being kept 'like caged animals'.

The inspectors, it said, had visited a cross-section of jails – male, female and young offenders – and reckoned the long-term consequences could be profound, given how over 90 per cent of a prisoner's day was spent in their cell, without family visits, education classes, gyms, anything. The chief inspector of prisons, Charlie Taylor, said they had heard suggestions that 'the restrictions and a subsequent reduction in recorded violent incidents have made prisons safer. Clearly, with so little time out of cells, prisoners had less opportunity to be violent or fight.' But he went on to say that this was not the full picture.

Prisoners passed time rearranging their possessions or, 'varying when they sat on their bed or a chair'. Doubling up was also a problem: prisoners often fell out while sharing cells. Violence, intimidation and bullying had not stopped, prisoners had told the inspectors; they had just taken other forms. 'The accrual of debt persisted. And some had turned to using drugs and other unhelpful coping strategies as a way of managing their isolation and boredom.' An anonymous governor of one adult men's jail said that prisons were 'at a point of absolute crisis. Morale is at rock bottom.'

I spoke to one lad only today, a very young kid who has just done nine months inside for arson, the whole time during the Covid lockdown. For weeks, he told me, they had a shower every day, collected their meals, and that was it. Imagine. Nelson Mandela must have got out more than that.

The bottom line is, prisons need to attract and retain more staff and for that to happen there need to be better conditions, better pay, better pensions and better training, so they can start opening people up in a civilized way again. It needs a return to a prison regime such as we had at Strangeways in 2010, before the place went tits up. Back then, although we'd already started losing staff, we had enough to run the place in such a way as prisoners knew they could leave their cell, phone loved ones, get under a shower, order their canteen and get to know one another while we, the officers, could also get to know them.

In fact, right across criminal justice the rules of policing are always changing, probation is always changing; the entire system needs stability. We need a long-term plan, taking in the next twenty-five years at least, but I doubt we've got enough leaders with the vision or ability to implement that, unless it came with a chance to funnel lucrative contracts the way of family members or ex-public school muckers.

As usual, we go on hearing loads of fine words about law and order when what the prison estate actually needs is direct action.

Make no mistake, at the moment the situation is grim. It makes me feel ill just thinking about it.

As with dynamic security, this book has only come about through the building of relationships, trust and honesty with the people in its pages. Those we've heard from have trusted me to put their stories out there so that you, the reader, can get a better understanding of the realities of British criminal justice.

I hope you agree with me that their different perspectives have made for some fascinating reading, and hopefully thought-provoking insight into what makes a criminal in the first place.

With their help, I've tried to paint a picture of the various types to be found across our prison estate, the better to show you how jail really is. By getting to know these characters and learning how they came to be in the position they did, I've also hoped to get a few pointers as to how the service might be improved.

After all, that would be in all of our interests, wouldn't it? Not just those banged up inside, whether inmates or prison staff.

So now, before the credits roll, let's have a brief look back at the cast and sum up what we can glean from their experiences.

Johnny Mo is the man who brought us into Strangeways, showed us around and introduced us to the joint. A prison first-timer, I could think of no one better equipped for the job.

Johnny is a normal working-class guy, worked hard all his life. Okay, so smuggling fags and a bit of booze on the side . . . I've got mates who have done that. Illegal, sure, but it's hardly the Brink's-Mat robbery, is it? Then a family member wants to borrow a vehicle, he's lent it him and bam! Strangeways here we come.

Next we had Lee Robson and his cousin Harry, white-collar crooks as events transpired, but every bit as naive about jail and their own actions as Johnny in their way, neither of them natural-born convicts. Their stories epitomized bad choices.

Super polite, easy to get along with, a dry sense of humour and a real grafter, Johnny was absolutely loved by the staff on our wing. And I don't know about Harry, but Lee seems to have been no bother either, getting on with what was in front of him. In both cases, their saving grace was a friendly and trustworthy nature. However, that also let them down: Johnny in actually answering questions thrown his way instead of saying 'no comment', and for Lee, being led astray by those with experience they trusted.

Johnny's honesty put him in prison, although given how he landed a job inside straight away, it might just have saved him as well. And how many businesses like Lee and Harry's go bust? Their tales should send a shudder up the back of any reader. There but for the grace of maybe one dodgy decision go we all . . .

Johnny and Lee contacted me after reading book one, as did

everyone else in these pages. But while I remembered Johnny from inside Strangeways, Lee I would otherwise never have got to know at all. Others like him not in the book also got in touch, a sign that such outcomes are far from unique. That ought to make us wary of jumping to conclusions about the sorts of people who wind up behind bars, because it could be you, me or someone we love.

But empathy shouldn't begin and end with customers you wouldn't expect to find inside or those convicted for white-collar crimes (although some argue that they cause most damage). Even career criminals like Mr Subtle in chapter three deserve at least a little sympathy when we look into their backgrounds. Not that he would either ask for any or want it.

The first point about Mr Subtle is that he is not a man for excuses, won't blame his childhood or upbringing. And yet when you look at it, what person with a normal past could even imagine the horror? Yeah, we all have choices, but his journey shows how we ought to hear the full account before we cast judgement. The experiences of someone growing up and into their teenage years will affect the likelihood of him or her going inside, quite definitely. And Mr Subtle's tale shows how the effects of 'a misspent youth' extend well beyond HMP Manchester, should anyone doubt it.

Mr Subtle, like Lee Robson, I've since got to know through writing *Strangeways: A Prison Officer's Story*. Marv, from chapter four, is another I ran into while working inside. Otherwise his story is similar. Actually born in a jail – before growing up alongside the gangbangers and drug pushers of Moss Side – he too seems to have had no chance of avoiding life behind bars.

Strangeways and the mean streets of Manchester became his natural environment.

How do you police what was happening on those estates? The coppers know where all the drugs are sold, there is a road that might as well have market stalls on it. They know the addicts and those touting for business yet seem powerless to change it.

So when it comes to discussing ideas of rehabilitation, as we did with Frank – another one born to the life – in chapter seven, we can surely see how the problems we face are as much about society in general as they are about what goes on behind bars.

Sure, a few hardened criminals like Marv and David, who we've just met, end up making a go of it on the out, but in both cases we saw how nothing that happened in jail 'cured' them. In fact, fucked-up lungs and a broom handle in the eye suggest the opposite, don't they? No, what turned these guys around was a sense of belonging, of family, of having a pukka reason to become a law-abiding citizen. Looking back, I remember one other time . . .

In 2019, I was doing my shopping in Walkden and this little lad, seven or eight, runs up to me in the supermarket. 'All right, Mr Samworth?' he says. I looked down at him, then looked around and thought, *Mr Samworth? It's got to be a con's lad, this.*

It was then I saw him, a former young offender from Forest Bank who we also had for a spell at Strangeways. So I pushed my trolley over and shook him by the hand. 'All right, lad?'

'Yes, Mr Samworth, how are you?'

I said I was fine and asked if he'd been inside lately.

'No,' he said.

'Is this the reason why?' I said, nodding at his boy.

'Yeah,' he said. 'I've got him now. You've got to change.'

Not that such a touching scene as this will be the destiny of everyone. Frank, for instance, has been with his missus forever, but that doesn't deter him from his life of crime, does it? In fact, since we spoke for this book, he has been in and out of jail again. Don't ask me why, it's hard to keep up with him!

'It's me life, Mr S,' he chuckled. 'While I'm on this planet I'll be up to something.'

But what it does come back to is that however well or badly our prison service is run, finding ways for society to stop churning out damaged people is a primary issue if we want to see proper lasting change. As I've said in two books now, this country's prison estate can quite definitely be managed in a more productive and safer way, but the bottom line is, a load of issues could be avoided before it got to that if we better raised and educated our kids.

Sure, there will always be the Hugh Pinkmans and Dale Cregans of this world, psychologically damaged or just down-right evil. Even kids like Lucas, with childhoods moved from pillar to post and never settled, may well slip through the net. But as we saw with the impact of Daz's imprisonment on his kids, if we don't at least try to get a grip on the root causes of criminality, there will always be a new generation ready to suffer mental health issues down the line, many on course to give the likes of Strangeways even more to think about. And right now, as Mr Subtle described, the juvenile estate is in many ways even more brutal and violent.

It's clear that when he first went to what back then were called borstals, he loved the boot camp feel of the place, its almost military style, enjoying the parameters of discipline. So we don't have to be talking only about promoting a touchy-feely sense of belonging, do we? Sometimes a kick up the arse will do the trick – the important thing is to show our kids that as a society we care.

While, as should by now be clear, the prison service is too often its own worst enemy – I'll say it again: bring back dynamic security – it quite definitely cannot cure society's ills on its tod.

If we get to the teenagers especially, we might just be able to guide some of them off what looks too much like an inevitable path. Lately, I asked this lass I know why she stayed in an abusive relationship. 'I'll tell you why, Sam,' she said. 'It's normal to me.'

Marv, Frank, Mr Subtle, David, Lucas and a good few of their co-stars here would doubtless say something similar. If thee and me went on an armed robbery, we'd be terrified of being caught. None of them have that fear. And that's never going to be ideal if we breed a prison population too large to look after properly.

It's not called gang and drug 'culture' for nothing, is it? Some people grow out of it, but are then being replaced by young 'uns chasing status, excitement and money. It's engrained.

But Strangeways wasn't just about criminality. Mental health issues were everywhere too, for staff and prisoners alike – which is why I wanted to take you back to healthcare and in particular that year from hell. On reflection, although we staff tried to help people, tried to have a regime and do what we could, it was quite a dark situation. Some of the people we dealt with quite definitely should not have been in prison. For me, in the court system there ought to be healthcare professionals assessing these people and either managing them in the community or in proper forensic units.

Hugh Pinkman in some ways was a standalone – no pun intended – case. I doubt there'll ever be another like him in the service. To begin with he was able to walk but chose not to; the mind boggles at how he then took it to such extremes. Lying in bed long enough for your legs to bend physically to a state where they would require numerous operations and years of physiotherapy to put right . . . how do you even begin to make sense of that? We as a prison were complicit. Everyone knew he could walk really, but when it got to the point where he refused, if we needed to get him to reception to take him to court, we'd put him in a wheelchair. And that became the norm. Prison just weren't right for him.

He may well have been one of those who aren't mentally ill when they come in, but get that way inside. Being locked up and taken away from your loved ones . . . I've tried to imagine what it would be like. The things that would get me are the things that got Lee Robson – not being in control, not being able to speak to or see your family when you want. Plus the absolute boredom, you never get away from that. Despite all the high drama from time to time, prison is more often than not an extremely boring place.

On healthcare, I now realize, there was genuine fulfilment to be had in trying to help people. But it was otherwise such a grim place, where people who should be in hospital would languish for months on end. It shows you how underfunded such units were. And speaking of mental health leads us back to IPP sentences . . .

For me . . . anyone who is over tariff, get them out. Give them a twelve-month or two-year licence, if you must, but the only reason you send them back to prison is if they commit a crime and go in front of a judge. Do what you can to keep them out.

If I had one final wish, though, regarding how we improve the prison service, it would be to make being a prison officer a role to be proud of. We would employ well-paid people in that position who have the street smarts, presence, intelligence, call it what you will, and appropriate training to make a proper professional job of it, all overseen by people promoted on the basis of talent and experience – such as the great Bertie Bassett – rather than those who just mark time and won't rock the boat. And there would be enough officers not only to keep a growing population under control, but also to operate a regime that was fair, disciplined and as civilized as it ought to be in the twenty-first century, while recognizing that the folk in there have often committed the most heinous crimes.

Until then, at the very least those in charge of our jails ought to be planning for the return of, you guessed it, dynamic security.

Because at Strangeways and elsewhere across Britain, that is the only way we will make prison a safer place.

And right now, staying safe is the best we can hope for.

Acknowledgements

It's time to thank everyone who helped me to bring *Strangeways Unlocked* to life.

As ever, top of the list is Amy, and our daughter, the two most important people in my life. I love you both. Here's a bark out to Stephen, too, my regular four-legged sounding board.

I'm grateful for the input and support of my agent, Martin Redfern at Diane Banks Associates; Tony Hannan, who once again helped me to tell the tale; editors Lorraine Green and Graham Coster, our editorial director Ingrid Connell and the rest of the staff at Pan Macmillan, my lovely publishers.

This time, though, I would mostly like to thank all those people I got to visit (socially distanced when lockdown permitted, of course), without whom this latest adventure could not have happened. Thanks as well to those who missed the cut; we didn't have room to include everyone's story, but please know that your contribution is appreciated. By reaching out and sharing your experiences, reading the books and watching the *Real Porridge* podcast, you inspire me to keep going.

Now, get out from behind your door.

Discover Neil Samworth's first book

STRANGEWAYS

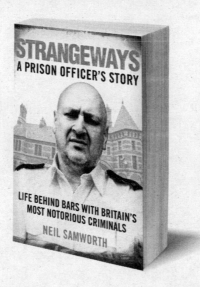

Neil 'Sam' Samworth spent eleven years working as a prison officer in HMP Manchester, aka Strangeways. A tough Yorkshireman with a soft heart, Sam had to deal with it all – gangsters and gang bangers, terrorists and psychopaths, addicts and the mentally ill.

Strangeways is a shocking and at times darkly funny account of life in a high-security prison. Sam describes being attacked by prisoners, tackling cell fires and riots, and reveals the problems caused by radicalization and the drugs flooding our prisons.

This raw, searingly honest memoir is a testament to the men and women of the prison service and the incredibly difficult job we ask them to do.

'A fascinating insight into the workings of a prison . . . a frequently shocking read'
Daily Express

'Authentic, tough, horrifying in some places and hilarious in others'
Jonathan Aitken